I Remember Eden

Holly Chandler Christy

In loving memory of my parents,
Howard Chandler Christy and Elise Ford.

Acknowledgments

First and foremost, I want to thank my husband Jim who forfeited many a home-cooked meal in good humor by quoting from *The Stepford Wives* in which Jon Lovitz is shocked to find his favorite cupcakes were yet unbaked--to which Bette Midler exclaims, "But I wrote two chapters!"

A special thanks to Zara Morton, Amazon's Senior Project Manager, for her brilliant expertise, her never tiring readiness to answer questions and her warm personality that made me feel as if I were dealing with a friend. Without her and her team of experts there would be no book.

Many thanks to Judy Goffman, owner of the magnificent American Museum of American Illustrators on Bellevue Avenue, in Newport, Rode Island in which she has enshrined Poppy's art. Thanks to Elaine Stomber, archivist at the Skillman Library at Lafayette College in Easton, Pennsylvania for taking such good care of all things pertaining to Howard Chandler Christy, and, in particular, my deepest appreciation for my mother's love letters to my father which she sent me. They have meant so much to me as they helped me understand my mother in ways I never could have as a child.

Heartfelt thanks to Caroline Briggs, Esq. for suggesting that our Book Club read my book, and Caroline's mother Anne Briggs, our amazing Attorney at Law for telling me she liked my book so much that she read it from beginning to end in one sitting. Thanks to all those Book Club members who took the time to read it: Mary Ann Uchrioli, Kathy Hicks, Cindy Gerlach, Teresa Owens, Mary Lundstrom, Janet Alsup, Carolyn Jacacinski, Meg Waclawik, and a special thanks to Teresa Sekine who told me, "The name of this book should be 'Reclaiming Eden'" which is the title I ultimately gave it.

A big thanks to my cousin Lieutenant Colonel Tom Leonard for reading my book and exclaiming, "That's my Dad's voice. It's exactly what he used to say." And thanks to his daughter Karen for telling me what he said. There's nothing like having a relative's verification. Tom's father was my Uncle Jim in the book, then Fire Chief of the City of Greenwich, Connecticut.

A special thanks to NASA's Systems Analyst Engineer Judith Herman with whom I worked in Caltech's Galileo Flight Software Lab. During that time, she tirelessly boosted my confidence by telling me, "You're a good writer." I also want to thank all my Jet Propulsion Lab buddies who believed in me. Because of them, I look back on my JPL experience as my alma mater. Thanks to Bret Huggins and his talented artist mother, Bonnie Porter, who read everything I wrote through the years and told me the way to protect my creative works was by writing a book first, not a screenplay as Bret's father, the famous screenwriter, Roy Huggins, author of *The Fugitive* always did. Thank you Cat Spydell and Donna Slone for your many helpful comments.

Thanks to Cindy Ebert who also took the time to read my book and comment on it as well as Professor Alina Alexeenko for taking a copy of my book to Europe on a conference after which she has never ceased to encourage me to get it published and who said reading it was like watching a movie.

A special thanks to my screenwriting teacher, Robert McKee, author of *Story*, for asking me what it did to me to grow up not being told the truth about the identity of my father. When I told him, he said, "That's the story you should write." Without Bob McKee, I never could have put the first few words on a page.

Last but not least I want to thank Tristine Rainer for her wonderful book, *Your Life as Story* which puts everything into perspective like "pearls on a necklace."

Then there are those people in my daily life who expressed such enthusiasm for this book that it spurred me on: my doctor's wonderful nurse, Susan Greene, and my Pilates teacher, Shirley Payne, both of whom have shown an eagerness to see my book reach completion. All these people urged me on. In so doing, they kept me going lest I let them down.

My sincere apologies if I have forgotten anyone through the many years it took to complete this book.

Most of all, many thanks to Paula and Gianfranco Sorrentino, owners of the famous New York restaurant my father decorated with murals of my mother for setting up a press conference for me at what is now called *Leopard at the Café des Artistes* and for putting me in touch with Steven Heller who wrote the wonderful review of my book in the *Atlantic* magazine, *My Dad, the Famous Painter?*

And to my children, many thanks for believing in me and for the joy they bring when I recognize traces of the man I called Poppy. With Rick, it's his positive, never give up attitude that has made him such a big success. For

Christina, it's her love of people that has made her beloved by so many. She also seems to have inherited my parents delight in the many antics of all those sentient creatures with whom we share this planet. Over the phone, some thousands of miles away, she tells me how the blue jays on her deck shake every peanut to make sure the nut inside is big enough. If not, they toss it to the side—that is, until the red woodpecker shows up. That's when all the nitpicking stops, and it's every bird for himself lest that woodpecker get more than his share. Oh, the laughter these birds bring into our lives.

Thanks to Helen Copley who made it her mission in life to introduce me to what she called "our Christy Family" which were all those people still alive who remembered Poppy about whom she wrote in her book, *The Christy Quest*. Without those wonderful people, like Joselyn Green and Olga Steckler, both of whom are now sadly deceased, some of the stories in this book would never have been told.

Thank you James Head, Esq. for helping me get information I never could have gotten on my own. He too has been writing volumes of books called *An Affair With*

Beauty about Howard Chandler Christy whom so many admired for his amazing talent.

Last but not least, thanks to Governor and Mrs. Voinovich for their kind invitation to the governor's mansion in Ohio to see Poppy's immense portrait of my mother and me titled *The Summit* hanging in their stairwell.

-Holly Chandler Christy

CONTENTS

CHAPTER ONE

Scent of Hyacinth

I glory in a little girl
So pure and sweet is she
Fresh as the scent of the hyacinth flower
Unfolding God's beauty in thee
The breath of the spring so tender
Telling of glory to be.

- Poem to Holly by Howard Chandler Christy

Mother had a secret. And it had something to do with me. I could tell by the whispers and furtive glances that she and Nanna exchanged if they thought I was listening. And

I would try to listen harder; what I couldn't understand, I stashed away to memory.

To Mother's chagrin, I remembered things she wished I did not.

Mother was an artist with a studio at 54 W. 74th Street on New York's Upper West Side. Too busy to care for a toddler, she often left me with her parents in Freeport, Long Island, where her father, Carl T. Forsberg, was building fishing vessels for what would become the Viking Fleet, a booming family-owned charter fishing business still in operation today in Montauk, New York. On those days when Mother left me with Nanna, I would cling to the broad back of Bubby—Nanna's black Lab mix—and cry as I watched Mother hurrying away down the leaf-strewn country road in her high heels, veiled hat, and grey fox coat with padded shoulders. Mother's secret and frequent abandonments made me feel there was something wrong with me, and I grew to resent her for it.

On one of my stays at my grandparents' house, Nanna sent Mother a typewritten note. Long after Mother's death, I would find it tucked away in a grey tin file box where Mother kept her important papers and family photographs.

Elise dear,

Be careful what you say around Holly. She is so adorable with that face, so pure and sweet. She looks like a little angel. Dad came home early today, and we both noticed how she listens to everything we say. She stands in her playpen, holding onto the bars, and watches us with those big, serious, brown eyes of hers. Dad says she's as smart as a two-year-old. He swears she understands everything we say.

In haste, love, Mother

Oh, but Nanna was wrong about one thing—I was no angel. There was a gnawing question about my identity I was determined to resolve, and to my way of thinking, I came to wonder if the only person standing in my way was Mother. Mother's secret was a burning ember that would one day erupt into a blazing flame.

Mother went by the name Elise Ford whereas mine was Holly Morris. When I asked her why I didn't have a father like other children, she gave me her Christian Science answer. "God is your father." But Mother had a father I called Papa. So why didn't I have a father?

When I asked her why my name was different from hers, she told me Elise Ford had been her New York modeling and stage name which she now used to sign her paintings.

There was no getting around Mother.

She was a skilled photographer, yet she had no pictures of my father. As I grew older, this put scary thoughts in my head. Like Error, a term Christian Scientists dismiss as "Nothing" but negative thinking, I came to wonder if I were Mother's "Error" to be ignored.

A huge 17th century silk Flemish tapestry set the stage upon which my self-awareness began. Reaching from floor to ten or twelve feet high ceiling, this woven depiction of the Archangel Gabriel heralding the immaculate conception of the Christ child to the Virgin Mary took up an entire wall of Mother's art studio as if it were a set design in a religious drama in which we were the actors. By day, rays of light beamed down on it from a northern skylight. By night, it glowed like burnished gold from a big lamp on a Giovanni Bologna table.

Was Mother like the Virgin Mary?

If God was my father, who was the man with the wild, white hair who came to visit every day? And why did he make me feel like the center of his world?

It wouldn't have been hard to imagine Mother as the Virgin Mary. Soft-spoken and shy, she drew no more attention to herself than a gentle zephyr moving through lace curtains. Angelic in face and figure, she didn't drink, smoke, or swear. Abrasive behavior was unknown to me. Nor did she ever lose her temper. To all appearances, she was a woman without human stain. Perhaps—like the Virgin Mary on our 17th century tapestry.

***

Every Saturday, Mother and I listened to the Metropolitan Opera on the radio. During intermission, Milton Cross described scenes of illicit love ending in tragedy. Like doomed operatic lovers, Mother was a soprano—a soloist at the 68th Street Christian Science Church on Central Park West, a short walk from her studio.

Opposite the Immaculate Conception tapestry hung three life-size portraits, all by the man with wild, white hair. One was of Mother in a blue satin gown. Another was of me in a yellow bonnet. The third and largest was of Mother and me sitting on a mountaintop. In it, Mother is trying to tell me something as she points to the clouds beyond. She called it *Mother and Child*, but fifty years later, I learned its real name when Governor and Mrs. Voinovich invited me to their Columbus, Ohio mansion to see it hanging on their stairwell wall with a new name of *The Summit*.

***

Mother's studio was my sanctuary, far from the World War II bombings in Europe. Like a cathedral, the richness of its paintings and antiques gave me the impression that no harm could ever come to me until the day when fear threatened my sense of safety when, for the first time, the white-haired man didn't show up as he usually did.

That was the day that would shape the rest of my life.

Mother was painting a still-life. The smell of turpentine and rancid linseed oil overwhelmed the delicate fragrance of the purple hyacinth she had arranged in a Tiffany vase. I looked up at the northern skylight. Daylight was waning. Soon it would be bedtime. *Where is he?* His visits were like clockwork. Every morning he walked the five blocks along Central Park West from his art studio at the Hotel des Artistes at One West 67th Street to our place. He was the only person in my little world who paid attention to me. Unlike Mother, who was always preoccupied with her art, he would pull me up on his lap and tell me stories about his "barefoot boyhood days" in Ohio. Mother called him Poppy, and so did everyone else. It was obvious to me that he was famous and admired by all. Even the elevator man and garbage collectors whom he joked with as if they were family called him Poppy. Everyone loved Poppy. But isn't Poppy what some people call their fathers? I wanted him to be my father. Not anyone else's.

It was no secret that Poppy lived at the Hotel des Artistes with his wife, Nancy, and a cat named Winky. Mother and I never went there. But I felt like I knew Winky because Poppy told me all about him—how Nancy feeds him his can of cat food on top of a Spanish shawl spread over the grand piano. I even know about the bust of Mussolini on the piano next to where Nancy puts his cat food. What I didn't know about Mussolini was that Poppy went to Italy to paint his portrait, and the bust was supposed to be a reminder of the good times they had singing Steven Foster songs together—something I will learn more about many years later in a book on great American Illustrators. Other than stories about Mussolini, the man with the wild, white hair tells me lots of things.

Without him, all I would know would be operatic tragedies.

Mother tells me nothing. She is always quiet, except when she bursts into song or whistles while she paints. What is she hiding? And why is the Hotel des Artistes out of bounds when it's only a few blocks away? We walk past that street every time. Mother and sometimes Poppy take me to Central Park through the entrance next to Tavern on the Green.

I languish on the oriental rug, half listening to the sound of Mother's brush rubbing paint from her palette into the canvas propped up on a paint-splattered easel. Burnt sienna, raw umber, and cerulean blue. "Colors of the earth and sky," Mother calls them. "The great outdoors I love," she likes to say.

She swipes her paintbrush over the Tiffany vase on canvas, and magically a watery green stem appears through the crystal.

Unlike Mother, who cares more about her art, the man with wild, white hair makes me the center of his attention. He brings me Indian beads and relics he collected as the son of pioneers. Arrowheads and Civil War bullets. He tells me he once swallowed a Civil War bullet to keep his big brother, Bern, from wrestling it away from him. A day later, he pooped it out. That made me laugh. I love his stories about a time when steamboats and horses were the only means of travel.

Mother only talks to me at bedtime when she reads me stories about Peter Rabbit and Br'er Fox. The man with the wild, white hair tells me stories about his family. His parents, his pets, his first wife, his second wife, his daughter, his granddaughter, his brothers, and sisters. He talks about his many friends at the Café des Artistes in the lobby of the building where he lives. Oh, how I wish I were part of his happy world instead of my lonely one with Mother.

It's as if I have no family or friends other than my grandparents, with whom Mother drops me off when she wants to get rid of me.

Mother's studio darkens around me as the light from the skylight fades. Fumes of turpentine fill the air as Mother pours the acrid liquid into a coffee can and starts cleaning the paint from her brushes by dipping them into the can and wiping them clean, after which she wipes her palette down with a turpentine-soaked rag.

Where is he? He's been gone all day. What if I never see

him again?

Oblivious to my concern, Mother whistles *Beautiful Dreamer* as she inspects her day's work.

She is happy.

I am not.

From Columbus Avenue, six stories below our three large windows, the muffled drone of city traffic reminds me that the man I love is out there somewhere in the bustling city streets of New York instead of here with me. I scramble to my feet and trudge over to the tapestry. Beneath Gabriel's foot, strands of silk have come unraveled. Combing through them with my fingers, I pretend it is angel's hair. My heart aches for the man with the wild, white hair. He lives in a place where I cannot go. There is a wall of separation that I am unable to tear down. I'm all ears when he talks about his friends. *Why doesn't he ever take me to the Café des Artistes? Is there something wrong with me that he and Mother must hide? Doesn't he want me to meet his friends? Does he like them better than me? Is that why he isn't here? Such thoughts fill me with fear.*

I want him to be here with me, not his family and friends. I want him all to myself.

Mother fixes me shad roe for dinner and puts me to bed. In her melodious voice, she sings me the Brahms lullaby until I fall asleep.

Lullaby and goodnight, with roses bedight. / With lilies o'er spread is baby's wee bed / Lay thee down now and rest, may thy slumber be blessed / Lay thee down now and . . .

I awake to his familiar rap. A drum and bugle corps rap. *A-rat-a-tat-tat. A-rat-a-tat-tat.*

He is here!

I leap out of bed and bound for him as he swings open the front door. I reach up, and he scoops me up into his arms.

My whole world bursts with joy.

"Look what I brought you," he says, holding out a brown paper sack. I peer inside. "Strawberries and cream," he says. I did not know that World War II had made fresh fruit a luxury reserved for the privileged.

He seats himself on an antique bishop's throne beside the tapestry. Like the tapestry, this chair is one of the treasures he brought back from Italy after painting Mussolini's portrait. Threadbare, its crimson velvet is faded with age.

Mother slips out of her painter's smock and into a Japanese kimono, which is white with splashes of green leaves and orange blossoms. She pours him a cup of coffee. She comes alive for him as she dances around the table, then returns to her paint-splattered sink, where she pretends to dry a plate on her swiveling hips while belting out an Irish ditty from her days on a New York stage. *"When I was at home, I was merry and frisky / My dad kept a pig, and my mother sold whisky."* It's totally out of character for Mother, but the man with wild, white hair throws back his head and roars with laughter.

I climb up on his knee while he peers through a magnifying glass at the *New York Times* while Mother washes the strawberries in a paint-stained sink. She then places a bowl of the bright red fruit on the table. My bedtime has been forgotten as I become the center of attention. After smothering them with cream and sugar, the man with the wild, white hair scoops a strawberry onto a spoon and aims it for my mouth. "Mmm," he says, "Open wide."

I shake my head and push his hand away. "I want coffee."

"No coffee," scolds Mother. "It's bedtime." But he

ignores her and tips his cup to my lips. It's creamy and sweet.

He takes it away. "More," I demand, but he places the cup back on the saucer.

"That's enough. Now eat your strawberries. Look how juicy and red."

I shake my head. "I want coffee."

"Don't you want to make Kelly the Clown happy? Now, eat your strawberries like a good girl, and make Kelly proud." I had felt sorry for Kelly from the first time I saw him when Poppy and Mother took me to the Barnum and Bailey Circus. He had such a sad face it made me think he was like me.

I loved Kelly. He was sad like me, so I wanted to make him happy. He writes me letters that Mother reads to me from Ringling Brothers Barnum and Bailey Circus. Thirty years later, I will find these same letters, brittle with age, on letterhead stationery that reads: *Howard Chandler Christy, Hotel des Artistes, One West Sixty-Seventh Street*, and I will recognize the unmistakable scrawl of the man I loved more than anything in the world.

After more coaxing, I open my mouth, and Poppy

pops a strawberry in. Its sweet juice seeps out between my lips and runs down my chin. He takes out his handkerchief and wipes the juice from my face. "Rosebud lips," he says. "You have rosebud lips like your mother."

Oblivious to my future fate, I bask in the warmth of his love. I have nothing to fear as long as he's near.

After eating the strawberries, I set out on a foray over his Santa Claus tummy beneath the crisp lines of his three-piece, navy blue suit. I dig my fingers into his breast pocket behind a colorful silk pocket square handkerchief and pull out a black comb. Standing on the arms of his throne, I swing my legs over his shoulders. I am now higher than Mother and everything else around me except the Archangel Gabriel on the tapestry. From my lofty place, I run the comb through his hair the way I did the strands of silk on the tapestry. His hair is long in front and always looks as if it got caught up in a gust of wind. To me, every inch of his scalp is familiar ground. The hair at his nape is cropped short. Coarse and gray, it stubbornly curls under, refusing to obey a comb. All these details are familiar to me even now.

I feel as if I am sitting on the shoulders of God as I twist his white hair into braids while listening to him read the front page of the *New York Times* to Mother. As usual, it's about the war. The conversation grows somber. He tells Mother he is going to make her the symbol of America, fearless and victorious. He will call his World War II poster *I Am An American*. "If we're going to win this damn war, we've got to know who the hell we are!"

When I tire of combing his hair, I slide down to his lap and onto the floor. As I scamper away, I hear him thunder, "God damn it all to hell! We gotta fight for our freedom. Without freedom, life's not worth living." He is the only one who swears, which gives him a more powerful heir than Mother, who is soft-spoken and sweet. She doesn't swear. She never uses bad words like "damn" or "hell." Only the man with the wild, white hair wields what I perceive as masculine power.

Freedom is a word he uses often—a word I don't understand. But I do know about war, which I act out when I flop down on the red Oriental rug and separate my marbles into two camps. Black and white ones on one side, red and white ones on the other, with two big marbles as generals—Blacky and Red at the head. With a wide swing of my arms, I clash them together.

That's war.

"Saw Tunney last night," he tells Mother. I have no way of knowing that Gene Tunney is the world heavyweight champion, nor do I know that the man with the wild, white hair used to box. "Tunney, Babe Ruth, and I, we had a grand old time. Then Claire Booth Luce showed up."

Although I don't know who any of these people are, I will remember their names for the rest of my life. Years later, I will learn that Luce was famous for such pithy statements as, "The trouble with this world is that men can't live together. So, what do they do? They go out and die together."

***

I feel as if Poppy and his wife and friends exist in another realm—one I am not worthy to enter. Something is wrong, and that something has got to be me. My thoughts churn with sudden urgency. I pull myself off the floor and pad toward the great man on his throne, who everybody calls Poppy. I have a question that makes me tremble with fear as I suspect the answer might give away Mother's secret.

Like approaching the Tree of the Knowledge of Good and Evil, I knew what I was about to do was wrong.

I remember every detail. Above him, the Archangel Gabriel's wings are spread. Across the table, Mother is seated beside the kneeling image of the Virgin Mary.

My insides knot up. Words I want to speak lodge in my throat, almost making me choke. I'm about to reach for the forbidden fruit.

Seeing me standing there looking as if I'm about to cry, the man with the wild, white hair leans in close.

Against the warning voices in my head, the words burst forth.

"Why can't I call you Father?"

An uneasy silence follows. I recoil as if from an impending storm. I have crossed a line. I feel myself alone in forbidden territory.

I shoot Mother a worried look.

She turns away.

I draw back in dread.

I want to belong. More than anything in the world, I want to belong. Not just to some ghost in the sky. I want to belong to him. The man with the wild, white hair is the only God I want to worship.

Then comes the answer that will curse the rest of my

life.

"You can call me Poppy," he says, blue eyes twinkling beneath bushy white brows.

My chin quivers with the pain of rejection.

Everybody calls him Poppy. I want to be his little girl. Special.

I shrink before him. Tears blind my eyes. Small and helpless, a little over two feet tall, I feel smaller than my pet mouse, Squiggles. My thoughts are a snarl of conflicting emotions, a chaotic mix of love and suspicion—a rough sketch gone wild, twisted, and distorted.

I want him to be my father.

Poppy gives me an impish grin. The same grin he gives me when he tells me how happy Kelly the Clown will be if I'll be good and eat my strawberries. With a chuckle, he gathers me up on his knee. "Holly," he says with a chipper voice, "Remember the bagpipes in the park? The men in their kilts? Did they sound like this?" He tucks his chin into his neck and bellows from deep down in his throat. Grabbing the loose skin on his neck, he shakes it to make the halting whine of a bagpipe. And he looks so silly that—

—along with my sniffles—I start to giggle.

"Dewlaps," he says, jiggling his neck. "You know—that's what the black-and-white cow has under her chin. Like they say back on the farm—up to her dewlaps in clover."

He continues to make the twang of an ancient windpipe instrument while tapping out the rhythm with his fingers. *A-rat-a-tat-tat-tat.* And together, we bob our heads to the beat of a one-man, marching bagpipe band.

For the time being, he has thrown me off track. His ability to distract and entertain me makes me forget how much I want to be Howard Chandler Christy's girl.

***

For the next ten summers, he will teach me the most important lessons in life. But my desire to know the truth about my identity will smolder through my childhood until puberty when it will burst into an all-consuming fire.

CHAPTER TWO

Smiley

Scarcely ever have I known a man so filled with the joy and delight of life.

He had an indomitable quality, and his happiness was infectious.

- Norman Vincent Peale on
Howard Chandler Christy in
The Power of Positive Thinking

As a child, I never thought of Poppy as old. Though his hair was white, he was as young in spirit as the stories he told of his youth. What child doesn't love someone who fills her head with enthusiasm and expectation of joy?

"Tell me a story," I would squeal as I climbed up on

his knee. "About when you were a boy called Smiley." It was easy to see how Poppy could have earned that name.

He was born in a log cabin in what was then the wilds of Ohio, all of which sounded wonderful to me. Storytelling was our special time together. Through story, he shaped the way I thought life should be—chock-full of family love and good humor around the warm glow of a stone fireplace.

Mother jotted his stories down in shorthand as he told them to me. Later, after Poppy returned to his other world at the Hotel des Artistes, Mother would transcribe them into print on a clattering old typewriter. Years after her death, I will stumble across her grey, tin file box abandoned in the corner of her sister's Massachusetts moldering garage. In it, I will find Mother's journal with Poppy's stories in his voice, just as he had told them to me.

Always worried that someone would suspect that Poppy and Mother were more than business partners, Mother transcribed everything he said into the third person. Fifty years later, while reading Mother's journal, I will accidentally slip into the first person. To my amazement, Poppy came alive. Replacing Mother's "he's" with "I's, I will hear his voice speaking to me from the page. Reading his stories will take me back to those happy days where I always wanted to be, on Poppy's knee.

"Tell me about when you were a boy," I beg.

"Well," he says, "I was three years old, my father sat me outside under the shade of a tree while he plowed. I loved it there, surrounded by flowers. There were hummingbirds and buzzing bumblebees and the smell of warm freshly turned earth and weeds. Suddenly, a man with a black handlebar mustache came riding up to the fence and yelled out to my father, 'Did you hear the news? Custer's just been massacred by Indians!'"

Poppy was the second son of a farmer who, when he was seventeen, fought on the Union side of the Civil War by lying about his age.

"Tell me about your father," I beg. Hearing about his father made me feel like I had a father too.

"Dad was a good-natured man," said Poppy, leaning back in his antique throne beside the tapestry of Angel Gabriel and the Virgin Mary. "The only thing that upset him were thunderstorms. They were frequent in the summer and seemed to follow the river with terrific winds. He would bundle us children up and take us down into the cellar till the winds passed. I peeked out once during a tornado. The sky was green. What a sight! After it was over, debris were scattered over the lawn. Some of it had been blown there all the way from Philo, which was a mile away. I loved storms. The blowing of the wind. The clap of thunder. Seeing the sky light up. Feeling the vibrancy of the air. The scent of rain. I always wanted to be right there—in the middle of the storm, but my mother wouldn't let me. She told me she didn't want me 'exposing' myself to the weather. So, I had to stand up on a chair and watch through the window. One day during a storm, I followed my big brother Bern out the door. My mother stared at me—dismayed at my disobedience. I said, 'Look, Mama, here comes Bern dra-a-a-gin' me out again.' My father had a droll sense of humor. He just stroked his mustache and observed me with a teasing scowl. But Mother, she wasn't about to let me get away with it. 'No, he's not dragging you out. You get right back in here.'"

"More stories," I begged, bouncing up and down on Poppy's knee. Through his stories, I came to see the world as he saw it. Filled with love of family and the beauty of Nature.

"My dog, Scout," said Poppy, "he would be stretched out on a rug in the glow of the fire. His nose would twitch as he dreamed about the day's hunt in the snow." To Poppy, even his dog's thoughts were an important detail. And if Scout wasn't in the picture, it was his horse, Nelly. "My mother would be rocking while she knitted sweaters to keep us kids warm," mused Poppy as if reliving those cozy nights with his family gathered around the hearth. "We lived in that log cabin till I was four. It was two stories high with a great chimney and a large fireplace inside. It was up on a hill with a beautiful view of Meigs Creek. In summer, the front porch was shaded by an arbor of tangled grapevines that stretched the full length of the cabin."

"Where was Nelly?" I asked, remembering how Poppy had trained his horse to come galloping over the hill whenever he blew his bugle.

"She came later when I got a bit older."

"Someday, will you buy me a horse?"

"Well, that's not so easy. Not anymore. You see, when I was a boy, horses were the only way to get around. That and riverboats. Oh, how I loved those steamboats.

"When I was four, we moved to a farm on a hill

overlooking the Muskingum River. My favorite thing was to sit in the grass and watch the steamboats plow up and down the river. I got to know each boat by name as they carried passengers and freight in and out of the valley. *The Lorena* made weekly trips between Zanesville and Pittsburgh. *The Lorena* provided excellent food and good beds. Only nine dollars a week. Quite a deal, right, Kid?" Poppy glanced at Mother, whom he always called Kid. She smiled as she flipped over a yellow page on her shorthand pad and jotted down more notes with weird-looking squiggles.

Tired of telling me stories, Poppy began chatting with Mother about the war poster he wanted President Roosevelt to give him permission to paint. "Now that we're at war, more than ever, this nation needs a sense of identity. I'm gonna make you the symbol of America," he told Mother. "And I'm gonna call it *I Am an American.*"

"Poppy," I whined. "The story. You were telling me a story."

"Oh, yes. Let's see. Where was I?"

"*The Lorena.* You were talking about *The Lorena.*"

"Oh yes, the steamboat. Well, it was my ambition to get a job as a waiter or a cabin boy. It paid good money.

Five dollars for the round trip. Just saying her name, *The Lorena*, brings back memories of those happy days when I'd hear her whistle blow. I'd know it was her because it was the most tuneful one of all the packets that plied the Muskingum. It would echo from hill to hill, and I'd drop whatever it was I was doing and run like hell to watch her coming up that river. Oh, those steamboat days—they'd breed romance into any youngster's life—never to be forgotten. Our farm was on the crest of a hill overlooking the lock and canal. Those big Ohio riverboats had to pass through it, and no matter what time of day or night it was, I never missed the thrilling sight of seeing them lock through. I knew all the captains and pilots, and they would never fail to look up and give a wave of the hand to the small boy looking on.

"Sometimes, the morning boats would steam up the river carrying picnickers. Out on the hurricane deck would be a beautifully uniformed band. There was one in particular with musicians playing horns all bright and silver in the sun, and oh, how that band could play! It sent joy and enthusiasm out on the clear sparkling morning air. It made me think, 'God is on his throne. All's well with the world.' Oh, it was grand!"

Poppy shifted his leg and hoisted me onto his other knee. "There, that's better," he said, stretching out his right leg and shaking his foot. It never occurred to me that Poppy was in his seventies, but how could a man so filled with the love of life be old? Like God, I thought he would live forever.

Poppy's storytelling filled my head with memories of a past I'd never lived. A past in which I was part of a loving family. A past that would almost come to pass at a place called The Old Red Mill in Pawlet, Vermont, then disappear like a dream when I turned twelve.

Poppy continued his story, "At night—miles down the river and echoing from hill to hill—*The Lorena's* beautiful chimes whistled, and the deep sound of the bell drawing closer could be heard. It was just impossible to lie in bed, so out the window I'd go so as not to awaken anyone. And there, from the crest of the hill overlooking the lock, *The Lorena* would appear brilliantly lit up with activity everywhere. Sometimes her furnace fire would be leaping out of the tall smoke stacks—especially when two of these big boats would happen to be coming on together and racing for the lock. Taking chances in order to win meant nothing to the captains or crews. Everything went into the furnaces, which fairly roared as they came plowing up the river.

"I could well understand Mark Twain's saying that he was jealous of the cabin boy who shook the tablecloth out over the railing—for that boy had been places, seen things, and was going somewhere—while my big brother and I were working hard on the farm. So, one day, when I was sixteen, I boarded *The Lorena* and headed east to study art in New York."

Listening to Poppy made me want to go places and see things also, and one day I would.

As Poppy talked, I was right there with him in my dreams. On the sunny deck of *The Lorena*.

All too soon, Poppy had to leave. "Gotta get back to Nancy," he said. "Natalie and Carolyn are coming over." Even though I'd never met them and never would, I knew Natalie was his daughter, and Carolyn was his granddaughter.

I felt myself grow heavy on his lap as he slid me off and stood up.

No longer was I a part of Poppy's family.

He had a real family at that forbidden place called The Hotel des Artistes.

CHAPTER THREE

Only the Shadow Knows

"[T]he root of all fear is that we've been forced to deny who we are."

- Francis Moore Lappe, *O Magazine*

Humanitarian, lecturer, and author

Mother played the saxophone. Just one of her many talents. She had played it ever since her school band. It was during one of her practice sessions that I remember tugging at her skirt to get her attention. As Christian Scientists, we didn't celebrate birthdays, so I can only guess my age by my eye level, which was midway between the hem of her skirt and her waist, or my relationship to the tabletop, which I couldn't quite see over. She slipped the reed from her mouth and looked down at me. With an amused smile, she said, "And he told me nothing would happen. That he was *too old*?"

What Mother didn't count on was my ability to recall such events years later. Especially when I sensed it was a clue to my identity. Like pieces of a puzzle, I would one day put them all together.

***

My first day at an Eastside kindergarten began with Mother introducing herself as Mrs. Morris and me as Holly Morris. She was Elise Ford to everyone else. As for me, I had always thought of myself as Holly. Just plain Holly. But now, among other children, my last name became a matter of importance. It identified me as the daughter of a man I'd never met and didn't love.

In kindergarten, I learned something that scared me. I heard the children whispering something bad about a little girl named Lisa. What awful thing had she done? Her mother was divorced. My imagination went wild. Was Mother divorced? I visualized Lisa being ganged up on like the deer I'd seen in a Museum of Natural History diorama, with snarling wolves closing in with no place to go but over the cliff. I imagined us all on an outcropping in Central Park, preschoolers closing in, forcing Lisa to the edge for no other reason than not having a father. I imagined myself coming to her rescue.

Instead, I slunk off by myself lest I, too, become the object of their contempt.

It was there in preschool that I decided that——like Lisa——I was the hated Other who would never fit in. So I kept to myself and didn't join in the games they played.

During World War II, toys were scarce, so we had to make our own. One day, the teacher handed me a pair of scissors and asked me to pick out a piece of cloth with which to make a doll. I envisioned the Lone Ranger shouting, "Hi-yo, Silver, away!" and the sound of pounding hooves that I always heard on the radio. I picked a piece of white sheeting for my galloping steed and was happily cutting away when the teacher snatched the scissors from my hand. "No!" she barked, prying my chubby fingers loose. "That's wrong! You do it like this..." She forced the fingers of my right hand through the holes in the scissors. It didn't feel right. But who was I to tell the teacher she was wrong? So, I obeyed. But every time I tried to cut, the cloth got mangled in the scissors.

I looked around. All the other children were cutting away with no trouble.

Switching my left hand to my right was just one more proof that there was something wrong with me. I hadn't noticed that Poppy was left-handed. Nor did I remember that he bragged about being left-handed like Michelangelo.

Besides not having a father, I was a lefty.

Making my left hand right hobbled me to the point that my galloping silver turned out to be a two-legged flop with button eyes. But I loved him just the same. Instead of Silver, I named him Pony. And every night, after Poppy returned to the Hotel des Artistes, I hugged Pony tight until I fell asleep.

Poppy was left-handed. So why didn't he or Mother notice that I was too? He bragged that he was left-handed, just like Leonardo di Vinci or was it, Michelangelo? So why didn't they notice this about me? I clearly remember using my left hand to eat——something an old lady shamed me for, while I was sitting on the porch of a New England hotel after Poppy and Mother went inside.

"Don't you know you're supposed to use the other hand?" the old biddy snarled.

It made me feel bad enough to want to hide.

By then, I had come to accept myself as a child, about which a secret would keep me from ever growing up as a part of the adult world of gods like Poppy and Mother, who alone know things I can't and get to break the rules. I could hardly wait to grow up.

Mother and I lived a secluded life. Other than Poppy, Mother's sister Doris was our only visitor. Doris lived within walking distance at 36 Central Park South. Other than Doris, I don't remember a single visitor ever passing through our door. But Mother didn't seem to need anybody other than Poppy, with whom she shared her love of art. She was always absorbed in something: stretching canvases; typing Poppy's business letters; painting a still-life: cleaning brushes; repairing an electric cord; building a bookcase for her art books or a giant rack for storing paintings. Like her father, who was happiest off by himself building fishing boats, Mother was happiest while pursuing her creative goals. Like Snow White, Mother sang and whistled while she worked.

Sometimes Mother took me to the New York Public

library, where she perused books on art and biographies of great artists. Afterward, she would take them home and read them aloud to Poppy as they sat beside the tapestry of the Archangel Gabriel and the Virgin Mary.

I was awed by the New York Public Library. Majestic stone lions stood sentry at its wide steps leading up to its gates. Feeling lost in its palatial marble halls, I held tight to Mother's hand as I stared up at the religious murals on its walls and ceilings. Tugging me along, she entered rooms with bookshelves towering so high I feared they might topple over and crush me under their weight.

I was stunned to see how much there was to learn. I could never read that many books, even if I knew how to read, which I didn't. The thought so overwhelmed me that I had a nightmare about a book the size of the Hindenburg blimp falling out of the sky. I woke up screaming just before it was about to crush me. I think of that dream today as the books I buy pile up around me as I search for answers to the human propensity for unhappiness, violence, and war.

At home, Mother was never idle. While she busied herself with the love of her life, which was art, I sprawled on our oriental rug and drew pictures. Classical music was always playing softly in the background.

I wanted to be an artist like Poppy. Something he encouraged. I'd hear him brag to Mother, "Holly's a dreamer. Someday she'll be a great artist."

Poppy and Mother were Christian Scientists. Every morning, when Poppy came over, he would sit on his medieval throne beneath the outstretched wings of Gabriel on the tapestry while Mother set a pot of brewed coffee on the table. As Poppy sipped his coffee, Mother read aloud from Mary Baker Eddy's *Daily Lessons,* which she marked with soft blue chalk on the onionskin pages of her black leather *Science and Health with Key to the Scriptures.* Today, one of Poppy's quotes is being published in *Guidposts, Daily Scripture, and Reflections.* "Every morning, I spend fifteen minutes filling my mind full of God: and so there's no room left for worry thoughts." —Howard Chandler Christy, artist." It was what Poppy told Norman Vincent Peale while he was painting Peale's portrait, for which Peal included Poppy in Peale's 1952 bestseller, *The Power of Positive Thinking.*

Morning inspirational reading was Poppy and Mother's daily routine, after which she and Poppy would study art from books Mother had brought back from the library.

Poppy's God did not rain down fire and brimstone. Nor did He demand a blood sacrifice for sin. Poppy's God was a nurturing "Father/Mother God." Creator of the beauty on Earth that Poppy and Mother loved to paint.

One day, Mother brought home Elbert Hubbard's biography of Jean-Baptiste Camille Corot, the French impressionist painter of peaceful landscapes (1796-1876).

"A landscapist's day is divine. . ." said Mother as she read aloud from a letter Corot wrote to a friend. *"I see the river, like a stretch of silver ribbon; it weaves in and out and stretches away, away, away. The masses of trees, of the meads, the meadows—the poplars, the leaning willows, are all revealed by the mist that is reeling and rolling up the hillside. I paint, and I paint, and I paint, and I sing, and I sing, and I paint…!"*

Mother's eyes welled with tears as she read. *"Oh, would I were Joshua—I would command the sun to stand still. And if it should, I would be sorry, for nothing ever did stand still except a bad picture. A good picture is full of motion. Clouds that stand still are not clouds—motion, activity, life, yes, life is what we want—life!"*

"Yes!" boomed Poppy. "Life. That's what great art is

all about. Life!"

It was Poppy's love of life that instilled in me the desire to be an artist. Like him, I came to revel in rhythm, shape, and form. Early on, the creation of beauty and the preservation and celebration of "Life" became my reason for living.

Half a century later, I will find a typewritten copy of Corot's letter carefully transcribed in Mother's journal as if it were a piece of holy writ.

***

Mother didn't like to cook. Besides Thanksgiving turkey or pheasant——if pheasant happened to have been a subject for one of her still lifes——hamburger fried in bacon fat was the house specialty. Occasionally, shad roe was substituted for the hamburger. I loved it and still remember its taste, but it's impossible to find as I believe it is now extinct due to the damming up of the rivers shad lived in, so I haven't had any since I was a child. Funny how you can remember the taste of something you liked so far back in childhood and pine for it.

At the end of the day, Mother would turn on the kitchen radio while she washed her paintbrushes in the kitchen sink with an oversized bar of brown castile soap.

Out of that wooden box on a shelf above the sink emanated the menacing voice of Orson Welles. "Who knows what lurks in the hearts of men? The Shadow knows," followed by diabolical laughter.

I didn't know about evil. Up until then, all I knew was what Mother read aloud to Poppy every morning from Mary Baker Eddy's *Science and Health with Key to the Scriptures*. That God is good. And, since God is all in all, there is no such thing as evil.

So, what were these bad things the Shadow was talking about?

I wanted to know what the Shadow knew.

Like the world of *The Shadow*, mine was a world of shadowy mystery.

Mother's secret stood between me and the truth. I came to resent it more and more as I grew older.

One day when I was about ten, Mother was typing next to the Virgin Mary. Boldly, I marched up to her and said, "Who was my father?"

The irksome clatter stopped.

Silence followed as Mother stared blankly at her shorthand pad.

An ominous foreboding rose on the back of my neck.

Maybe I'd rather not know.

Mother was a gentle soul. Not easily perturbed. Christian Science's dismissal of evil had turned her into a woman of reassuring calm. So, this show of trepidation sent chills through my body.

Beside her typewriter stand sat a grey tin file box in which she kept photographs and important papers. Silently, without looking at me, she reached down. Lifting the lid, her *Cherries In The Snow Revlon* fingernails walked the labeled manila folders.

I watched as she slipped out a manila folder.

She opened the folder. Out came a faded mimeograph copy of one of Poppy's sketches of a man's head.

She held it up for me to see. "Holly dear, this was your father."

I stared in disbelief at the picture.

"His name was Frederick Morris," said Mother with convincing reserve.

Then she read aloud an autograph written below. "To Frederick Morris from Howard Chandler Christy."

I was bowled over. Flattened. *So this is why I can't call*

Poppy my father!

Feeling small and helpless, I felt myself shrink into the floor. I would never rise to Mother's stature. The I Am of America. No. I would always be just a little over two feet tall.

For the second time in my life, the answer to my plea for identity sent my thoughts into a snarl of conflicting emotions, a chaotic mix of love and suspicion, making me feel like a rough sketch gone wild, twisted, and distorted.

But there was more.

I recognized that face in the picture.

Yes, it was *The Huntsman* in Poppy's illustrations of Sir Walter Scott's *Lady of the Lake.* Mother kept his green coat and stockings and his long leather boots in our closet. I liked dressing up in them while pretending I was Robin Hood. Only I looked more like Disney's cartoon character, Dopey the Dwarf, in dangling sleeves and baggy tights in the movie Snow White and the Seven Dwarfs.

I was taken aback. Never had I dreamed Mother could produce a picture of a man named Morris. I ran to my room, screaming in my head, *I hate him! I hate him!*

When had this Morris fellow taken me to the park?

Held me in his arms? Laughed at the things I said? When had he shielded me from the evil eye of the wicked Queen in *Snow White and the Seven Dwarfs* when I dropped to my knees and tried to hide behind the theater seat?

The thought filled me with rage. *Why, oh, why do I have to be the daughter of a man I've never met? A man I don't love? A man no one ever brags about? A man whose picture Mother never bothered to take? A man no one ever mentions? A man everyone wants to forget?*

Whoever this man was, I wished I'd never heard his name.

But it was my name. A name I was stuck with that told everyone I was Nobody and Nothing, just like Christian Science's "Error."

I didn't want to believe it. But mothers don't lie, do they? To believe they lied felt like heresy. Downright scary. It threatened my security. Only wicked Queens and witches lie. Always with evil intent. Mother wasn't evil. She loved me. Didn't she? I had to believe what she said.

"Where is he now?" I whimpered as I came out from hiding.

"Who, dear?"

Unable to utter the word "Father," I spit the words out. "That man."

"He was a correspondent in the war," said Mother as if that explained everything.

I didn't know what a correspondent was, but I did know about war.

Men died in wars.

End of story.

CHAPTER FOUR

Rough Ride to Fame

A shell had struck one man in the face, carrying all below his eyes entirely away. His body, from head to foot, was a mass of clotted blood, and yet that poor fellow was able to stagger along toward the hospital, two miles to the rear.

- Howard Chandler Christy,
War Correspondent for *Leslie's Weekly*,
July 1898

War?

Correspondent?

Afraid to press Mother for details——secrets do that to you——it would take another thirty years before I would learn the truth about that "correspondent" Mother told me was my father, who was in a war.

In 1979, I was returning from work at NASA's Jet Propulsion Laboratory in Pasadena, California, when I spotted a "Sale" sign in the window of Dalton's Books on Fair Oaks Avenue.

No sooner had I entered the store than I spotted one of Poppy's illustrations on the cover of a coffee table book prominently displayed on a table in the center of the room. I rushed for it. Looking inside was like reuniting with Poppy, that loving man who had been just like a father to me until his death right after I reached puberty.

I could hardly wait to pay for Susan Meyer's *America's Great Illustrators* and take it home. In its pages, I discovered things about Poppy I didn't know.

Things too awful to tell an innocent child, which is probably why Poppy kept that part of his life a secret.

***

In 1898, Poppy was a young struggling artist in New York who had finally followed his dream and taken the Lorena to Pittsburg, from where he managed to get to New York.

War sold newspapers. And William Randolph Hearst

knew it. So, he whipped New Yorkers into a furor by publishing alleged crimes committed by the Spanish against the Cubans. There were rallies and torchlight parades. Thousands of angry New Yorkers came out to pledge their support for the Cuban rebels. Finally, Hearst sent a reporter, Richard Harding Davis, and the artist, Frederic Remington, to Cuba. Remington telegraphed back from Havana to Hearst in a seething New York: "Everything is quiet. There is no trouble here. There will be no war. I wish to return. —Remington.'"

To this, Hearst replied: "Please remain. You furnish the pictures, and I'll furnish the war. —W. R. Hearst. "

It reminds me of Claire Booth Luce's pithy statement: "The trouble with this world is that men can't live together. So, what do they do? They go out and die together." But Poppy, at the age of 26, had yet to hear Luce's words of wisdom.

On February 15, 1898, what is now thought to have been an unfortunate accident in the boiler room gave Hearst an excuse to get Americans to go to war. The battleship Maine exploded in Havana's harbor, killing over two hundred and fifty American men.

Hearst blamed the Spanish.

As I read the events that followed, I pictured newspaper boys on New York City corners hawking "Extra, extra—read all about it! Spanish sink the Maine!"

There were cries for war: "Remember the Maine! To hell with Spain!"

Thousands of men enlisted.

Poppy was one of them. Itching for a fight.

War was declared on Spain, and *Harper's, Scribner's,* and *Leslie's Weekly* clamored to snap up illustrators— enlisted men who were fast on the draw—with pencil and gun.

In 1898, cameras could only take posed shots. Soldiers scrambling through the brush with cannonballs and bullets whizzing overhead could hardly stop to say cheese. Besides, cameras were too heavy to lug through pouring rain and jungle mud. As for movies, the technology for filming action had not yet been developed. Today, any documentaries on the Rough Riders are staged re-enactments.

It was in *Great American Illustrators* that I learned what Mother was referring to when she said my father had been a correspondent in the war. Intimidated by Mother's secret, pressing for the truth made me feel guilty. Like asking for "forbidden fruit" of the knowledge of good and evil. And, as a child, I didn't know what questions to ask. Like "What is a correspondent?" and "Which war."

What I learned in Susan Meyer's book let me in on Mother's secret.

"Correspondents" were what the artist-writers hired to cover Teddy Roosevelt's Spanish American war were called.

I was overjoyed. It was the first piece of the puzzle that proved what I always wanted to be true—that Poppy was who I always wanted him to be. My father. The confounding doubt that had plagued my life began to lift in an explosion of emotion.

***

Poppy——a Rough Rider? That was a shocker.

It was one of the correspondents who coined the term "Rough Riders" for Teddy Roosevelt's First Volunteer Cavalry. And the name stuck. Out of 23,000 applicants, Poppy was one of the 780 chosen to be one of Teddy Roosevelt's Rough Riders.

According to Meyer, Poppy was thrilled. At the time,

disaster.

When the Rough Riders finally managed to drag themselves ashore, they may have still been rough, but riders they were not. The loss of their horses and mules had reduced them to a motley bunch of pack animals. Gasping for air in sweltering heat and humidity, they slogged through tropical swamps bent under their heavy packs.

Undaunted by the lack of horses, Teddy Roosevelt and his Rough Riders were determined to make it to the front line before the other regiments. The trek before them was grueling in the jungle heat. According to Brand. "...At each stop, the men sank to the ground to catch their breath, only to have to rise again, pick up their gear, and resume their pace." Their gear consisted of a carbine, a hundred rounds of ammunition, a canteen, a poncho, half a shelter tent, an army blanket, and rations to keep from starving.

I visualized Poppy stumbling through the swampy mire—his supplies slipping sideways on his sweaty back, catching on low-hanging branches—the weight of it forcing him to his knees in jungle ooze.

According to firsthand accounts, the men could stand

it no longer. First, they tossed off their blankets. Next went the cans of meat, followed by coats and underclothes until some were left with only their guns and ammunition to carry. When a nighttime downpour hit the camp, the men who had left their tents, ponchos, and blankets behind got drenched.

Nevertheless, Teddy Roosevelt's staggering efforts paid off. The Rough Riders arrived at Las Guasimas in time to start the action.

But who would fire the first shot?

Everyone agreed the honor should go to one man.

That man was Poppy.

Which takes me to another shocking disclosure.

One I might never have discovered if my friend, Cindy Eberts, a professor of statistics at Purdue, hadn't called me up one day and said, "Hey. Let's go antiquing."

***

It was a grungy-looking place smelling of mildew and dust. While I was eyeing a loveseat with a ratty cover, I thought I could get reupholstered. I heard Cindy yell from a cluttered, dark corner, "I found a book with your father's picture on the cover." I ran over to have a look.

It was *The Story of the Constitution* dedicated to "We the People—to the 138,000,000 who desire to know something about the Constitution" written by Congressman Sol Bloom in 1934. It was Bloom who gave Poppy the idea of painting the Signing of the Constitution painting now hanging in the Congressional stairwell of the United States Capitol. On the cover was one of Poppy's posters of Mother looking like a Greek goddess. As it turned out, this book would become very important to me later, but it was the series of events that happened next that were so amazing.

Turning to the store owner, Cindy said, "Holly's father was Howard Chandler Christy. And this is one of his pictures on the cover of this book."

"Is that so?" said the owner. "Well, in that case, maybe you'd better give me your phone number. Every now and then, one of his illustrations comes in. I'll give you a call."

I bought the book and went home.

A week later, I got a call.

"A book just came in. I think you'd better have a look."

God, how I love books. In them, you can find out things you never dreamed possible, and no one will ever tell you. If you want to know the truth, chances are it's hiding in a book.

I rushed right over.

When I got there, the owner handed me a dusty old book with a faded green cover with a lackluster title. *Book Buyer, Vol. 19—A Review and Record of Current Literature (August, 1899-January, 1900)* published by Charles Scribner's and Sons.

"Take a look at page 166," he said as he turned to the page marked by a scrap of yellow newspaper.

I gasped. The first thing I saw was a photo of a dashing young man in a three-piece suit. It was Poppy, as I'd never seen him before. Young, slim, and handsome with a head of curly hair slicked back like a country gentleman.

The article was an interview with Poppy when he was twenty-six.

I paid for the book and took it home, where I immediately began reading what turned out to be an interview with Poppy about his stint in the Spanish American War written by Regina Armstrong.

As I read, I could hear Poppy's voice as if he was speaking to me.

He was telling me things he had never told me before.

"Prior to the battle of Las Guasimas, the commanding officer turned to me and said, 'How about if you fire the first shot?'

"I thought that would be mighty fine, so I told him, 'I'll do it.' But after a time, I began thinking of it—that it might not be so fine after all. I was not a soldier. I was an artist representing certain periodicals and in no way pledged to offer myself up as a target for Spanish rifles, although in the capacity of artist I was constantly under fire. No man voluntarily puts his life in jeopardy. I decided that I didn't want to fire the first shot. So, I didn't. The man who did was struck by a cannonball, and his trunk and head were blown away, the legs standing upright. They had to sweep him up for burial."

I caught my breath. Had Poppy accepted that "honor," his life would have exploded into nothingness on the spot. I wouldn't be here. Nor my children. Nor my children's children, one of whom looks just like Poppy did at twenty-six when he gave that interview. By now, I even have a great-grandchildren. All that would have ended in nothing had Poppy not forfeited that "honor" and played macho by firing the first shot.

How monstrously destructive is war!

If Poppy had played macho and fired that first shot, none of us would be here. Several families would have never come to be.

But then, Poppy had a mission. A purpose far greater than male prowess.

"I'm going to do something big someday," Poppy told Ms. Armstrong. "And I don't know how I'm going to do it, either; you see, I haven't found myself yet, but I feel I have it in me to do something."

That something, I'm sure, would be the Signing of the Constitution painting. Weighing over one ton, it is the largest painting in the U.S. Capitol. In it, he left me a personal message and another one "for the American people."

In concluding the interview, Armstrong wrote, "It would seem that caution and level-headedness are his natural endowments."

***

At the end of the Spanish American War, Poppy had

fulfilled his commission as a correspondent, which included action illustrations drawn on the spot as they happened. A feat in itself.

The wounded "were shot in every way imaginable," wrote Poppy in the July 1898 issue of *Leslie's Weekly*. "[T]hrough the stomach, through the lungs; some had their legs and arms shattered; and there was one poor fellow, being assisted by a comrade; who was shot through the lungs, while his arm was shattered and a bullet had plowed a hole through his hand."

As I read Poppy's bloody accounts of the war, I understood why he chose to protect the innocence of a little girl still too young to face the ugliness in this world. I also realized why he shouted at me one day when I pointed my cap pistol at Mother. "NEVER point a gun at anyone. You hear me? Not even a toy one."

***

As I found through another remarkable coincidence, Poppy did tell Mother about his stint in the Spanish American War, probably at night after I'd been put to bed and gone to sleep. Like everything else about Poppy, she transcribed his words into her journal.

After the war was over, Poppy returned home, glad to

be alive. And who better to celebrate with him than his Dad? Francis Marian Christy, a Civil War veteran. "I brought him back some stogies thinking it would make him happy," Poppy told Mother. "They came in bottles from Cuba and were very long. After Dad smoked one, I asked him how he liked them, and he admitted he didn't. He just said, 'Oh, they're all right. You might like them, but as a matter of fact, they're not as good as a Wheeling Stogie.' I was disappointed as I always tried to make him happy."

That was Poppy for you. All transcribed by Mother in her journal.

He loved making people happy.

Never a negative word.

Except when it came to Communism and modern art.

***

As a correspondent, Poppy came to realize the importance of the arts in shaping hearts. As he told Mother, "I was beginning to see that culture is the master sculptor that shapes society. Artists, writers, and musicians are the creators of tomorrow. Vested in them is the responsibility for the happiness and well-being of society."

To Poppy's chagrin, the Spanish American War had typecast him as a military artist. And the love of war was not the vision he wanted to create for the future of America. He had seen the tragedy of bloody battles and wanted to leave it behind. He had even come to respect the enemy rather than hate him, an account of which Mother transcribed in her journal.

"I had climbed a tree to get a better view of the charging forces. Sketching fiercely to capture the details of the action, I found myself focusing on one man. A Spanish soldier. ...During the fighting, he kept pacing back and forth fearlessly out there in the open while shouting orders to his men who were entrenched." The closer Poppy came to bringing the image of this supposed enemy to life on his pad, the more he admired him.

To Poppy's amazement, this soldier remained standing through the entire battle with shots ringing out all around him. "I was up there in that tree when a shell burst alongside me, knocking me right out of the tree and damn near killing me."

When Poppy joined the other Rough Riders back at camp, he asked if anyone had noticed the courage of that

Spanish soldier giving orders. They had. Word had spread through the battlefield not to shoot him because he showed such bravery. "Like me, they couldn't help admire him," Poppy told Mother. "I drew him holding his sword and standing high, right out there in plain view. The thatched roofs of huts are in the background. I named the picture, *The Defense of El Caney.*

"I later painted that same tree I fell out of into another picture, making it smaller to fit into the design. Theodore Roosevelt is shown too with his men on duty, guns smoking, while beyond is glimpsed the Block House."[5] Poppy called this picture *Gun No. 1, Grime's Battery— Planting a Shell in front of San Juan Block House on July 1st.*

*** *

The war was over. But male lust for exploding cannons, fireballs blasting through palm trees, and sword-rattling brigades raged on. Because of this, Poppy—who had personally witnessed the action in Cuba—was in great demand for his depictions of war, which sated male fantasies of violence.

Life was pretty boring before the turn of the century. Imagine life without television, movies, or radio. Even the

Victrola had yet to be invented. Five years later, the first silent film, *The Great Train Robbery*, came on the scene, lasting only twelve minutes.

Because everyone loves a story, books and magazines brought drama into otherwise humdrum lives. Artists and writers became the spinners of fantasy before photography and motion pictures took over.

Naturally, publishers scrambled for Poppy's illustrations—all blood-and-gore action pictures for war stories. First, there were pictures of "high adventure and deeds of valor." Then soldiers. Then sailors, marines, and Rough Riders.

Poppy quickly tired of all this "soldier stuff." He wanted out. But how? The money was good, and he wanted to continue working as an artist. But not this way. Not by reliving the violence of war with every stroke of his brush.

He complained to his editors. As related in Susan Meyer's book, Poppy said, "Surely by now I have served my apprenticeship and have earned an opportunity of just one girl—any girl," he told his editors. "But they could not see it my way and handed me, this time for *Scribner's*, a story by Richard Harding Davis—a yarn, as you can imagine, about more soldiers."

That's when Poppy remembered a song the men had sung on the ship after the "Star Spangled Banner." With their hearts still crossed in reverence for their country, they had sung their reverence for *The Girl I Left Behind Me*. It was that song that gave Poppy a vision for the future that guided him safely through the war and later turned him into one of America's most famous illustrators.

"Traditionally, warriors must have loves, and those loves must be left behind and worn on ragged sleeves whenever guns stop popping," said Poppy, as quoted in Susan Meyer's *Great American Illustrators*. "So I portrayed this battle-scarred hero returning home, now that peace was in sight, to the girl whose features were radiantly discernible through the cloud of smoke from his pipe. She was everything my poor talent was able to make her—young, glowing, tender, and infinitely sweet. Thus, out of my own dreams was fashioned the first Christy Girl, whose reception turned me, almost overnight, into a painter of some of the world's most beautiful models."

"The Christy Girl became the artist's emblem," writes Meyer: "She was saucy but elegant, independent but sweet. A free spirit. Men were fascinated by her. Women copied her manner and dress. The way she wore her hat. Poppy, along with Gibson, Flagg, Held, and Rockwell, played an 'extraordinary part in shaping American cultural history.' All readers could confirm their American identity through these artists, and the thousands of immigrants pouring into the country each day would find here a common image of the ideal American type, patterning themselves after this model."

The Christy Girl labeled him a connoisseur of female beauty, and in 1921, he was made the first and only judge of the first Miss America Contest.

On the boardwalk of Atlantic City, a gaggle of reporters mobbed him, snapping pictures as they shouted questions, "Mr. Christy, Mr. Christy! How do you define beauty?"

Having been the son of a pioneer woman, Poppy knew better than to think of women as "the weaker sex."

"Beauty is strength," shouted Poppy over the boardwalk hubbub, "Why, even the boat that wins the race has the best lines."

***

In 1922, Norman Rockwell and other famous artists

were invited to judge the second Miss America Contest. In Rockwell's memoir, *My Adventures As An Illustrator,* he states:

"We entered the grand ballroom to find Howard Chandler Christy standing on the platform at one end of the room flanked by two enormous potted palms. His wife, a big, handsome, blonde woman who always reminded me of an 1890s burlesque queen, was leading the contestants one by one up onto the platform to meet her husband. It looked like a reception for Christy. I didn't care (as long as the guinea hen and burgundy held out, I didn't care if someone put a blanket over my head), but James Montgomery Flagg and some of the other judges, who had tasted fame and liked it and wanted more, were miffed. 'Why, that no-good, conceited publicity hog,' said one of them, referring to Christy. 'Who does he think he is?' Christy had scored off us.

"He continued to score off us the rest of the week. We were helpless. At the right moment, when the photographers were clustering around trying to get a good picture and shouting at us to smile, move in, move out, stand up, sit down, Christy would appear in a white suit and broad-brimmed Stetson with a beautiful contestant on each arm, and the photographers would leave us milling about and run to take his picture. During our frequent parades up and down the boardwalk behind the girls, someone in the crowd would invariably yell, 'Which one is Mr. Christy? Which one is Mr. Christy?' Then the parade would halt, and Christy's wife would lead him out to the edge of the boardwalk. The crowd would rush to shake his hand, and the photographers would snap pictures of him."

***

Until Poppy came along, women were expected to button up and cover every curve responsible for causing men to sin. They were to remain silent and obey their husbands as taught in the Bible. Looking back, Poppy's desire to bring women out of the closet and elevate them to shameless leaders of men, which he felt they should be, was what made him famous.

Poppy's attitude toward women can best be summed up in his last admonition to me the summer before his death. "Never let anyone make you ashamed you're a woman. Remember, You can do anything a man can do. And better!"

As demonstrated in all of Poppy's war posters, he saw

women, not men, as the saviors of the world.

Ironically, Karl Marx also understood the importance of women in the outcome of a nation. "Anyone who knows anything of history," said Marx, "knows that great social changes are impossible without feminine upheaval. Social progress can be measured exactly by the social position of the fair sex, the ugly ones included."

Through his art, Poppy had been given the power to shape a nation by freeing women from the shackles of shame.

**

With the popularization of his Christy Girl, Poppy was well on his way to participating in a mission. He was to help cause a national upheaval that would dramatically change our culture.

CHAPTER FIVE

Winky's Secret

One of the most striking differences between a cat and a lie is that a cat has only nine lives.

- Mark Twain

Poppy had a black-and-white cat named Winky. Long after Winky's departure from this world, Poppy continued to talk about him as if he were still a beloved member of his des Artistes family.

So it was. I came to love Winky as if he were my own.

Half a century after Poppy's death, Winky's ghost would resurface.

This time, as the purveyor of a secret.

***

Mother was Poppy's favorite model. I came to understand this after watching her pose for his *I Am An American* World War II poster. Soon after its completion, her image appeared on every dimly lit subway wall as a reminder of who we were, Americans fighting for our freedom against Hitler's Nazi Germany. Watching for it flash by through a grimy subway window became a game I played with myself. No matter how fast our express blasted through a station on the opposite track, I could always spot Poppy's image of Mother—an angel of light shining out from dingy tile walls. The American flag she was holding aloft paled against the nipples of her breast, showing through the white see-through veil I had watched Poppy drape around her.

There was no missing it.

In those days, no one but Poppy could get away with a public display of a thinly veiled naked woman. Much less on a government poster. But then, in those days, artists were like gods. As a world-famous artist, Poppy's creativity was above reproach.

On one of these trips on the New York subway, I was startled by what I saw as Mother and I bustled up from the subway dungeon into the glaring lights of Broadway.

There she was. Poppy's poster of Mother on a blown-up billboard as big as King Kong above the blinking Coca-Cola sign. "Mommy, look," I squealed, pointing to her iconic figure towering from the center mast over Broadway and Times Square, from which the New Year's ball drops to the cheers of millions on New Year's Eve.

"Shhh!" Mother cautioned as she shouldered her way through the stone-faced throng hustling toward us on Broadway.

How could Mother think she could keep something that big and glaring a secret?

Silently, I gazed up at Poppy's muse, looking like the guardian Angel Gabriel shielding New York and all of America against the onslaught of Hitler's Nazi armies.

Could Poppy ever love me that much?

***

Mother was a Thanksgiving baby born on November 27, 1912, to Sophie and Carl Forsberg, Nanna, and Papa to me. Her father was a man of few words. Firm but tender. His only vice was his pipe. If it weren't for his serious demeanor, he could have passed for Cary Grant.

Carl's wife, Sophie, had been a school teacher, an

artist, and a concert pianist, but marriage put an abrupt end to her creative dreams when the children began to arrive, one right after the other. First Carl. Then Audrey. Then Doris. And—a year later, Elise, my mother.

Four months before Elise turned two, World War I broke out. Reminiscent of the Spanish American War, it began with a single incident. Only this time, the whole world erupted in what was called the most-cruel war in history. As in the Spanish American War, faces were blown off, only this time by shrapnel from bigger, more destructive weapons than ever before. WWI claimed the lives of seven million and caused worldwide despair.

With the loss of men during the war years, women took on jobs previously thought of as man's work which gained them what they'd never had before. Independence.

Then——as if massive death and destruction by war weren't enough——the world was hammered by a plague that killed ten times more people than in WWI. Worse than Black Death, the 1918 flu pandemic was dubbed "the greatest medical holocaust in history." Infecting 28 percent of the world's population, it killed 50-100 million. This H1N1 virus started with dark blotches on the face. Within hours, the whole body turned blue as bloody froth oozed from facial orifices, causing suffocation.

Elise was six when Americans started dying in droves. Worse than Ebola, death came quickly within hours after infection. So many people died at once there was no time for coffins or the dignity of funerals. Mass graves were dug by steam shovels into which bodies were dumped like garbage.

Mother was born into a world afflicted by disease and death.

During this time, Papa continued to build boats and fish in the open sea. If it hadn't been for the Forsbergs' seclusion on their quiet waterfront street, they might not have survived.

No one visited anyone for fear of catching the flu. To survive, people were forced to stay at home in isolation. During this time, Sophie gathered her family around the piano to sing. Soon, Elise, the baby of the family, was showing a talent for rhythm and song.

Growing into her teens in the country, Elise preferred the great outdoors and would join her big brother, Carl, in hunting pheasants by leaving the household chores to her two older sisters.

As for her mother, after suffering years of worldwide disaster, who wouldn't long for the gaiety of theater and the bright lights of Broadway? For Nanna, relief from fear must have felt like rebirth. So——while Papa hunched silently over his nautical blueprints beneath the glow of a Tiffany-style lamp——Nanna took a train to New York, rented servant's quarters in the Hotel des Artistes, and enrolled Elise in the Alviene University of Theatrical Arts on West Seventy-Second Street.

These were times of rapid change for women. Three months before Elise turned nine, women were granted the right to vote. Corsets were out: the roaring 20s were in. Having gained independence during the war, women's fashions changed from cinched-in, bodacious curves to a flat-chested, short-haired boyish look. With the Jazz Age, in shimmied the fun-loving, frivolous Flappers out for a joyride through life.

After the move to New York, Nanna had no more children, proving abstinence is, after all, the best birth control. Good-natured as he was, Papa didn't complain. He just kept doing what he loved—building boats and testing them at sea while Mother's two older siblings, Carl and Audrey, watched over Doris until Nanna and Elise returned on weekends.

Nanna became Elise's "stage mom," and by the age of ten, Mother was tap-dancing across a vaudeville stage, dressed as an urchin boy with a fake cigar clenched between her teeth. People loved her solo comedy skit as much as they loved Elise. *Elise, you most wonderful child!* Wrote the owners of the Alviene School of Theatrical Arts: *Please know that your great spirit, cheerful cooperation, and untiring application to your studies have been an inspiration to your classmates and teachers alike. May success—big success, shower your every effort.*

Signed, *Mr. & Mrs. Alviene*

***

The end of WWI brought prosperity. The stock market was booming, filling the future with hope. With the loss of fear, women's hemlines took a hike, showing off legs that had, for centuries, been concealed as objects of lust beneath layers of crinolines, ruffles, heavy stockings, and layers of cloth.

By 1929, Mother had grown into a graceful sixteen-year-old of exquisite beauty and had started modeling for New York's famous John Robert Powers Agency. Photos of her during that time show her in wide-legged trousers that clung sensuously to her hips, a sailor middy top, and a big floppy hat, which was attire her corseted grandmother could never have envisioned as permissible. Besides modeling, Elise was on her way to a successful career on stage.

Then came yet another worldwide disaster.

One month before Elise turned seventeen, the stock market crashed.

Having lost everything in the Great Depression, previously successful businessmen either jumped to their death from tall buildings or fell into line with the starving masses at the soup kitchens. At the same time, worldwide unemployment rose by 25 percent.

What next? It seemed anything could happen, and something probably would.

Nanna's aspirations for Elise were wiped out. No longer able to pay the rent, she was forced to give up the room at the Hotel des Artistes and return home, where Elise returned to honing her skills as a marksman pheasant-hunting with her big brother, Carl.

In those days, seventeen was marrying age. During the Great Depression, women lost the independence they had gained during the war years. Once again, they were dependent on men for their survival——if and when those men could find work.

Hard times set in with no end in sight.

At twenty, Elise was still unmarried. The Depression was at its height and lasted ten long miserable years. At some point, Elise's parents moved to New Rochelle, the oldest community closest to New York that was accessible by rail. *Forty-Five Minutes from Broadway* was a musical written by George M. Cohan. "Only forty-five minutes from Broadway," go the lyrics. "Think of the changes it brings / For the short time it takes / What a diff'rence it makes / In the ways of the people and things."

Resourceful as she was, Nanna took Elise on that forty-five-minute ride to New York and introduced her beautiful daughter to the world-famous artist Howard Chandler Christy, whom she knew lived in the building where she had once rented a servant's room. Had Christy not made women famous through his illustrations and his World War I posters? Introducing Elise to Christy was a survival tactic Nanna hoped would give her daughter exposure to men of means, hopefully, a Rockefeller or a Vanderbilt. Someone who could lift Elise above the masses now groveling like chickens trying to scratch out a living.

As it turned out, Elise would get more exposure than Nanna anticipated.

***

Poppy had been one of the first tenants to move into the Hotel des Artistes——a neo-gothic building that housed an illustrious crowd: Noel Coward, Isadora Duncan, Fannie Hurst, Rudolf Valentino, and Norman Rockwell, to name a few. The des Artistes was a hub for world-famous artists, writers, and entertainers. In spite of all that talent and creativity, the general mood was glum during the Depression. Patronage to the Café des Artistes dwindled. Hoping to restore it to its former glory, the Hotel's board of directors held a meeting in 1932. Out of thirty-six famous artist residents—which included Norman Rockwell—they picked Poppy to come up with an idea that would brighten the Café's atmosphere and attract more business.

Ever since he started his art career at the turn of the 19th century, Poppy had had an aversion to Victorian prudishness. At that time, a Calvinist named Anthony Comstock rose to power. As an influential postal inspector and politician, he labeled the invention of the car and the telephone "instruments of the Devil" that would lead to "unholy acts."

Alarmed over the rapidly increasing potential for sin, Comstock organized a religious Gestapo. His New York Society for the Suppression of Vice (SSV) put Poppy in jeopardy of being nabbed as one of the "sinners" Comstock vowed would be "hunted down like rats."

Determined to purge America of illicit sex along with its use of condoms and the teaching of sex education, Comstock rallied the FBI to his aid.

"For Comstock, sex was a controlled substance," states James R. Peterson in *The Century of Sex*. He was a man who "had the government at his disposal; no one would stand up in favor of freedom for fear of being next on his list."

Things didn't get better until WWI. But, even then, some artists depicted democracy as a vulnerable, flag-draped woman in the arms of Uncle Sam. To Poppy, any depiction of women as weak was abhorrent. As a comeback, Poppy painted a WWI poster of a revolutionary beauty charging into battle, her long, wavy black tresses blowing in the wind. I believe the woman portrayed in that poster was his first wife, Maebelle.

WWI provoked an internal battle against puritanism. It took women out of the home and gave them jobs previously belonging to men, which only served to prove women could do anything. Something Poppy wholeheartedly believed. Many years later, Poppy would tell me, "You can do anything a man can do——and better!"

While Comstock claimed sex education was tantamount to pornography, World War I drove the young into a live-for-the-moment-for-who-knows-what-will-be-tomorrow frame of mind and shook people's faith, derailing puritan shame. At least temporarily.

During this time, Billy Sunday made himself famous by preaching that civilization rests on the morals taught in the Bible and that "God hates beer."

Really?

In 1919, under the leadership of Billy Sunday (later to become Billy Graham's hero), the Eighteenth Amendment of the Constitution was ratified, making the sale, production, transportation, and/or imbibing of alcohol a crime punishable by imprisonment.

During this tidal wave of powerful evangelists, Poppy defiantly continued to paint high-spirited women who, by their attitudes and appearance, showed that they had no intentions of buckling under to allowing themselves to be shamed for their gender.

Failing to stop the consumption of liquor during the Great Depression, Billy Sunday's following dwindled, and——fourteen years later, on December 5, 1933—— Prohibition was repealed by the Twenty-First Amendment.

It was during the year that Prohibition was repealed that Poppy painted the nudes that——to this day—— continue to adorn the walls of New York's elegant Café des Artistes. Although Poppy had several models for the murals, Elise's face and figure appear more often than any other.

Brendan Gill, the legendary New York author and critic, described the outcome of Poppy's Café des Artistes murals in his foreword to *The Café des Artistes Cook Book* as follows:

"He [Howard Chandler Christy] painted a total of thirty-six pert nudes in a variety of seductive but not very naughty poses, counting on an abundance of foliage, feathers, and falling water to conceal what Adam and Eve, egged on by an angry Jehovah, grew unaccountably ashamed of as they made their sorry way out of Eden.

"The nudes, says Gill, have been described as reflecting 'the artist's splendid sense of design, and the use of color and form,' and that may well be the case; what matters more to us is that they do honor to his randy old evergreen heart. The Café is a happier place for the relish with which he carried out the commission of the board of directors; his pinkly silken hamadryads instruct us by their wanton rompings in how far we have come from those dour Dutch burghers and buttoned-up Britishers of the seventeenth century.

"We are lucky to visit here on West Sixty-seventh Street, to find ourselves among artists and writers whom their fellow New Yorkers regard not with suspicion but with adulation."

In Elise, Poppy saw everything he idealized in a woman: intelligence, strength, talent, and hard work. She was slim and athletic. The summation of his statement thirteen years earlier when he was the sole judge of the first Miss America pageant.

"Beauty is strength."

With Elise as his favorite model, Poppy set out to counter the legacy of Comstock, which was still very much alive in American culture: the idea that the female body was the cause of lust that led to sin.

Knowing history explains why Poppy painted Mother the way he did in his World War II *I Am An American* poster. Having been the son of a pioneer woman, he thought of women as the mothers of our nation. He knew full well that without their strength of character, we would never have survived as a nation. He had seen it with his own eyes.

Through art, Poppy strove to elevate women to their rightful place, deserving of dignity and respect.

Not shame.

***

Poppy was so inspired by Mother's beauty that he continued to paint nudes of her after the Café des Artistes murals were done——filling his studio with her face and form. So much so that his wife Nancy finally told him, he could no longer paint "that woman' in our studio." At the time, Poppy was working on a self-portrait of him painting a nude of Mother.

He never finished it.

Although I don't know for sure, I suspect that Nancy's

protest was what prompted Poppy to secure the studio at 54 W. 74th Street, which became Poppy and Mother's love nest. A brisk six-and-a-half-block walk from the Hotel des Artistes, it also served as Poppy's daily exercise and adjunct office and art studio.

***

Out of the grim Depression years, Poppy had found his muse, and Mother had found her love of art and the love of her life. The man everyone called Poppy.

In one of the des Artistes murals, Mother is holding a finger to her lips as if to say, "Shhh. Don't tell anyone, but we're having fun."

Seven years later, I was born.

***

In 1993, Judy Goffman Cutler invited me to her 77th Street brownstone, off Fifth Avenue, halfway between the Frick and the Metropolitan Museums of Art. Judy began her career as an art dealer with Poppy's paintings, which were auctioned off after Nancy's death. When I met her, she already owned the largest collection of Maxfield Parrishes and Norman Rockwells in the world. They are all now on display at her magnificent mansion on

Belleview Avenue, in Newport, Rhode Island—The National Museum of American Illustration (NMAI)

After showing me the many paintings of Poppy's she had collected over the years, Judy said, "I have your portrait in my bedroom. Want to see it?"

Of course, I wanted to see it. So, I followed Judy upstairs. As I entered her bedroom, my attention was immediately drawn to the huge portrait prominently displayed across from Judy's massive empire bed. The painting was enormous—the kind of thing you only see in a museum like the Metropolitan. Memories long dormant returned. I remembered standing on the Giovanni Bologna table while Poppy painted. The black velvet hat with yellow satin lining, the organdy dress I was wearing, and the black patent leather shoes all popped back into memory. I even recognized the ornate Pancani frame Poppy had bought for it. As I stood there staring at it, I felt as if I were back in Mother's studio on 54 W. 74th Street.

"And over here," said Judy, interrupting my state of rapture, "Is Christy's painting of your mother, 'Nude with Cat.'"

"That's Winky!" I exclaimed, recognizing the black-

and-white cat curled up on Mother's naked stomach. Winky's eyes were as wide as saucers. I could almost hear him growl as if to say, "Enough posing. I want out." I told Judy why I recognized Winky. That Poppy had talked so much about that cat; I felt as if I had stroked the fur on his arched back and heard his purr as he rubbed against my leg. I even knew details about his life, all of which I shared with Judy. The way Winky scarfed down his cat food on the Spanish shawl spread over the grand piano. I even told her about the bronze bust of Mussolini next to where Poppy's wife served Winky his can of cat food. "Not that Poppy was a fascist sympathizer or anything like that," I assured Judy. "He hated fascism, but he and Il Duce would sing Stephen Foster songs together while Poppy painted his portrait. Apparently, they got along great. Lots of laughs. But that was before the war. When Poppy and Nancy's visit came to an end, Mussolini gave Poppy a bust of himself in memory of the good times they had together."

Judy laughed. "Poppy," she said, repeating the nickname everyone used when referring to this affable artist who was loved by all.

Returning to Poppy's nude of Mother, I did a double-take. Mother was reclining with her arms up as if stretching after having just awakened from a pleasant nap. Unlike Poppy's Café des Artistes murals, this was different. The seductive look in Mother's eyes made me uneasy.

Then I saw the date at the bottom of the painting.

1925? I did the math in my head. *Mother was born in 1912. She would have been thirteen?*

I was shaken by this troubling possibility that Mother...

But wait. If that were so, Winky would have had to have been thirty years old in that picture.

Feeling uncomfortable and confused, I shared my concern with Judy. "Winky was no longer alive when Poppy told me those stories about him. Something's wrong with this picture."

"Besides," I told Judy, "In the photographs I have of Mother when she was twelve and thirteen, she had a bowl haircut with bangs and looked like Tom Sawyer in overalls."

The date puzzled me for years. Even made me feel queasy.

Only recently did someone solve the mystery.

My friend, James Head, Esquire—a trust lawyer in the D.C. area—told me that *Nude with Cat* was painted on Claessens (Belgian canvas), which Poppy didn't start using until the 1930s. Mr. Head also explained that Poppy's threes often look like twos.

It's true. Poppy had terrible handwriting. Mother was one of the few people who could decipher it. I still can't.

So, the date on *Nude With Cat* had to be 1935, which means it was painted two years <u>after</u> the murals in the Café des Artistes, and the way Mother looked matched up with the way she looked in the murals.

Last I heard, *Nude With Cat* was hanging over the fireplace in the Howard Chandler Christy Drawing Room of Vanderbilt Hall in Newport, Rhode Island. Below it, carved in big letters on the white marble mantel, is Mother's name: "ELISE."

By 1935, something was definitely going on between Poppy and Mother.

As Poppy used to say, "The cat was out of the bag."

CHAPTER SIX

Sidekick

"Beauty is exuberance."

- William Blake

Four years before my birth——when Mother was twenty-three——Poppy publicly declared her to be one of the most beautiful women in the world. The title of the article in which Poppy made his claim was *"WHO Are the Beauties of Today?"* The article appeared in the June 1935 issue of Movie Classics Magazine and was subtitled: "HOWARD CHANDLER CHRISTY, America's foremost illustrator, portrait painter and judge of feminine pulchritude, selects ten." The author, B. F. Wilson, interviewed Poppy in his

Hotel des Artistes studio. He began with an introduction of Poppy that would have made any artist glow with pride.

"Howard Chandler Christy has been painting beautiful women ever since he began his famous career as an illustrator and portrait painter. He has seen all the great beauties of the past forty years. He has known them all. He has painted them all... He has painted hundreds of nationally famous posters featuring beautiful girls... For five years, he picked 'Miss America.'

And at his studio in the Hotel des Artistes in New York, surrounded by life-size portraits of gorgeous women, he told me:

"There are no great beauties today. If I thought for a week, I couldn't name a half dozen women who are what we used to call 'raving beauties' —and neither could you. Beauty has become a commodity, more than a quality, to the extent that no individuals stand out."

Poppy went on to explain,*"...[F]amous beauties of the past fulfilled a need that made the world brighter, happier—a more desirable place to live in. They were legends; and around them, men spun dreams."*

"His keen blue eyes twinkled merrily," states Wilson.

"He ran an impatient hand through his shock of his snow-white hair and said: 'Perhaps it's the movies that have done it. I don't know. But most of the girls who are stars look alike to me. I can hardly tell one from another."

Poppy then named eight women he considered beautiful and gave his reasons for naming each one: Mary Pickford, Whitney Bourne, Marion Davis, Barbara Hutton Mdivani, Mrs. Harrison Williams, Doris Duke Cromwell, Elisabeth Bergner, and Claudette Colbert.

And the next thing he said should make women today think twice before electing to get plastic surgery:

"You don't have to have perfect features to be a great beauty,"

Poppy said, giving Elisabeth Bergner as an example.

"'The most beautiful woman on the New York stage today has, in reality, a plain, almost homely face. Her name is Elisabeth Bergner, and I defy anyone to witness her acting without feeling that he is looking at the most radiant, the most vibrant, the loveliest female he has ever seen.' He [Christy] got up from his chair and went over to the telephone. 'I'm going to have you meet a young girl who has the requirements for beauty,' he said. 'She is only nineteen, and her face is unusual. She is my model—you must have

Shipment Summary

Return to:
Lulu.com

P.O. Box 12018
Durham, NC27709
United States

Received by:
Holly Longuski

277 White Street
Combined Book Exhibit
Buchanan, NY10511
United States

Shipment Date : 02/19/2024
Order Number : 18694951-1.1
Ship Method : fedex overnight

QTY	Item ID	Item Description	Pages
		Holly Longuski (Cody Baker)	570

seen her on the President's Birthday Ball poster. Her name is Elise Ford, and she lives in this building with her father and mother."

The article went on to say that Poppy called the number, and Elise said she would be right over.

"Mr. Christy went back to his seat and filled his pipe. A fox terrier and a Siamese cat played running games up and down the length of the studio. He watched their antics."

Wilson continued by describing Mother as she walked in:

"The door opened, and a girl walked into the room. She was tall, slim, and lovely. Her black hair was caught back and revealed two small ears. A cluster of short curls graced the slim nape of her neck. Her eyes were huge and almost as dark as her hair."

I was surprised by the "black" hair. Mother had brown hair. Maybe she had dyed it.

"'This is Elise,' said Mr. Christy in introduction. "She is really an unusual type. How much do you think she weighs?"

"I looked at the trim, boyish figure. About one

hundred and two pounds, I guessed."

"She weighs one hundred and thirty pounds," said Mr. Christy. "She's all bone and muscle, and yet see how slender her ankles and wrists are. She is a fine swimmer, a great little athlete. Yesterday she walked nine miles in the country 'to get a breath of air,' she said, and she has won eight cups and medals for excellence in her studies, and athletic competitions. She is learning how to be an artist, and has no desire to go in the movies. She wants to paint."

"How tall are you, Miss Ford?" I asked.

"Five feet, six and three-quarter inches," she answered. Her voice was low and charming.

"With my shoes on, five feet, eight inches," she added.

"Have you ever done any screenwork?"

'Oh, yes,' she answered indifferently.

'I have been in several short features for different film companies—modeling clothes and things like that. Then I was in a news picture with Mrs. Roosevelt that we made for the President's Birthday Ball. I liked that,' she said naively. "Some of the companies have made tests of me, and I've had some offers—but I don't want to go into pictures. I'd rather learn how to draw."

Mother left to get a photograph of herself for the article. Meanwhile, the interview with Poppy continued.

"You see how unusual she is, don't you?' asked Mr. Christy. 'She has something more than just a beautiful face and body. She has sincerity. Intelligence. Ambition. And a decided talent. I think she will make good as an artist. Her sketches are remarkable for a beginner."

"On the high walls [of Poppy's studio], there were several unusually beautiful portraits of the same model. The face was lovely with its purity of line and delicately cut features. She was tall and blond. I kept finding my eyes attracted to the portraits. Mr. Christy, noticing, said, 'She is one of the beauties of today on any Christy list."

"What is her name?" I asked.

"He smiled. 'Mrs. Howard Chandler Christy.'

In Poppy's portrait of his wife, Nancy, were her two Irish wolf hounds that she used to take running in Central Park alongside their limousine.

"On my way out," said Wilson, he [Mr. Christy] showed me the hotel dining room whose walls glow with life-size figures from his brush—a room that has created a furor in New York because of its beauty. He turned to me and said with a laugh:

"When I brought Will Rogers in to show him this room, he looked all around very carefully without saying a word. Finally, he scratched his head and grunted: 'Well, Howard,' he said, 'you don't have to go out to Hollywood. You've got it all right here.'"

Wilson claimed that, in 1932, Christy's "life-size figures" in the Café des Artistes prompted a New York furor, making Poppy's effort to increase business in the Café during the Depression a screaming success. Most of the nudes on the murals capture Mother's unique features, which made it impossible for Wilson to ignore——yet Wilson never mentioned it in his article.

Why?

Something else Wilson chose not to mention was the odd photograph Nancy presented to Wilson to include in his article. In it, Nancy is dressed in a nun's habit as if she were Saint Agnes, the patron saint of chastity. Not only is she wearing a black wimple, but her eyes are rolled toward heaven as if to proclaim that she, like Saint Agnes, would prefer death to sex.

In Wilson's article, Poppy and Mother both lied about their ages. Mother wasn't nineteen. She was twenty-three.

In those days, an unmarried woman of twenty-three was considered an *"old maid."* Either she was trying to avoid this label or perhaps another less flattering one, considering all the nudes for which she had posed.

This wasn't the only time Mother lied about her age by declaring herself younger. As a child, I remember her gleefully stating she was *"27+"* on her driver's license and any other document presumptuous enough to ask personal questions.

Mother was twenty-seven when I was born. I wonder now, did she see my birth as the end of her life? Is that why twenty-seven was the oldest age she would admit to?

As for Poppy, he lopped off three years for Wilson's article in an attempt to narrow the yawning forty-year gap between him and his pretty, young model.

***

Aside from their love of art, Poppy and Mother were as different as a redwood is to a red rose. Poppy's lineage was straight out of American history. Born in a log cabin, he was the seventh-great-grandchild of Myles Standish and John Alden of Mayflower fame through the marriage of their great-grandchildren, Joseph Chandler III and Elizabeth Delano. There was also a Sam Houston connection on Poppy's father's side, as documented by the *Society of Mayflower Descendants.* Poppy's father had fought in the Civil War on Lincoln's side.

By contrast, Mother's background is enigmatic—at least on her mother's side, and the changes of names and outright lies make them impossible to trace. Her family on both sides were newcomers to America. Her father, Carl T. Forsberg, was a swarthy, dark-haired son of Swedish immigrants who had a recorded genealogy all the way back to seventeenth Century Lapland. A self-taught naval engineer, he built boats that became and still are famous to New York weekend fishermen as the Viking Fleet. One of them is eighty feet long.

Mother's mother, Sophie Louise Maxmann, was the daughter of immigrants from Saxony, now called Dresden. When Mother's grandmother and great-grandmother left Saxony, it was the center of European culture, home of Meissen porcelain, great libraries, and academies of art and music. Its Baroque and Rococo architecture are now mere echoes of past splendor. Royal palaces and a promenade along the river Elbe called Bruhl Terrace Royal and a wide boulevard lined with majestic statues of prancing horses testify to a once-glorious past before it was bombed into senseless ruin by the Allies during World War II.

But World War II was not what drove Mother's family out of Dresden. Of the real reason, Mother was silent, and the changes of names makes it impossible to trace a single one of them.

Despite the gap between their ages and the disparity in their pedigrees, Mother and Poppy had one thing in common. An exuberant love of life and a driving need to celebrate it through art.

Two years before I was born, on December 13, 1937, Mother wrote Poppy a letter. He was in Washington, D.C., fighting to get a bill passed that would commission him to paint the *"Signing of the Constitution."* This painting now hangs in the Congressional stairwell of the United States Capitol.

DEAREST "POPPY",

Closest to my heart—in fact—all that is in my heart is what you put there. You and painting. And an abundance of love of the beautiful, which you have showed me. And an intense desire to express it in painting, which you have taught me. And, no matter how you fix it, it all points and centers around you.

So, is it any wonder that I am completely at a loss without you?

Lots of love to you again,
Your Sidekick

* * *

The Great Depression lasted ten years, ending in 1939. The year I was born. It had been seven years since Poppy painted the Café des Artistes murals.

As for Mother, she would remain Poppy's "Sidekick" until his death in 1951.

CHAPTER SEVEN

The Ford Sisters

Of two sisters one is always the watcher, the other the dancer."

- Louise Glück, *Wild Iris*

Stories are what bind us together as a family. Without them, we lose the ability to understand one another. And without understanding, there can be no love. No empathy. No compassion.

Mother and I were strangers on the train of life. Everything I know about her past today, I learned from books after her death. Only now, equipped with the knowledge of the past, can I appreciate the forces that compelled her to remain silent.

Unlike Poppy, who loved telling stories about his family, mystery surrounded Mother's past and her relatives. It would take me half a century to unearth the intrigue that sealed her lips. And then only by accident.

****

Mother's sister Doris was the "ugly duckling" of the three girls. She was clumsy and not all that smart—or so I was told years later by Adel, the aging sister of Mother's brother, Carl. Although a year older than Elise, Doris showed no talent for song or dance. Probably this is why Nanna entered Elise alone in a New York drama school at the age of nine. A photo of Doris given to me in recent years confirms a gangly girl with bangs in a boxy haircut. According to Adel, "Everyone called her Dodo." But, unlike the Dodo bird, Doris had no intentions of fading out of sight or memory.

Then something happened no one saw coming.

Doris transformed herself from an ugly duckling into ravishing beauty with a sophisticated Park Avenue accent. Who would have thought?

Perhaps she acquired her sultry voice and appearance

by mimicking the appearance and mannerisms of movie stars she saw on film. Whatever it was that transformed Doris into the statuesque elegance of Joan Crawford and smoldering sensuality of Marilyn Monroe, it was a fairytale come true. One with which I was enthralled.

Whereas Mother was a gentle presence, Doris was loud and boisterous, a siren calling attention to herself. A head-turner even in the jaded city of New York, where world-famous people are as common as Jewish delis on the street. As a child, I was enthralled with Aunt Doris. Her boisterous flaunting of her beauty was far more exciting than Mother's angelic innocence. Doris turned heads. This made Doris a woman I wanted to emulate when I grew up.

How Doris ended up in New York, I don't know, but about twenty years ago, while visiting the Café des Artistes, a long-time resident of the Hotel surprised me by pointing to Doris's likeness on one of the nudes dancing around an oak tree. "They were known as 'The Ford Sisters,'" the woman told me. It was then that I remembered finding an old library card in Mother's file box with the name "Doris Ford" on it. At the time, I was confused. It was Mother who went by Elise Ford, a truncated version of Forsberg. Why would Doris use the same name when she had no acting career?

Years later, I would discover the answer to this question in a most unlikely place.

Doris and Mother became New Yorkers during the Depression years when the only way to survive was to land a big catch and marry him. Women went to college to get their Mrs.—not their MS or Ph.D. As my friend Bonnie, wife of a famous screenwriter, who lived during those times, said, "In those days, the only jobs available to women were, secretary, hairdresser, waitress, and WHORE."

On the other hand, as a little girl, I liked to think——if you were beautiful like Mother and Doris, you could aspire to marry a handsome prince and live happily ever after. I had no idea such women were called *"gold diggers."* Either way, whore or Cinderella, a girl just couldn't win.

Or could she?

From newspaper articles in which Mother and Doris appear, it appears Poppy showcased both Ford sisters for success. First in the Café des Artistes murals, then as the centerpiece on the only float in the biggest parade in American history—Franklin D. Roosevelt's NRA (National Reconstruction Act) Parade in 1933.

Over a million and a half people cheered the float with a standing Doris dressed as Miss Liberty that day. Draped in royal blue velvet, Doris held the torch of freedom aloft. Sitting regally beside her on a throne was Mother as Miss NRA clothed in a white satin gown. Both wore laurel wreaths of victory, like conquering goddesses out of Greek mythology. As their float came into view, mighty roars went up, and a blizzard of confetti rained down on their float from open skyscraper windows.

With the Café des Artistes murals and the NRA parade, both Ford Sisters were well on their way to being recognized as the most beautiful women in New York, if not the world. And that was something that couldn't have been missed by the discerning and——I might add—— leering eye of a European world-famous New York painter of nudes, Tadeusz (Tade) Styka (pronounced *Tah-day Stee-ka*).

How Tade approached Doris, I'll never know. But the two began to date.

Escapades followed between the foursome of Doris and Styka, Elise and Christy. One of which almost ended in tragedy. Years later, I would find an article about it written by none other than Mother.

Though gentle and withdrawn, when necessary, Mother could show the strength and courage of a lioness, a trait she was called upon to demonstrate one cloudy day on a desolate beach along the Atlantic coast.

On that day, Mother's Christian Science faith in mind-over-matter was put to the test by thunderous breakers rolling onto an abandoned shore.

Following is Mother's testimonial, which appeared in the *Christian Science Sentinel,* which I found years later in her grey tin file box. As was her custom to conceal her ever-increasing age, she excised the date from the article, so I can only guess that it must have been written about six years before I was born. Perhaps in 1933, after the Café des Artistes murals and the NRA parade lured Styka toward Doris like a hungry shark.

"It was a hazy, rainy day," wrote Mother, who was a strong swimmer and a certified lifeguard. *"And some relatives and friends decided to go for a swim."*

Notice the "some relatives and friends." Sounds innocent enough. But it wasn't.

Ambiguous, as usual, Mother's use of "relatives and friends" had to be Doris and her fiancé/lover——the world-famous European painter of voluptuous nudes——Tade

Styka. Undoubtedly, the other "friend" whose identity Mother also concealed was the other world-famous artist I would come to call Poppy.

As was her habit, Mother began the day by studying the Daily Christian Science Lesson to *"prepare the way in my consciousness to receive Divine Goodness."*

That morning I had carefully gone through the entire Lesson. When I went out to join my friends, I saw that the sea was very rough and was suddenly filled with fear for the moment on hearing my sister and her escort calling for help. They were out in the ocean, unable to swim or hold out longer against the swift current which was carrying them seaward in spite of their struggle. Mortal mind whispered that there was no one to help, no one being in sight and that I alone could not save them. This fear was overcome with a deep sense of love. Courage and faith came to me, because from God comes our strength and power. Running back over the sand I knocked at the door of the cottage for those who might help. Not waiting for response, I raced back to the water and swam through the breakers until I reached my sister and her friend calling words of encouragement as I approached. I took my sister's hand and swam vigorously, shouting to her companion to follow, but he seemed to have lost hope and become powerless. We backed-watered, I caught his hand and continued toward the beach and soon found that we could touch bottom and were safe. I thanked God, whose Divine Power had brought harmony… Lifeguards arriving on the scene expressed the opinion that my assistance had been most opportune, for with a few minutes delay, it would have been too late to help.

In gratitude for saving his and Doris's lives, Tade Styka gave Mother a topaz ring—the biggest I've ever seen. Cradled in 14-karat gold, it was about two inches long and one and a half inches wide. Mother wore the ring for the rest of her life. She is wearing it in the portrait Poppy painted of her in the blue satin gown, which now hangs in the Ohio Historical Society.

***

In 1933, the Depression was still in full swing. During this time, Nanna was acting as Mother's counselor. One of her admonitions to Mother, which I remember hearing was, *"The only way to keep a man from straying is to be everything he needs, including his secretary."* So, along with her voice and tenor sax lessons, her singing, dance, acting, and modeling career, Mother enrolled in business school. Before long, she was skilled in Gregg's shorthand and typing—two more skills she could add to her already-burgeoning repertoire.

There were things I adored in Mother. Her love of life, especially the out-of-doors. To her, the smell of dry leaves was cause for ecstasy. Like Poppy, she loved animals and treated them as family. We were never without a dog, which she treated with the utmost gentleness and care. When not focused on her work, she was as playful as a child. Full of fun. On snowy days in New York, Mother pulled a red sweater over our Dalmatian and hooked her up to a sled for a two-mile Iditarod along Central Park with me on the sled. Afterward, we'd stop at a corner drug store, climb up on a stool, and order Nestle's hot chocolate with whipped cream on top. I will never forget these good times with Mother on a drug store stool, the taste of hot chocolate and the scent of radiator heat warming us from the outside cold. We left the sled outside, but the dog got to come with us inside from the cold. No New Yorker would leave their dog outside shivering in the ice and snow.

At home, Mother was totally focused on whatever she was doing, which I selfishly felt was at my expense. I resented being left to myself and ignored like a dust bunny in the corner. We had no television, and the only toys I had were my marbles and a log cabin set. My main source of entertainment was drawing, which may be why I surprised myself and my teachers years later in my first life class at the Pasadena Art Center College of Design. Looking back now, I realize that must be why I'm never bored. I have my imagination.

Years later, I was able to look back and admire Mother for all those things that once annoyed me. Her industriousness, her tenacity, and dedication to creating something beautiful in life. She was always happiest while at work. She never complained. Never gossiped. She seemed to be perpetually in a good mood. Like the song in *Snow White and the Seven Dwarfs*, which was so popular on the radio at that time, Mother whistled while she worked. To this day, I can't hear that tune without thinking of Mother. *Just whistle while you work. . . So hum a merry tune. . . And soon, you'll find you're dancing to the tune./ When hearts are high, the time will fly./ So whistle while you work.*

That was Mother.

Happy and good-natured.

Mother was never showy in her attire. She had only

two suits. Both tailored and serious, which she dressed up with silk scarves and sometimes a fox fur stole for her art exhibits. Doris was exactly the opposite. An inch taller than Mother at 5'8, she wore turbans which—combined with high heels—made her tower above the New York crowd.

I would watch with amazement as Doris took two long strips of two-toned jersey and wrapped them around her head, twisting them into a peak in front. I suspect she learned this from her eccentric artist husband, Tade, who sometimes dressed up like Ali Baba. He once had a professional photograph taken of himself wearing eyeliner and lipstick as he stood on the steps of his palatial Isle of Capri villa. In the photograph, a plush carpet is spread over the steps beneath his "princely" feet, giving him the red-carpet treatment. Large tapestry pillows in exotic fabrics are flung here and there on the steps as if to emphasize the extravagance of his lifestyle— and libido. A huge ostrich plume standing erect from his turban gives him a Priapic air. There stands Tade in nothing but a loincloth, his bare chest and arms draped in jewelry. He resembles Yul Brynner in *The King and I*. Next to him, almost hidden by tropical vegetation, is a bronze bust of his equally famous father, Jan Styka.

✳✳✳

Unlike Tade, who was bald, Doris wore her turbans on bad-hair days when she was in too much of a rush to untangle the mane of auburn tresses that tumbled over her shoulders and down her back. On such days, she'd say in her breathy voice, "Oh, my hair. I must make an appointment at the Sherry Netherland Hotel salon."

Doris's turban made her look like a Sikh. Only she called it *"chic."*

As if the turban weren't enough to call attention to Doris's towering glamor, she pinned a large broach—designed by her famous artist husband—at its front. It was a leaping fish with golden scales inlaid with precious gems. An ogling turquoise eye seemed to jump out at you like a third eye as she swished by. With the broach as a permanent fixture in her couture, Doris always wore a matching choker—two strands of enormous chunky pearls mixed with equally chunky turquoise stones. Gay men would have loved Doris. Too bad they were all still in the closet. But I'm not so sure about Tade, as I would find out years later.

Doris looked as if she had sailed in on a magic carpet.

With or without her turban, she was a head-turner, even in Manhattan, a city of wealth and fame. Her racy laugh exuded animal magnetism, which I found fascinating. As sensual as Doris was, the word "sex" was never mentioned. As for four-letter words, so common today, they were non-existent in my world.

When it came to lipstick, Mother wore Revlon's *Cherries in the Snow*, whereas Doris wore *Love That Red*, which she slathered over her lipline. Joan Crawford's lips were another one of Doris's trademarks. In fact, Doris's resemblance to Hollywood's most glamorous movie star— especially when she wore her turban——might have been what made people turn and look.

Every time Mother snapped her picture, Doris would thrust her head forward, part her lips and do a Marilyn Monroe pose as if in the throes of orgasm. That was Doris. Tall and glamorous, carefree and vivacious. And to me, very mysterious.

Mother was demure and withdrawn, happy to fade into the background. By contrast, Doris was out there. She upstaged Mother with her antics, and I loved every minute of it. I'd watch her with studied concentration. Her self-assertiveness, her lusty laugh. She was as enthralling as a movie star on widescreen.

***

Like Poppy, Tade Styka was a portrait artist and painter of nudes. However, that's where the similarity ended. Whereas Poppy painted nudes, Tade painted naked women. Whereas Poppy's nudes were engaged in innocent fun, Tade's naked girls were voluptuous, seductive, and carnal.

Doris and Tade lived in two separate apartments at 36 Central Park South, next to the Plaza Hotel. Tade's two-story art studio was on the same floor just down the hall. Stepping into Tade's place was to sink into cushy white wall-to-wall carpeting. A balcony looked down at the horse-drawn carriages across the street from the Plaza and the lake in Central Park. Doris's apartment was small, carpeted in chintzy gold shag with a view of a fire escape. The only thing remotely elegant was a mirrored bedroom wall which miraculously enlarged the whole room.

Like Mother, Doris was fun-loving, always cheerful, and never angry. Unlike Mother, Doris never worked a day in her life, as far as I could tell. At home, she seemed to while away the hours dressed in a see-through negligée doing nothing other than typing an occasional letter to the recluse copper heiress Huguette Clark who lived a few blocks down Fifth Avenue. Doris had met Huguette through Tade, who was teaching her art at his studio. At her death, it was found that Huguette had left Doris's daughter Wanda 60 million dollars in her will.

Mother could be as distant as the planets silently floating overhead and as mesmerizing as the spatial sounds in the Hayden Planetarium. Her dreamy look and soft brown eyes contributed to her mystique, which left me feeling like I could never be a part of her world.

As different as they were, Doris and Mother were the same when it came to secrets.

They both lived by a code of silence.

***

While Doris enjoyed a life of leisure with trips to Europe on the Queen Mary and long stays at Tade's villa in Capri, Mother was working hard to become a successful artist while raising me—— the brat who sometimes tipped the studio with toilet paper to get attention. My resentment toward my mother for keeping what I knew was a secret about me only grew as I got older.

For first grade, Mother enrolled me in Broadway's

Professional Children's School, which was literally packed with talent. It was easy to spot the kids in the longest-playing Broadway hit in history——*Life With Father*. Their dyed orange hair identified them as belonging to "Father."

I developed a crush on one of them. Dean was twice my age and never even glanced my way. Still, my heart throbbed every time I saw him.

In art class, Mr. Berkowitz had us draw a picture. Considering my drawing talent proof of some vague relationship to Howard Chandler Christy, I was eager to prove my skills. When finished, my picture was of the boy next to me—which I thought was a pretty good likeness. We all sat quietly while Mr. Berkowitz strolled up and down the aisles scrutinizing everyone's work.

Eagerly I awaited the praise that would prove my link to Howard Chandler Christy the way Dean's orange hair linked him to *Father*.

Eyeing my picture, Mr. Berkowitz snatched it from my desk and held it up for the class to see. I held my breath—my identity at stake.

"This is NOT art," barked Mr. Berkowitz as he waved my picture before the class. He then dropped it back on my desk, where it slid to the floor.

I was mortified.

"This is what I want," he said, snatching up a boy's drawing and holding it up.

It looked like a temper tantrum on paper.

"This," said Berkowitz, "has passion."

That evening, I told Poppy what happened.

All I remember after that is Poppy's back as he stormed down the school hallway like a mad bull, with me racing behind him, trying to keep up. He burst into the Principal's office. BLAM and slammed his fist on the counter. I couldn't see over the counter, but I heard him bellow, "I'm taking Holly out of this school. You've got a goddam Communist teaching art."

Yes, it was the McCarthy era, but there was some truth to the Communists' effort to corrupt our culture through art. In fact, most modern artists were card-carrying Communists. To Poppy and Mother, art was like religion. It was supposed to uplift, inspire and make us more human. Beauty does have a reassuring effect that releases one's imagination to do better in life.

That was the end of Professional Children's School on

Broadway.

The next thing I remember is being introduced to the teachers at Daycroft School in Stamford, Connecticut. I recall a large sunny room with French doors while hearing myself introduced to a little girl my age named Felice, who had big smiling teeth.

I was being sent away. And I hated it.

All because of modern art.

Poppy hated modern art as much as he hated billboards along the highway. Although his landscapes were Impressionist, he disdained vulgarity and what he viewed as contempt for women and life itself which appalled him about Picasso's "Peeing Woman" and Salvador Dali's severed penises and breasts. As for Salvador Dali, I remember hearing Poppy say, "If I had thoughts like that. I sure as hell wouldn't want anyone to know it."

To Poppy, modern art was an expression of contempt for humanity and for life itself. "There are no sharp edges in Nature, he would say. These pictures are taking us somewhere I don't want to go." He saw modern art as a declaration of war on human sanity and decency. Picasso, who was a card-carrying Communist, openly admitted that he used art as a weapon, and, as I would find out years later, Mussolini used Futurism to coarsen culture starting with contempt for women——something Poppy had witnessed for himself in Italy's streets while there painting Mussolini's portrait.

Poppy could get really worked up over modern art. "If ever this nation is destroyed," he boomed, "it won't be by war. It'll be through our culture!"

Pleased with what they saw at Daycroft, Poppy and Mother enrolled me on the spot, and I would spend the rest of my school years in boarding school. I wouldn't get out until I turned sixteen.

* * *

Always feeling like I didn't fit in and painfully shy because of it, I threw a fit at the first mention of being sent away to school. To assuage my terror, Mother had me commute to Daycroft on the Boston Express for several months—maybe even a year. I can't remember. During that time, when I was at home, Mother tried hard to turn me into a lady, perhaps hoping it would give me more confidence. She put a book on my head and told me to glide when I walked. She taught me manners from Emily Post's etiquette book and told me to wear kid gloves and curtsy when shaking hands with adults. Especially men. It was Emily Post this-and-that, all of which instilled in me the superiority of adults as gods I had to pay homage to.

She took me to Riverside Drive for piano lessons with a teacher whose husband was a Philharmonic conductor. I rebelled at practicing for hours on our Steinway and became all the more stubborn after the teacher rapped my hands with a ruler. Intent on turning me into an admired virtuoso, Mother wouldn't give up. She carted me off to Julliard, from which I was promptly ejected. Mother remained determined. Realizing I would never be a pianist extraordinaire, she scoured antique stores for a Stradivarius violin as if, by magic, a Stradivarius might turn me into a Fritz Kreisler. None being found, she bought me an ordinary violin and entered me in the Diller-Quaile School of Music, near where we lived. While I screeched away, Mother practiced her do-re-mi's in a class next door.

"Why can't I take dancing lessons?" I asked one night as we walked home from Doris's place.

"Such a hard life," Mother mused as if remembering her own past.

So, I contented myself by dancing around the studio to music on the radio—that and drawing pictures. As much as Mother loved to paint, she gave me no encouragement when it came to art. Perhaps she saw an increasing trend toward modern art, the painters of which were drug addicts and alcoholics living in what was then sleazy Greenwich Village, which was at that time a hotbed of communism. It was becoming clear to Mother that to make a living at art—let alone become a famous artist—you had to be male.

Looking back, I'm glad Mother discouraged me from pursuing art.

The world was changing. Agents had inculcated the art world, making themselves rich by convincing the public what was and what wasn't "art." Like the Nigerian Prince who promises to make you rich, many people fell for it. In so doing, appreciation for the kind of art Mother and Poppy saw as a celebration of life was overrun by drips of paint and angry splashes. And, to survive in the art world, you must have appreciators. To succeed in this new culture, you had to look and act crazy like a clown. Somehow that gave people the idea that you were other-worldly.

If Mother was disappointed in my musical failures, she didn't express it. She wasn't one to criticize, berate or use harsh words. She simply gave up.

Failing to direct my interests in a more cultured direction, Mother settled for a professional photograph of me instead. In it, I am wearing a pink taffeta dress with a white lace collar. My long, dark braids are looped up and tied with pink ribbons. In my lap, I am cradling a violin.

I refused to smile for the picture, which gave me the appearance of a child prodigy deep in thought.

Ultimately, Mother's efforts to turn me into a princess who would one day find my prince failed miserably.

CHAPTER EIGHT

A Force of Nature

How inappropriate to call this planet Earth when clearly it is Ocean.

- Sir Arthur C. Clark, 1917-2008
British Sci-Fi author and inventor
Geologica Ultraiectina, 1957

I must have been about two or three when I remember playing in the rocky shallows of the Housatonic River. At the time, Poppy and Mother were looking for a good spot to paint. I remember Poppy coming over to check on me. Shocked by what he saw, he swooped me up in my sopping wet underpants and shouted, "God dammit all to hell! Look, Kid!" he called to Mother. "Somebody upstream is polluting the river." That's when I saw the oily green and yellow swirls pooling around the rocks where I was playing.

"Damn fools!" thundered Poppy, "Don't they know? Water is life!"

To Poppy, life was beauty, and water was what sustained the health and beauty in life. Consequently, he headed for water to paint, which made it imperative that I know how to swim. I have a home movie of Poppy teaching me to swim in the Chesapeake Bay when I was six months old, which may be why I don't remember learning. It seems as if I always knew.

***

Our first summer retreat was Captain Allen's Clam House in Westport, Connecticut. I must have been about four. What had once been a restaurant, the Clam House, was built on stilts over a saltwater inlet. Our front porch was a dock connecting Captain Allen's house on the right to our house, which was now an abandoned restaurant on the left. Every morning, I bounded out onto the dock, eager to greet the day by feeling the dock's rough planks warmed by the sun beneath my bare feet. Inhaling the smell of brine from the marsh, I was thrilled by the cry of seagulls in the air, the hypnotic sloshing of water against the dock, and the creaking of row boats moored to posts. It was a world filled with the sights and sounds of artistic beauty.

There was no such thing as television back then. Nor were there roaring speed boats riling the water and creating the threat of danger. Nor was there the roar of traffic or the pounding beat of loud, jarring music—just the still, sweet strains of Nature. To me, it was a love song.

The slow melodic creak of oars alerted me to Captain Allen's return, and I'd jump down onto the clam boxes to greet him as he pulled in his oars, floated in, and moored his rowboat to the dock. His boat was always loaded with waterlogged grey baskets full of clams, which he heaved onto the dock.

During those summers, a partially submerged clam box was my playpen. In the corner of one end, prehistoric horseshoe crabs with dull grey eyes climbed clumsily over themselves as they tried to get away from me as I jumped in. They looked like army helmets with creepy-crawly orange legs inside. I called the biggest one Snooky. I was sure he loved me as much as I loved him. Fearlessly I would wade out to him, pick him up by his spiked tail, and haul him into the house, where he'd scare the dog by clopping across the floor using all his legs. At the sight of this strange creature, Cutie, our little Fox Terrier, would run and hide.

In the evening, Mother and Poppy, and I would sit out on the dock in wicker chairs and feast on steamed clams dipped in melted butter. On moonlit nights, the ripples glittered like diamonds as the evening breeze swept in from the sound.

When it was time for me to go to bed, it was the lapping of water that lulled me to sleep.

***

"How much longer?" I pined from Poppy's knee as I leaned out the window of our Studebaker, eager to catch the first glimpse of the ocean blue beyond the dunes. "There it is!" I screamed at the first glimpse of the Atlantic stretching all the way to the horizon. The crack of thunderous breakers filled me with excitement as they rolled up to shore in a foaming fury.

I was the first one out of the car. Already in my bathing suit, I raced ahead as Mother and Poppy hauled blankets, towels, a beach umbrella, and a picnic basket to a sheltered spot beside a grassy dune. How I loved the smell of cocoa butter melting in the heat as Mother slathered it over my back and shoulders before letting me loose to dig in the sand. Pounding surf. Hot sun on my back. The smell of salt water. It was euphoric.

With Poppy, I fell in love with life.

It was a different world in 1940. There were over three billion fewer people on this Earth. The beaches were not crowded. Nor were there any towering glass-and-steel resort hotels to block you from entering private beaches for paying visitors only—just miles of openness and wind-swept sandy dunes.

Having rescued Tade and Doris from a riptide, Mother was aware of the dangers lurking in those breakers looming in the distance. Yet she allowed Poppy to take me by the hand and lead me into the Atlantic's deep blue swells. Perhaps it was her Christian Science faith in the protection of Divine Love. Or maybe it was her confidence in her life-guarding skills that allowed Poppy to coax me into those ominous waves.

I hung back as Poppy plunged headfirst into the churning water barreling toward him. It fizzled and washed up around my legs, leaving a momentary rim of foam along the beach. Meanwhile, Poppy plunged deeper and deeper into the dark watery abyss as wave after wave pummeled his seventy-something-year-old chest.

"Come on, Holly, be a sport," he called, looking back at me over his shoulder.

Surely, he didn't expect me to wade beyond all that churning froth swishing around my legs. As the wave pulled back, feeling its pull, I bolted for the beach, afraid it would drag me out to sea.

Beyond Poppy, all I could see were dark mounting swells. Each seemingly higher than the last. Curling over at the top, they crashed with the crack of thunder. Poppy's white head would disappear into their cavernous curl. Then pop out on the other side.

How did he do it?

"Come on, Holly," he called from way out in the blue.

Wading in up to my waist, the pull grew stronger. I wanted to turn back, but Poppy urged me on.

"Come on, Holly, if I can do it, you can too."

It never occurred to me that Poppy might have only a few years left on Earth. To me, he was as eternal as the sea. Filled with the love of life, he was my personal sun shining down on me. My summer happiness.

I followed Poppy until my feet lost contact with the

sandy bottom.

Dog-paddling to keep from sinking, I felt the pull of a mighty force wrap around me.

"Never fight a riptide," Poppy warned as the tide pulled me toward him. "The current's too strong. Always swim with the current. Never against it. You gotta ease your way out." Many years later, it would occur to me that not swimming against the current was why he and Mother kept secrets. Although I didn't know it then, he was teaching me an important life lesson.

Riptide? I was about to turn back when I saw the spectral shape of a jellyfish pulsating next to me in the murky depths.

"Come on, Holly, be a sport," called Poppy as a giant swell mounted behind him.

"Wait," I cried as the wave loomed before me.

"Swim through it," yelled Poppy as it crested above my head. Then he disappeared through its dark crevasse. Too late to go back. I felt myself being sucked in. Too scared to do nothing, I ducked my head and swam through it. To my surprise, all I felt was a blip.

"We'll take the next one," said Poppy as we rose and

fell with the swells in the after-lull. "Now, when you see the curl, you swim like hell to the top before it breaks, or you'll be forced under and thrown around. If you can't make it to the top, swim through it."

The water rose like a mountain before us.

"We'll take this one," shouted Poppy as he swam for the monstrous wave rising before us. "Now! He shouted, "Swim to the top. Swim like hell!'"

I remember fighting to make it to the top of its curling lip. Turning to face the beach, I felt the wave lift me up in its watery arms and heave me forward. Looking down at the beach in the distance, I felt it arch beneath me with a powerful surge, then break. With a mighty crash, it rocketed me toward the beach on top of what felt like a watery barrel of rolling force and churning fury.

Never had I felt such a thrill.

After depositing me on the sandy shore, it ebbed back to sea, leaving me in its fizzling froth.

A tiny crab pushed out of the smooth wet sand and skittered sideways along the beach. Nearby, Poppy hauled himself out of a pile of seaweed and ambled back to Mother, who had been watching from the shade of our striped beach umbrella.

I continued body surfing all summer long. Sometimes I waited too long and got thrown head over heels by a wave, my head shoved into the sand. Once I even got caught in an undertow. As I felt myself being swept out to sea, I did what Poppy said. I swam with it and eased my way out, ending up far down the beach. The long walk back was far better than being swept out to sea.

Poppy had given me the gift of confidence.

And with confidence came freedom.

***

Poppy was my strength—the giver of all good. More than ever, I longed to call him Father.

But it was not to be. Like the ocean breakers, he was a force of nature. Nothing could turn him from his course.

CHAPTER NINE

The Aristocrats

"Our families are where we first learn about ourselves.
Healing the Shame That Binds You In"

- John Bradshaw

There was competition between Doris and Mother over which artist was greater: Styka or Christy? The rivalry was palpable whenever they got together. My-god-is-better-than-your-god was Doris's game. She bragged about her world-famous husband as if he were of Divine origin. She was always playing my Tadeusz Styka is greater than our Howard Chandler Christy. Like Moses and the Egyptian magicians, Styka's rod was bigger and longer (reaching all the way to Europe). Styka's rod could turn into a snake and gobble Poppy up.

Four years after I was born, Tade and Doris had a baby. They named her Wanda. At her baptism, copper heiress Huguette Clark—whose life story is told in the 2013 book *Empty Mansions*—made Wanda her godchild. With big dimples on both cheeks, Wanda was so adorable that Huegette left her $60 million dollars in her will which resulted in a highly publicized court battle and a sizeable reduction to just $3 million in the settlement.

***

I scarcely noticed Wanda until she turned six.

Then something happened that changed everything.

I was ten years old when Wanda pranced into Mother's studio and gave my already topsy-turvy world a spin. She waltzed past me, wearing a white fur coat and matching fur hat. I was sure it was ermine—the sort of thing I'd seen princesses wear in swashbuckling movies that Mother took me to see for a quarter in the many theaters that lined New York streets during the 40s and 50s.

I felt the chill of a dusting of snow from Doris's bulky mink as she brushed past me down the narrow hallway without so much as a hello. In fur that fell to her ankles, she looked like a Kodiak bear in stilettos. Doris loathed to be called "Aunt," so she was always just Doris to me.

In her arms was a wooden box that looked like a radio with a six-inch glass screen.

"What's that?" I asked.

As usual, she ignored me.

I was used to Doris snubbing me, which had the effect of making her that much more intriguing—a Goddess beyond my worldly reach—a star that sparkled so much brighter than Mother.

"Lee Lee, Oh, Leee Lee," squealed Doris in a departure from her usual Park Avenue accent. She sounded like she was calling one of her seven miniature white poodles, which, thankfully, she'd left at home as they would go potty on our rug.

"Come see what I brought!" said Doris with overly dramatic enthusiasm. "A television!" She plunked the brown wooden box on the Giovanni Bologna table and flung off her coat, burying the divan in fur.

I'd heard about televisions but had never seen one.

I peered into its small grey window.

Doris called to Wanda, who was still prancing around

the studio in her snow-white fur coat. "Wanda, dear. Come to Mommy. Let me help you take off your coat."

Wanda twirled round and round, showing off her new coat as her doting mother paced helplessly behind her. "Wanda dear. Please. Let Mommy take off your coat."

Unable to control Wanda, Doris laughed it off. "Oh, Lee Lee," she squealed, her voice reaching a high rasp. "Look! Isn't Wanda adorable?" Doris gave a little cry of delight. "Just look at those dimples."

Wanda had dimples, alright. Big dents on both cheeks, even when she wasn't smiling. Doris cupped her hands as if in prayer, her face contorting in reverence. "Oh, Lee Lee. Isn't she the image of Shirley Temple in those curls? I set her hair in rags for her television debut."

Wanda was on television? "When?" I piped up. But Doris was too enthralled with her darling Wanda to even acknowledge my existence.

"Lee Lee," said Doris, looking past me as if I were invisible, "I bought this television so we could watch Wanda's exhibit on Park Avenue. But now that it's over, we don't need it anymore."

Wanda? An artist? My attention turned to Wanda,

who was still twirling around the studio like a whirling dervish. *Wanda had an exhibit? On Park Avenue? She's only six! I'm ten, and I've never had an exhibit.*

I thought *Park-Bernet,* remembering the woman who accosted Poppy on the street with all that "You must be Howard Chandler Christy" stuff without ever looking at me. *Now Wanda? On Park Avenue? That BRAT.*

I imagined Wanda's chubby hands reaching into the Park-Bernet display window and replacing Poppy's landscape with *her* picture under the spotlight. I wanted to smack her right on her dimpled cheeks.

Doris glanced at Wanda and cooed, "My precious." Then she gave Mother a sidelong glance and said in a hushed voice, "Lee Lee, there are just too many shows on television unfit for delicate eyes and ears."

What? The implication was clear. Doris was giving Mother that naughty box because I wasn't as "delicate" or "precious" as her "adorable" Wanda.

Doris gave one of her gamy laughs, which implied she was in possession of some sort of forbidden fruit. Blinking lights went off in my head like the neon signs I'd seen on Broadway Adults Only marquees: "

"Oh Lee Lee," raved Doris, "I did so love watching *The Loretta Young Show*. Really, Lee Lee, you must see it! The way she swishes through the door in those luscious gowns." I didn't know it then, but Loretta Young had an illegitimate child with Clark Gable that she went to extremes to keep a secret lest her life be ruined by incrimination by the harsh judgement of the public.

Doris pirouetted to demonstrate how Loretta Young entered on the TV screen as her satin dress ballooned out like a parasol. "It's marvelous!" crooned Doris. "Simply marvelous!"

I don't remember Mother saying anything while all this was going on. Doris did most of the talking while Mother busied herself brewing a pot of coffee in our kitchenette. She then lifted the heavy lamp and spread a tablecloth over the Giovanni table.

Doris fell into Poppy's medieval throne next to the tapestry and prattled on and on about her talented cherub. Mother smiled in her quiet Mona Lisa way as she set cups and saucers on the table. Mother was like the morning fog—cool and hard to see through.

Other than Doris's flamboyant personality, no two sisters were more alike. They both worshiped two world-famous artists. But rivalry divided them into separate camps. I could feel the tension. I turned my reception to high as the competition mounted.

Like me, Wanda had grown up in an art studio, the only child of a world-famous artist. Unlike me, Wanda had a "Daddy." To make matters worse—for me, that is—Wanda was the proud bearer of her famous daddy's name: Tadeusz Styka. Tade for short. The man Mother had rescued from a riptide. Mother called him Toddy.

Tade was a Duke. This made Doris a Duchess, I suppose. At any rate, I sensed that Wanda was special. Not that I knew about her noble blood. I didn't. Not then, anyway. But the feeling was strong. Wanda was something I wasn't. She was *"amazing!"* and I was—well, nothing to brag about. More like something to be ashamed of, but I wasn't sure why.

Doris could boldly brag about Wanda's pedigree, which made Wanda privileged in a way I could never be.

Wanda's father was an aristocrat from a dynasty of European artists who consorted with royalty. The Styka fame began in the late 19th century with Tade's father, Jan (pronounced *Yahn*). Jan's reputation soared to artistic sainthood with his massively powerful works, *The*

Martyrdom of Christians in Nero's Circus, The Iliad, The Odyssey, and the *Crucifixion,* which is the largest framed painting on canvas in the world. One-hundred-ninety-five feet long and forty-five feet high. Today, this monumental panorama is still a big tourist attraction at Forest Lawn in Glendale, California. Several times a day, the lights dim in the auditorium built specifically to house it, and heavy curtains roll back to reveal the spectacle of Christ on the cross before 800 tiered seats. A spotlight moves from one scene to another as a speaker narrates the crucifixion story. Doris liked to brag that *she* was the one who brought the *Crucifixion* over from Europe to be showcased at Forest Lawn, where it remains today.

Doris always came well-armed with plenty to brag about. On top of it, her "precious" could do no wrong. Wanda was an aristocrat with distinguished European roots. The real thing. Not some worthless cur of unknown origin. And—on top of all that—she was adorable.

Doris tackled Wanda and wrestled the white fur coat and hat off her wriggling, giggling body. Having added one more fur to the heap on the divan, an exhausted Doris flopped back onto Poppy's throne next to the Archangel Gabriel. Meanwhile, Mother sliced the remaining lemon meringue pie Poppy had picked up at the bakery on our walk back from the Second Church of Christ Scientist, where Mother was a soloist. It was our custom on Sunday morning to walk down Central Park West to its big stone edifice on the corner of the same street where Poppy lived. After church was over, we'd walk down Sixty-Eighth Street (never Sixty-Seventh, where the Hotel des Artistes was) to a bakery on Columbus Avenue. There we picked up the lemon meringue pie. This was our Sunday ritual. Church and lemon meringue pie. I liked the meringue pie best.

While Mother poured coffee, I peeked into the six-inch window of the television. What was in there that was so bad for "delicate eyes and ears" but so titillating to grown-ups? I yearned to know the secrets of these gods.

Doris was like a mother bear when it came to shielding her precious little darling. Wanda was, after all, the offspring of a dynasty of pure genius. Her Uncle Adam, her father Tade, and her grandfather Jan had all achieved fame and fortune as European artists, more for their lecherous portrayal of naked women with pubic hair and big boobs than their serious portraits and religious works that made Popes and Cardinals, their benefactors.

Although Doris kept the lascivious fame of the men in her family under wraps, her asphyxiating airs of superiority were hard to ignore. Her presence sucked oxygen right out of the room.

I was never told how Doris met Tade, but it had to have been through Poppy's murals on the Café des Artistes walls for which they became known among prominent New Yorkers as "The Ford Sisters." Men of status were captivated by their charms.

My cousin Tom Leonard—retired Air Force Lieutenant Colonel—told me that Tade frequented expensive restaurants in search of beautiful women. I can see it now, Tade, with his fixated stare and European panache, propositioning women to pose for him nude.

"They always accepted," Tom told me. "Tade kept this up even after he was married to Doris. He must've been one horny bastard," Tom told me years later. "Gee, I musta seen at least sixty of those nudes with every detail painted in. I was just sixteen, and it would embarrass me when Dad and I helped Doris pack them up and take them to storage."

Tade and his brother Adam carried themselves with royal pride, and women found their European accents and deep voices irresistible.

Although both were world-renowned New York artists, Poppy and Tade were worlds apart when it came to background and upbringing. Poppy was a rustic American—the son of pioneers. A farm boy and former Rough Rider in the Spanish American War. Poppy was tough. He took up boxing and practiced with heavyweight champions. Unlike Tade, who preferred castles to cow dung and pastures, Poppy loved nothing better than being outdoors. Tade, on the other hand, brandished his aristocratic European heritage by strutting down Central Park South in white spats while wielding a gold-handled walking stick. An eccentric dandy, Toddy—as Mother called him——he even went so far as to powder his face white and don a foppish Victorian black top hat. Sometimes, he even wore lipstick.

I didn't have to know the details of the Styka dynasty to sense the importance of the Stykas and the unimportance of Poppy when it came to Doris. Whenever we were together, it was as if Poppy didn't exist. His name was never mentioned. Yet we all lived within walking distance. At 36 Central Park South, Doris and Wanda lived at the ritziest spot on Earth—next door to what is now Donald Trump's domain.

In spite of our close proximity, Doris never showed up when Poppy was there, and Poppy never went with us to visit Doris.

A chilly divide separated our two tribes, but it would take me until I was in my thirties to find out why.

"I want a piece of pie," cried Wanda rushing up to the table. "Yes, dear," said Doris scooping a piece onto her plate. "And dear, after you eat your pie, why don't you and Holly run along and play so Mommy and Lee Lee can talk."

That gave me a sinister idea. I would call Wanda's bluff. Prove her a fake. I knew how easy it was to fool the public when it came to art. I had entered a poster contest put on by my Christian Science Sunday school. Poppy drew it for me, and I won first prize. I wasn't about to be fooled by Wanda's shenanigans.

I watched Wanda jab her fork into the frothy white meringue and yellow custard. There was no question about who her father was. Unlike me, who looked like my Mother, Wanda was the mirror image of the great Tadeusz Styka. She even had his flared imperial nostrils. But yes, I could see a likeness to Shirley Temple, too, in all those curls and organdy frills. Wanda was everything a mother could be proud of.

As a child, I had no idea Doris might actually be jealous of Mother. Mother was, after all, the talented one. An accomplished artist and member of the Grand Central Gallery, she was a musician, dancer, soprano, former New York model, and actress. As far as Poppy was concerned, it was through his influence that Doris was Miss Anything in Roosevelt's National Reconstruction Act Parade.

Doris's only claim to fame was her husband. When she married Tade, she married into the Stykas cloistered priesthood. As a family, they were above everyone, beyond reproach.

Doris frequently bragged that Ignacy Jan Paderewski—celebrated New York composer, pianist, and former Prime Minister of Poland—was Tade's "best friend." The way she talked, you'd have thought Tade and Igy were lovers. Maybe so; for all I know, Tade's friendship with Paderewski may have had something to do with Tade's having been made a Duke. What I do know is that Doris felt the need to name-drop around Mother. At any rate, Tade was a man of great wealth exceeding anything he could have earned as an artist, which was already substantial. How he came into such wealth, I will never know. He was richer than Poppy. And Doris flaunted it.

Besides their use of translucent color and lifelike style, all three Stykas had a penchant for raw carnality. Poppy painted nudes while the Stykas painted naked women with big tits and bushy pubic hair—sometimes in the very act of making love. That sort of thing was too shocking for the times, but then, as European aristocrats, the Stykas were given the license to do—well, anything they wanted. Tade was the friend of Cardinals and the Pope. Something I would find out about much later in life.

As for Adam, he developed his own unique genre after touring the French colonies in Northern Africa. He was a master of sex in the sand with dirty, old men in turbans and voluptuous Arab women.

Recently I saw some of those paintings when a friend e-mailed me pictures of them. Both were vivid portrayals of giggling Arab women offering their ample breasts to grasping Bedouins. My friend expressed shock that Adam could have gotten away with painting such erotic pictures of naked women in Saudi Arabia, where the entire face and body of women are concealed beneath black veils.

However, in *Oriental Erotica,* a book I picked up at Barnes & Nobel, the pages are filled with Islamic pornography of the sort that cheapens the male-female sexual relationship. Some of the pictures are sadistic. According to that book, these paintings are on display in museums in Bagdad, Amman, Istanbul, Tehran, and the Metropolitan Museum of Art in New York. *"Love is my religion, and the religion of love is like no other,"* said the Islamic mystic and scholar Jalal al-Din Rumi (1207-1273).

Sexuality is central to Islam, at least in some sects. Apparently, this was a secret Adam penetrated in the Sahara.

***

Finished with her duties in the kitchen, Mother took her seat beside the Virgin Mary on our silk Flemish tapestry. Across from her, Doris dug into her enormous leather bag and produced a photograph. "Look, Lee Lee," she said, passing it across the table. "Here's a picture of Wanda on TV. Oh, Lee Lee. Isn't she amazing?" To Doris, everything was "Amazing!" or "Marvelous!" or "Wonderful!" But it made life exciting, and I loved it, always hoping those words could be directed toward me.

Mother smiled sweetly and nodded as she viewed the

photograph.

"Let me see," I said, moving in.

And there she was. Wanda smiling out from the television screen—dimples and all— with that mop of Shirley Temple curls as she held up a drawing that looked like pictures I'd seen in the Egyptian Art Exhibit in the Metropolitan Museum of Art.

"Lee Lee!" cried Doris. "She's a child prodigy. Just like her father. A genius. You know he painted that amazing portrait of his father when he was only twelve."

At that time in my life, I wasn't smart enough to ask, "If Tade was twelve when he painted his father, how come his father looked like the Ancient of Days with that long white beard when Tade was only twelve?" I just took Doris's word as gospel. Adults don't lie, do they?

The painting she was referring to was Tade's Rembrandt-like rendition of his father—Jan Styka. The last time I saw it was at Forest Lawn. It was hanging adjacent to Jan Styka's massive *Crucifixion*.

"I'll make more coffee," Mother said, smiling in graceful quietude as Doris continued to brag about her genius husband and his little offspring. "Amazing! Oh, Lee

Lee, isn't she amazing?"

"Let's go draw pictures," I said, remembering my wicked plan. Wanda finished her Sunday pie and followed me into my bedroom, but just before we disappeared behind a closed door, Doris puckered her big, red lips and threw her darling a kiss. "Muuaah! My precious." Doris shook her head in ecstasy. "My angel. Mommy's treasure."

Why wasn't I someone's treasure? Was it because I was four years older and not as cute? Or was it because I hadn't had an exhibit at the Parke-Bernet?

Inside my bedroom, Wanda and I plopped down on the floor, and I handed her a pad and crayon. "Now, let's see you draw a picture like you did for your exhibit."

Wanda looked down at the pad in her hand, then put the crayon back in the box. I grinned triumphantly. "Here, I'll draw a picture first," I said and drew Mother wearing a halo and wings.

Wanda cheered and clapped her hands in glee. "Yes, yes! Lee Lee is such an angel."

"Now it's your turn," I said.

Wanda dug around in the box as if looking for a lost

crayon. I was sure she was stalling for time to stave off my discovery of her shameful trick. Finally, she found what she was looking for. Royal purple. With it, she drew an Egyptian-like line drawing. A profile of a woman, highly stylized, with Egyptian eyes. It looked like Nefertiti. To this day, I still have Wanda's drawing along with the photo of Wanda's beaming face on a television screen.

My spirit fizzled like a deflating helium balloon.

Not only was Wanda cuter, she could draw better. She was everything Doris was so proud of. A genius. Just like her father.

I wanted to forever rid myself of Wanda and her superior birthright.

While Mother and Doris chatted over coffee, I plotted Wanda's downfall as we innocently drew pictures in the other room.

An hour later, I could hear Doris preparing to leave as she threw on her fur coat.

"Wanda dear. Time to go. Come let Mommy help you on with your coat."

"No!" wailed Wanda. "I don't want to go home."

"Wanda, darling. We must go. *Now.*"

"No," boohooed Wanda. "I want to stay overnight!"

I heard the click of Doris's stilettos coming toward us. Wanda shrieked as Doris swooped down on her trying to stuff Wanda's flailing arms through her coat sleeves. Wanda kicked and screamed in a flurry of fur.

"No!" sobbed Wanda throwing her coat on the floor. Her adorable face turned red hot with rage. Breathing hard from the struggle, Wanda glared up at her mother.

A perverse kind of pleasure crept over me as Doris retreated back to the kitchen with a sigh of defeat. Ah, but it made me feel grand.

I had the power to incite rebellion.

I quickly devised a plan to sully Wanda's glowing image. I'd show Doris, once and for all, that Wanda wasn't the precious little darling her mother thought she was.

I leaned in close to Wanda and whispered, "Tell her, 'God damn it all to hell! I'm not going." They were the worst curse words I could muster. Something Poppy reserved for Communists and modern artists, oh yes, and polluted rivers and those awful billboards that marred "God's beautiful landscapes." If there were any words worse, I didn't know them. And, if I could get Wanda to say them, surely it would permanently smear her image.

Wanda's bawling snuffled to a stop. Her lower lip trembled as she contemplated the bad words. Then her eyes grew large and round with surprised revelation.

"Wanda!" Doris's voice had grown more impatient as she bustled toward us.

"Go ahead, say it," I goaded, hardly able to believe I was capable of such evil. "You'll see, she'll leave us alone. Then you can stay overnight."

"It'll be curtains for me," snuffled Wanda, lower lip protruding.

The word "curtains" conjured up visions of Wanda disappearing behind a big, heavy curtain as it closed with a thud—the way it did when the *Rockettes'* show at Radio City Music Hall was over. Made me want to gloat.

"Wanda, don't be naughty!" called Doris, exasperated as she stood in the doorway. "Did you hear me? We're going. Now!" Wanda burst into another flood of tears as a flustered Doris rushed in and wrestled Wanda's arms into her white princess coat. Doris then pulled the fur hat over Wanda's violently twisting head. In a fit of fury, her curls in a snarl, Wanda yanked it off. Doris forced it back over Wanda's head, plastering her-once springy Shirley Temple ringlets to Wanda's sweaty, red face. Rumpled and wailing with her hat askew, Wanda struggled to twist herself free as Doris dragged her out the door and down the hall toward the elevator.

Not a single door in the building hallway opened that night. Not even a crack.

You would have thought the building was vacant.

Wanda's ear-piercing screams for help were suddenly silenced as the elevator door closed, only to resume again moments later, six stories down, as Doris dragged Wanda around the corner to Columbus Avenue.

Muffled noise of traffic in heavy snow only served to increase the decibels of Wanda's howls. I scrambled to the window to watch Doris hail a yellow cab while clinging to her struggling "precious."

The cab pulled away, and all went quiet in the glow of the city lights through the gently falling snow.

Minutes later, the phone rang.

From where I was playing, I could hear Doris's frantic voice as Mother held the receiver away from her ear. "No!"

Mother exclaimed. "Are you sure?"

I ran for cover.

Mother hung up the phone and tore after me.

Never had I seen her so angry.

I dove under my bed for safety. I remember seeing the bristle side of a hairbrush swinging wildly back and forth, just missing me as I scrunched up against the wall. Then Mother got down on all fours and hauled me out.

What happened next comes to me in flashes.

I see the inside of the bathroom sink—ivory soap in Mother's firm grip. I open my mouth to scream. My head in a hammerlock, Mother forces the soap between my teeth. Pieces of soap break off in my mouth and stick to my teeth.

I'll always remember the taste of that Ivory Soap, "99 and 44/100s % pure."

"Doris says she's never letting you play with Wanda again," shouted Mother. "She says you're a bad influence!"

That night, I threw a temper tantrum. I screamed so loud everyone in the building must have heard. I remember Mother's weary face as she chanted her

Christian Science mantra. You'd have thought she was exorcizing demons. "That's not my little Holly. That's Error speaking. And Error is Nothing!" She closed her eyes tight and repeated, "Error is Nothing. Error is Nothing."

"I'm *NOT* Nothing," I screamed till my throat was raw.

Squeezing her eyelids shut, Mother reassured herself of Mary Baker Eddy's Truth about the Omnipresence of God in everyone—everywhere. "You are God's Perfect Child, God's Perfect Child, God's Perfect Child."

All the rage I'd ever felt toward Mother exploded. "I'm not God's Perfect Child!" I screamed. "I'm not God's Perfect Child! I'm not God's Perfect Child!"

In a moment of rage, what I had instinctively had known from the beginning came gushing out. God was not my father, as Mother had said. I was what Mother's Christian Science called, "Error," which Mother's Christian Science denied as "Nothing."

Mother

Elise Ford doing Interview with Admiral Richard Byrd,
first to fly his Fokker tri-motor plane over the North
Pole on May 9, 1926

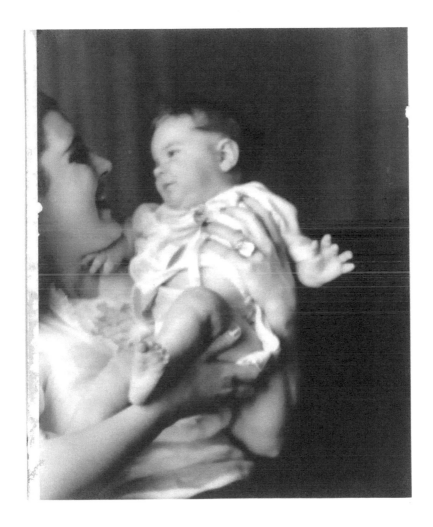

Elise Ford and baby Holly

Poppy playing harmonica for Holly on the beach

Holly in boys bathing suit playing inside clam box at
Captain Allen's Clam House

Holly holding Lamkins in Vermont

Poppy and Holly at her grandparents' house

1936 Sketch of Elise to "My Side Kick"

Howard Chandler Christy with palette and paintbrush

Poppy with wild, white hair. Photo signed to Elise and
Holly by "HCC"

Elise and Poppy on the beach

Captain Allen brings in the clams with Holly

Our Old Red Mill

Poppy and another man standing before "Signing of the Constitution" painting really shows the size of each signer and the immensity of the painting by contrast

Elise in Vaudville on Broadway

Mother as a child actress on the New York stage as a
street urchin

Tade Styka and cousin Wanda in his studio with an
unknown woman. His painting of Doris on the easel and
his father on the wall

Sketch of Poppy signed by James Montgomery Flagg of
"Uncle Sam Wants You!" poster

Collage of Holly at Captain Allen's Clam house, living
the childhood Poppy chose for her

Poppy painting in his studio

COLLAGE: Mother on CBS News; Old Red Mill dam
when Poppy bought The property; his illustration of
Elise; The Old Red Mill; Poppy painting on the beach;
Poppy standing in front of his Signing of The
Constitution painting in Navy Sail Loft

Poppy and Elise standing before the Constitution
painting at Navy Sail Loft

Elyse and Doris as Miss NRA and Miss Liberty in
Franklin D. Roosevelt's
NRA (National Reconstruction Act) parade in NYC

Aunt Doris and Uncle Tade Styka in his studio at 36
Central Park South

Photo of HCC with a pipe when he was a young man
with a painting of a woman in the background. Signed to
someone else

Poster of Elise waving holding the torch of freedom aloft

CHAPTER TEN

The Old Red Mill

I see the river, like a stretch of silver ribbon; it weaves in and out
and stretches away, away, away. The masses of trees, of the meads,
the meadows—the poplars, the leaning willows, are all revealed
by the mist that is reeling and rolling up the hillside.
I paint and I paint and I paint, and I sing and I sing and I paint! . . .

- Corot

I was five or six when Poppy clambered through the front door hauling a bulky canvas.

He was jubilant. "Holly!" he said as he propped a

painting up against the wall for me to see. "Remember the story about Hiawatha and Minnehaha? I painted a picture of them for you." I looked at the painting. It was like stepping into a watery world. Hiawatha and Minnehaha were standing behind a waterfall, arms outstretched, palms up as if accepting the blessings from the cascade of water plunging over the falls. In shades of muted blue and green, it was like looking through a blue mist into paradise.

To Poppy, living in harmony with nature was a moral obligation, an ethic he admired in the American Indians. Unlike the white man, the Indians had not polluted the land nor had a shoot-em-up love of killing animals needlessly for sport. Poppy especially liked Sitting Bull, who saw the Great Spirit in Nature. He believed in giving animals the same respect as humans. Reverence for the Earth is what Poppy impressed upon me.

He often brought me beaded bracelets and moccasins made by the Indians. He once brought me a grainy photograph of him as a young man sitting in a circle of Indians. "That Indian chief with the full feather headdress is Sitting Bull," he said. Ironically, it was Chief Sitting Bull who defeated Custer at the Battle of Little Big Horn, and it was Custer's widow who wrote a letter of introduction for Poppy that helped him get into art school in New York.

As I looked at Poppy's painting, he said, "In Dakotan, *minne* means water. And *Ha-ha* means falls." He then went to the Victrola, cranked it up and lowered a vinyl record onto its spinning turntable. "Now listen," he said, cocking his head. "I want you to hear the sound of laughing water."

Wish, wish, wish went the needle as it slid back and forth on the rim before it slipped into the groove. "Shhh," said Poppy, holding up his finger as he gazed upward toward the light beaming down from the skylight. At first, all I heard were faint orchestral sounds. "The water is trickling out of the side of the mountain," Poppy explained. The piece he was playing was the *Moldau River* by Smetana. Violins were making faint rippling sounds as if in the distance. Gradually, the rippling grew louder, flowing into undulating tones. "The mountain spring has become a river," said Poppy. "Hear it swirl as it tumbles over the rocks? It's getting deeper now. We're coming to the falls." He closed his eyes as if in prayer. "It's always the calmest before the falls. See the reflection of the willows along the bank?"

I closed my eyes too, but all I saw was the dark side of my eyelids.

"Now!" shouted Poppy in ecstasy. "The water's crashing over the falls. You can hear it surging down the rapids. Swirling around the rocks. Oh, what power!" The music softened. "It's winding down now." He raised his hand to his ear and cocked his head. "It's rolling along toward its final destination before it joins the ocean swells."

I was mystified by Poppy's effort to convey his love of this musical river.

"Holly," he boomed as if about to explode with joy. "I want you to run wild and free like the Indians. Like Minnehaha and Hiawatha the way God intended it. I'm going to take you to a place where you can do that."

I was seven years old when I first got to see the "laughing water." I remember because I had not yet learned to read, something Poppy told me he would have to do something about.

The trip to Vermont started out like any other search for serene places to paint. Mother and Poppy packed up their paint boxes, canvases and easels and hauled them down to the marble lobby, where Poppy and I waited while Mother got the Studebaker out of the parking garage near Amsterdam Avenue. When she pulled up, she and Poppy loaded the back trunk and seat with their painting paraphernalia, a picnic basket, a plaid blanket and Cutie——our little brown-and-white Fox Terrier. As usual, Poppy plunked himself into the passenger seat. Poppy never drove. Something to do with his vision, I think. I scrambled up on his lap, straddling his right leg so I could feel the wind in my face blowing through the open window.

I loved these trips, but as I grew older, I began to worry about the day when I would grow too big to sit on Poppy's lap. As yet, there was no hint that his life would be over by the time I turned twelve.

Traveling down the Hudson River Parkway, the New Jersey cliffs jutted upward from the opposite shore. Belching New Jersey smoke stacks looked so ugly I could hardly wait for them to disappear. Even the Palisades Amusement Park, which boasted the highest roller coaster in the world, could not compare with my expectation of the laughing water ahead. Like the garish billboards along the road, man-made ugliness filled me with dread.

Noticing my somber mood, Poppy piped in with a cheery voice, "Let's sing the *Yankee Doodle* song." Waving me on with the flourish of a Philharmonic conductor, he belted out his made-up words to the familiar song. "Oh... Yankee Doodle went to town... Come on, Holly, sing with me." I joined in, and together we sang at the top of our lungs, "Upon a load of lumber / He let a poop behind the car / And blowed it all to thunder!"

Poppy and I burst into gales of laughter.

Traffic thinned, and Mother pulled off the highway onto a serene tree-lined country road. As we reached the crest of a hill, she gave Poppy a mischievous look. "Here we go," she said, shifting into neutral.

"Careful now, Kid!" cautioned Poppy gripping me tight. "Keep both hands on the wheel."

"Wheeee!" squealed Mother as the Studebaker barreled downward, jouncing over ruts in the road. Coasting down hills was how Mother conserved gasoline, which had been rationed until I was five years old after World War II ended.

"Hey, Kid," shouted Poppy. "Stop the car. There's a

Metty!"

Metty is what Poppy called a landscape that looked like something Poppy's contemporary, Willard Metcalfe, would paint. Poppy lauded other artists whose work he admired.

Mother pulled off the road and rolled to a stop on the grass. I slid into the weeds as Poppy swung his legs out.

Irritated by this distraction that slowed our progress, I grumbled, *"Oh, PLEASE!"* as I traipsed along behind Mother and Poppy, dragging my heels and kicking at sticks. They ignored me as they headed for the clearing. Surveying the scene, they peered through imaginary frames shaped by their fingers.

"Can we go now?" I whined, forgetting that Poppy's celebration of beauty was responsible for the beautiful life he had created for me.

He paid me no heed. I kicked at a rock.

Mother clasped her hands in joy and scrunched her face up as if she wanted to cry for joy. She gave a little gasp. "What a glorious vista. And just look at that cerulean sky!" She then held a finger up as if listening for the voice of God. "Hear the wind rustling through the leaves?" She breathed in deeply, eyes closed in reverence. "Isn't this fresh air glorious!?"

"Glorious" was Mother's favorite word. I looked in the direction of all the fuss. A red barn. Black and white cows in a pasture. The cows weren't even close enough for me to pet.

I tramped back to the car while Poppy and Mother kept right on marveling at God's splendor. We were on our way to a place called The Old Red Mill, which I thought was a restaurant like the Log Cabin Inn. Thoughts of crunchy Southern fried chicken, all juicy inside, made me all the more impatient.

"Let's go!" I shouted.

When they finally returned, Poppy was ecstatic. "Elbert Hubbard was right! 'How much finer it is to go out in the woods, lift up your heart in song and be a child, then fight human inclination and waste good God-given energy endeavoring to be proper——whatever that may be!'"

I was no longer the center of Poppy's attention. Even after we got back in the car, he and Mother chatted endlessly about summer hues of green, billowing cloud formations, canvas weight and size.

Angrily, I scrambled into the back seat, my arms folded across my chest. *"There they go again. Talking about their stupid old paintings!"* I didn't like it when their art took precedence over me.

***

The trip from New York to Vermont took all day with me pinned between paint boxes and a picnic basket in the back seat of the Studebaker. I wrestled to get comfortable as my sweaty back stuck to the itchy wool seat while Cutie slept on the blanket Mother had spread over the picnic basket. By late afternoon, the liverwurst sandwiches had all been eaten, and I was very hungry. Looking out the window at the green mountains, Poppy got to talking about Ethan Allen, the rebel leader of the Green Mountain Boys. "To hell with the Divine Right of clergymen," Poppy bellowed, quoting Allen. "Where the hell do they get the right to tell us how to live?"

"Early one Sunday morning," said Poppy, reminiscing about his barefoot boyhood days, "I fed Ol' Nelly all the oats she could eat, then rode her to church and tied her up by the open window. As soon as the sermon started, Nelly let fly. One fart after another all through that preacher's sermon." Poppy and I thought that was uproariously funny. But Mother didn't seem to think so, which made it all the more fun for me.

To Poppy, Ethan Allen's "Life, Liberty and Property," which got written into our Declaration of Independence as *Life, Liberty, and the Pursuit of Happiness,* was what made life worth living. "I'm buying the Old Red Mill for you, Holly," he said, turning around so he could see me in the back. "So you can run wild and free in the mountains. Naked if you like. Like an Indian. The way God intended it."

"How much longer to the Old Red Mill?" I asked, picturing thick white tablecloths, folded napkins, and water being poured from silver pitchers into glasses over tinkling ice cubes.

By now, I was all sweaty, my back was sticking to the itchy seat, and my stomach was gnawing hungrily at my bones.

The Studebaker trundled around a sharp mountain curve, pitching the paint boxes sideways and hurling Cutie into my lap.

"We're here!" chirped Mother, pulling up to the steps leading to Mach's (pronounced "Matches") Market—the only store in Pawlet, Vermont.

"Is this the Old Red Mill?" I asked, catching a whiff of cooling pine-scented misty air.

"No, dear," Mother said as she opened the back door to let Cutie out.

"Then, why are we stopping?" I said, eager to get to the wonderful Old Red Mill.

Cutie skittered around at Mother's feet, excited to be let out of the car while Poppy unfolded himself from the passenger side. "Here's a nickel," Mother told me. "Get yourself something in Mach's Market." Then she and Poppy headed up the steep stone steps toward a house on top of a hill. A wooden sign over the door creaked in the mountain breeze: "Andrus Realty." Not that I could read it. I couldn't. From the back seat, I looked around. Not a flat place in sight. Nor a single living soul. Just mountains. And our car. The only one in sight.

Scrambling out, I climbed the steps to Mach's Market. Sprawled flat on the porch, looking like a bear rug, was a huge Saint Bernard. I'd never seen a dog that big. I stooped to pet his broad head. Jowls pushed up on a resting paw revealed enormous white fangs. I drew back.

"He won't hurt, ja," said a woman whose frame I could barely make out behind the screen door.

"What's his name?" I called to her.

"Sanka."

"Good boy, Sanka," I said, stroking the broad space between his ears.

Nickel in hand, I headed into the store. The screen door screeched open on rusty springs and banged shut behind me.

I asked for a soda pop, and the woman pointed to the red Coca-Cola box. I lifted the lid and looked in. There, clustered among big chunks of ice, were bottles of Hires Root Beer, Orange Crush, Cream Soda, Grape, Chocola, Cherry, Ginger Ale, Sarsparilla and Coca-Cola. I pulled out a frosty Cream Soda.

"New York license plates," said the woman. "I reckon your folks'll be coming in here a plenty. I hear they say they're buying the Old Red Mill."

I handed her my nickel. *Ca-ching* went the register as I trudged down a creaking plank floor toward the whirr coming from the back of the store. It grew louder as I strolled down the aisle toward the strange noise beyond the back, screen door. Workhorse bridles and harnesses hung like heavy coats along the wall permeating the air with the smell of leather on one side and laundry soap on the other.

Curious about the strange noise outside, I opened the back door.

The drone became a roar. From a tiny balcony, I looked down through blue mist into a rocky gorge. The depth of the gorge and the fury of the whitewater rapids terrified me. I slammed the door and darted back down the aisle, dodging Sanka as he lumbered toward me. Bolting from the store, I bounded up the stone steps to Andrus Realty, where I found Mother signing the deed to the Old Red Mill.

* * *

"I'm hungry. I want to eat," I demanded as I waited for Poppy to get back into the car.

"It's in the bag," Poppy told Mother, ignoring me as if I didn't exist as he and Mother crammed buckets, shovels, and brooms from Mach's Market into the already jam-packed back seat.

"How 'bout if we take a look at that church above the falls," said Poppy. "It might be a good scene to paint." He and Mother headed for a stone bridge. *They always put their work before me.* With a groan, I trudged grudgingly behind them. From the stone bridge over a waterfall, I watched them head for a wooded embankment above the falls, toward the water's edge. Although I could not hear Poppy and Mother over the roar of the waterfall, I could read their gestures. It was the language of art I knew all too well. They were extolling the "glorious" reflection of the willows and the white-steepled church in the still water above the falls. *How can they see beauty in something as frightening as that noisy waterfall?*

"I'm hungry!" I howled over the roar.

"Soon, dear," called Mother, her voice trailing off as she and Poppy extolled the beauty around them while leaving me to smolder by myself.

At last, they returned to the car. Feeling betrayed, I wrestled myself into the back seat, preferring the company of shovels and tin buckets to Poppy's lap. "I'd rather be in Mother Goose Park," I grumbled. At least it had swings." My griping fell on deaf ears as we pulled onto a dirt road. Fresh air was at last blowing into the hot, stuffy car.

"Oh, kid," exclaimed Poppy leaning toward the driver's side to see out Mother's window. "There's the

Mettowee."

I peered past the stack of paint boxes, broom handles, and teetering buckets. Way below, a river sparkled like a silver ribbon as it coursed through a mossy-green valley. Even from inside the car trundling down the road above, I could see grey and white marble stones at the bottom of the river as if I were looking through clear glass. Everything sparkled with freshness and life.

"We're almost there," Poppy said as we bumped over potholes in the dirt road. Ready to forgive him for his bad behavior, I scrambled over the front seat and slid onto his lap, straddling his knee. I could hardly wait as I pictured a fancy New England Inn on the village green with a steaming plate of Southern fried chicken being placed before me. Mmm. Hot buttered rolls and a glass of ice-cold lemonade never sounded so good. I could hardly wait.

I leaned out the window wanting to be the first to glimpse the Old Red Mill.

A cloud of brown dust billowed up from the road ahead. "What's that?" I asked, spotting what looked like a giant yellow caterpillar in the midst of a dust storm.

"It's a road grader," said Poppy. "It's leveling the potholes made by the rain."

Choking grey dust curled in through the open windows.

Mother slowed the car, lagging behind the road grader to keep from getting swallowed up in a cloud of dust.

"There it is," shouted Poppy. "The Old Red Mill."

Through the billowing dirt, I saw a line of buildings— —a stable, a garage and a grey, bare wood barn-like structure with a slate roof.

We pulled up in front of an unpainted, splintery barn. Poppy swung his legs out, sliding me into the freshly plowed dirt, which had banked up against a heavy plank door.

Mother got out and fiddled with the rusty bolt.

I was dumbstruck. Surely this couldn't be The Old Red Mill. No music. No sign of people anywhere. Just dead-looking ugliness.

Unable to unlock the door, Poppy took over, cranking the key in the rusty padlock. Managing to turn it, he heaved his shoulder into the big wooden door. It didn't budge. Together Mother and Poppy pushed with all their might until the door gave. It scraped through a hundred years of dust churned up first by horse-pulled wagons, then cars on Vermont's rural Route 30. It must have been at least six inches deep. I'd never seen anything like it. It was the sort of thing only a shovel could fix. Poppy bent down and scooped up some of the powdery stuff and rubbed it between his fingers. "Clay," he announced as if he were a sculptor eager to get to work.

I peered into the eerie shadows. *This is the Old Red Mill?*

It felt like the ultimate betrayal. In a huff, I got back into the car.

Poppy reached by me and grabbed the shovel. Reluctantly, I got out of the car and watched Poppy excavate a path to the back door of the mill, leaving a trail through a grey mantle of pulverized clay. Meanwhile, Mother got a crowbar and went to work prying boards off windows. Crack. Pop. And there was light. But it was anything but "glorious." It lit up menacing cobwebs draped in ghostly shapes over who-knows-what underneath.

"Look over there," exclaimed Mother pointing to a row of ominous shapes against the wall. All I could see was a dungeon with big scurrying spiders. "Restaurant booths," said Mother swiping the air with her broom as she cut through cobwebs.

"Well, I'll be damned," said Poppy. "The Old Red Mill was once a restaurant."

A restaurant! The idea gave me no succor. By now, my stomach was threatening to eat me alive. "It's uglier than Dracula's castle," I whimpered.

Off in a corner, Poppy checked out a horse-drawn sleigh. "We'll paint it blue with red trim," he said." And we'll leave it right there where it's been for a hundred years."

"I want to go home," I cried.

"Come on, Holly," said Poppy, "I've got something to show you."

I was in no mood to be jollied up, but he took my hand and coaxed me along with him through the powdery clay. Stopping in the center of the mill, he said, "A hundred years ago, this was a grist mill. That's why it's called The Old Red Mill. Right here in the center, there used to be two big mill stones that ground grain into flour for bread. The stones were turned by the force of the river through a mill wheel outside."

A history lesson on grinding flour was the last thing I

wanted to hear.

Poppy scouted around, poking at dust-laden lumps with his shovel. "Those two mill stones gotta be in here somewhere." Unable to find them, he headed for the back door, yanked a heavy bar from its cradle and shoved open the door.

We were greeted by the ferocious roar from a waterfall that stretched across the river.

Poppy stepped out on a tiny square balcony and looked down. "There's the millstone!" he shouted. I peeked around him. What I saw filled me with terror. Water plunged over a huge log dam that reached the entire width of a wide river with whitewater rapids surging toward the mill, crashing furiously up against its granite foundation. Directly below, Poppy pointed out the millstone. Big and round with a hole in the middle. Maybe five feet in diameter and twelve inches thick. Angry rapids swirled around it, frothing at the mouth as if the river wanted to tear the mill apart and take us and the millstone with it.

Where was the "laughing water" Poppy had promised? The *minnee* in water and the *Ha Ha* in the falls? To me, it felt more like a war zone.

"I hate this place. It's awful. It's awful."

Nobody gave me any heed.

Then Mother showed up, making a big fuss over that stupid stone.

"Holly," said Poppy, his voice uncharacteristically stern. "Don't you ever go near this back door. You hear me? You could fall into the river."

I plowed my way through the dust back to the car and hunkered down in the back seat while Mother unloaded the paint boxes.

"I have to go wee wee," I told her in a voice implying serious child neglect.

Mother looked at me as if I had taken her by surprise. "Well, all right, dear," she said. "Come with me." I followed her back into the mill, and she relayed the message to Poppy. He cocked his finger like a gun and shot it toward a door in a dark corner. "While you take her to the john, I'll unload the trunk."

Mother headed across the mill's dark interior. "Come on, dear, I'll show you the bathroom." I followed her down a narrow, musty-smelling staircase. At the bottom, I cringed around spider-webbed windows inhabited by big, furry black-and-yellow spiders the size of silver dollars. Through a door in the narrow passage, I saw "the bathroom."

A two-holer.

"Here, dear," said Mother as she swept a layer of dust from around the rim. Then she left me alone with those great big black-and-yellow spiders.

I looked into the chasm of the dark underbelly of the mill. Unable to hold it any longer, I plunked my bottom over the hole and exposed myself to the abyss. As my pee splattered into the slimy sludge below, I couldn't help obsessing over what goblins in the darkness might reach up and grab me. Finished, I yanked my pants up and bolted past the spiders and back up the stairs to Mother.

"I want to go home," I screamed as I reached the first floor of the mill. "I hate this place. Hate it. Hate it. Hate it! And I'm hungry." At that moment, I hated Poppy and Mother too.

"Don't be bratty, dear," said Mother. "Poppy and I have things we need to do. Then we'll go eat."

After what they'd just put me through, how could I believe her? Whatever they were up to, Mother and Poppy were keeping it to themselves.

I dashed for the car, threw myself into the back seat and slammed the door, preferring the scratchy wool seat to that haunted old grist mill. Snorting and sobbing, I squalled my displeasure to no avail until I wore myself out. When I woke up, we had pulled up in front of Hotel Equinox in Manchester, Vermont. Through a row of huge old oak trees, I saw the welcoming white colonial pillars and black-shuttered windows of New England civilization.

Dinner at last.

***

We made daily trips back and forth between the Manchester Inn and the Old Red Mill. For what seemed like forever, I watched Mother and Poppy shovel and scrape as if their lives depended on it. They got excited over the dumbest things, like the oak dance floor they discovered buried beneath a hundred years of filth.

"How long are we going to stay here?" I whined.

"Three *wonderful* months," said Poppy as he and Mother pried one of the restaurant booths loose from the wall, cheering as it broke free with a squawk. "We can put this by the kitchen window so we can look out over the dam," said Poppy. "And later, we'll put another one outside."

How Poppy could even imagine putting a booth out on that rickety balcony. Even I could see it would be too big to fit and would fall right into that awful river.

Once or twice a week, the ice truck came by. A man jabbed hooks into a slab of ice, hauled it into the mill and plopped it into the wooden ice box left over from the mill's restaurant days. This is where Mother kept our food. It was looking more and more as if we were there to stay. "How long are three months?" I asked.

"All summer long," said Poppy. To me, that sounded like a life sentence in prison. Why were they doing this to me?

"What do you think, Kid?" said Poppy dusting off a table. "We'll paint it white with red benches. Then we'll put it outside and eat our meals over the river." Mother clapped her hands with glee. *Eat outside? On that rickety balcony with no railing?* They got all giddy when they talked about it as if they'd made putting that ugly old booth outside their big goal in life.

"Holly, dear," said Mother. "Why don't you go

outside and play?"

"There's nothing to do outside," I grumbled.

"What the hell do you mean there's nothing to do outside?" said Poppy, slamming his hammer down on the table. "Tarnation! You got the whole damn Mettowee to play in."

"The stones hurt my feet," I whined.

"What are you? A tenderfoot?"

Coming from Poppy, it was the worst kind of insult. *Tenderfoot?* Nothing from Poppy had ever hurt so much. It meant I had failed to measure up to Poppy's barefoot boyhood days and all those Indians he admired. He was calling me a city slicker. *Well, I'll show him.* I stomped out of the mill and sulked down to the river bank above the falls, and took off my shoes. "Ouch, ouch!" The stones hurt so bad. *I hate this place.* I stuck one foot into the water. Gasp! It was freezing cold. Made my foot ache. I yanked it out and stormed back to the Old Red Mill. My foot was freezing cold as I shouldered my way through the Queen Ann's Lace.

Bleary-eyed, I watched Mother and Poppy throw themselves into restoring the mill. The whole thing was beyond my comprehension. Mother trilled Stephen Foster's *Jeanie With the Light Brown Hair* as she wielded her hammer. "Borne like a vapor, on the summer air / I see her tripping where the bright streams play / Happy as the daisies that dance on her way."

I resented every moment of Poppy and Mother's joy over this hundred-year-old wreck.

Then I got an idea.

Rummaging around in a dark annex of the mill, I pulled a board out of a pile of dust-laden rubble. *I'll pretend this is a ship full of people. Then I'll run as hard as I can and fling it out the back door, so I can watch it go over the dam.*

Feeling weak and helpless under the control of Mother and Poppy, the thought of creating such a spectacle of shock and awe felt empowering. What did I care that Poppy had told me to never to go near that back door? I would show them.

Poppy had propped the bar that had bolted the back door shut against the door to let the fresh air in while they worked.

My imaginary ship full of people in hand, I waited

until Poppy and Mother were in another room.

Ready, set, go! I bounded forward. As I burst onto the balcony, the bar gave way as I heaved my imaginary boatload of people toward the falls.

All I remember next is hurtling through space.

White water rapids below.

CHAPTER ELEVEN

The Sound of Life

Water is life's matter and matrix, mother and medium. There is no life without water.

- Albert Szent-Gyogyi
Nobel Laureate, 1937

Perhaps I blacked out when I fell from the balcony. All I remember is sitting in the middle of the millstone with frothing white water swirling around me. My legs were crossed in front of me as if I'd simply decided to sit down and rest. Fearing I might be dead, the first thing I did was reach down and pinch my leg to see if I was still alive. Fortunately, a waterlogged piece of cardboard flotsam had cushioned my fall.

Grateful to be alive, I scrambled up the granite embankment and back to the Old Red Mill. Ashamed of the evil thoughts that had caused my fall, I never told anyone.

As we drove back to Manchester for dinner, I slid from Poppy's lap to the floor under the dashboard. Curling up in the warmth of the car heater, I kissed every one of my toes and the bottoms of my feet the way Mother used to do every morning when she sang, "This little piggy went to market, this little piggy stayed home," to wake me up for kindergarten.

***

Until the day we moved into the mill, we must have spent every night in Manchester. However, I have no memory of this. What I do remember is the first day we made the Old Red Mill our home. Mother got the upstairs bedroom facing the road. I got the other upstairs room facing the waterfall. And Poppy got the big downstairs room off the former restaurant and dance hall. My bed was a fold-up Army cot with an Army green sleeping bag. Both from the Army Navy Surplus Store. The wide window above my bed gave me a view of the river plunging over the log dam and the mountain across the river that turned dark and ominous when the sun went down. There was no escaping the thunder of the waterfall.

Early next morning, Poppy and Mother slipped into their matching white canvas sneakers and waded across the shallows upstream. I followed them, my bare feet slipping and sliding over the rocks as the spring-fed river tried its best to pull me into its freezing clutches.

At the mossy base of the mountain across the river, Poppy held his bucket under a cleft in the rocks until it filled with the spring water that gurgled down the mountainside. "We need to build a basin here to catch the water," he said as the stream of crystal-clear water pattered against the sides of his pail. "We'll put a roof over it to keep the leaves out."

I sat down on a mossy rock in the shade of a clump of birch. Beneath my feet, a bed of Forget-me-nots had spread, covering the cold, dark mud. Everywhere, sparkling water seeped out through the moss and rocks. Poppy scooped a cup of water out of his bucket and handed it to me. It had never occurred to me to get excited over the taste of water. But this was different. Straight out of the side of the mountain, it was rich with minerals and had a taste I will never forget. Cold as ice, it was so refreshing in the summer heat.

As I listened to it babble down the mountainside, I suddenly understood what Poppy meant by "laughing water" and what he heard in Smetana's *Moldau River*.

Like the Moldau, which began with a trickle, the source of the Mettowee were mountain springs, the main one of which, I would later learn, was in Dorset, Vermont.

***

"This flag flew over our United States Capitol," Poppy told me as he unfurled the huge, heavy-duty red-white-and-blue symbol of our nation. Every morning, he would reel the American flag out over the Mettowee with the squeal of pulleys that he and Mother had rigged up from the side of the mill to a tree at the base of the mountain across the river. Today, I think of the red-white-and-blue of that big American flag as a symbol of our Old Red Mill as it danced over the water against a backdrop of a green mountain.

***

"Time for your bath, dear," called Mother blithely as she stuffed her long, dark curls into a white bathing cap. "Come on," she beckoned with a whole-body wave from a sloping outcropping of bedrock upon which the mill was built.

No. The water was ice cold, and I knew it. Curious, I trudged down to where Mother was lathering herself with soap. The Old Red Mill was built on a huge outcropping of smooth rock. Beneath my feet, the smooth mounds of stone felt hot from the sun. I dipped my toes into the pothole Mother was using as a tub. The water was warm.

I had just finished soaping myself when Poppy called to me from farther down. "Come on, Holly, let's go for a swim." Skittishly, I joined him at the edge of the log dam. I wasn't sure I could trust him after finding out that the Old Red Mill was the place he promised to take me where I could run wild and free. Wearing white sneakers, Poppy waded into the water.

Sneakers? Was Poppy a tenderfoot? Never mind. Like God, he had always been beyond reproach. But now I wasn't so sure.

With arms outstretched, Poppy splashed into the raging current close to the log dam; backing against the current, water swirled around his waist. He faltered, then pushed back against the waves to keep from being swept away.

"Come on, Holly", he called as he bucked the force of the river battering his back. White water churned around him. "Come on. The water's great," he assured me as his face and chest turned lobster red.

"Too cold," I shouted over the roar.

"No, it isn't. Just dive in. You'll see. You'll feel warm."

A likely story.

"Come on, Holly. Be a sport." That's what Poppy always said when he wanted me to experience some daredevil stunt he thought was fun, like riding the waves in the Atlantic.

I wanted to believe him, so I waded in where the current wasn't as strong and dipped down into the water. Bitter cold, I scrambled back onto the warm granite and scrunched up, hugging my knees and shuddering from the chill.

Poppy egged me on, promising it would be wonderful. I stood up and looked into the rushing whitewater. Although not deep, the current was strong.

"Come on, Holly, be a sport."

I couldn't let him down. I belly-flopped into the

waves. Struggling to get my footing, I tried to stand but got caught up in Poppy's backwater. The force of the river swept me off my feet as if it were dead-set on whooshing me into the boulders below.

I reached for Poppy. He grabbed my hand. With his help, I stood up. Shivering uncontrollably, I bolstered myself against the onslaught of icy water. Then, what seemed impossible happened. I felt a rush of tingling warmth, just as Poppy had promised.

It was as if the water had turned from cold to hot.

Poppy fought his way to the foot of the falls. Standing with his back against the surge plunging over the dam, he called out to me. "Come on, Holly, we're going under the falls.

Was he serious? The tumultuous roar. Algae-covered logs. Sheets of pounding water.

It was terrifying.

Cascading water beat down on Poppy's back, splaying out behind him like an angel's wings. Then he let go of my hand and disappeared to the other side of the deluge.

"Poppy!" I screamed as if I'd just witnessed him disappear into another dimension.

One I could not enter.

No answer. Only the thundering of water pouring over the dam. Then, out through the pounding waterfall came Poppy's hand. I grabbed it. The water shook me like a rag doll as he pulled me through the falls and sat me up beside him on an algae-covered log.

Like the blip I'd felt when I ducked through the ocean waves and came out on the other side. All was calm behind the falls. Rays of light beamed through from the other side. It was like looking through a crystal stained-glass window in a cathedral. Only instead of martyred saints, I saw life, not death. The American flag, the blue sky and the green mountain beyond. Under the falls, no water beat down on our heads. No current tore at my bathing suit as if wanting to rip it off and dash me against the rocks. Beneath us, the green algae felt velvet soft. Never had I felt so safe. It was as if I were in a sacred place. We were Hiawatha and Minnehaha under the waterfall, experiencing the blessings of the Great Spirit. Just like in Poppy's painting.

There in our secret place, Poppy told me something I will never forget. "Never build a house where you can't hear the sound of water. For the sound of water is the sound of life."

CHAPTER TWELVE

The Boston Express

To him, who is in fear, everything rustles.

~ Sophocles

Because of Poppy, I grew up unafraid. Because Poppy didn't believe in hellfire or Satan and his demons, I didn't grow up believing in ghosts, nor did I get spooked in the dark. However, all that confidence and security would end one day in 1947.

I was seven when Mother took me to New York's Grand Central Station. Before that day, I'd never even seen a train. Nor had I been in a train station.

"Please don't leave me! No, Mother, please," I pleaded

as Mother pulled me down the ramp into the dark underworld of Grand Central. A snake pit to me. Ahead lay a silver serpent in wait. The stench of rancid oil on metal filled me with horror as it hissed and spit.

It was my first day at Daycroft in Stamford, Connecticut, after Poppy yanked me out of Professional Children's School on Broadway.

"All aboard for Stamford. New Haven. Hartford. Boston," called the conductor as he paced back and forth beside the train.

We rushed in. Mother pointed me to an empty seat. I scooted in next to the window. She then dropped my school bag on the seat beside me and said, "The conductor will tell you when to get off." I flung myself back against the scratchy, blue seat as if to stave off sure death.

"You'll be fine," mother assured me. "Just remember—the first stop. You get off at the first stop. A yellow school bus will be waiting for you."

I couldn't possibly feel fine. I was about to be abandoned. Abandoned by my own mother in the belly of the beast——about to be taken far away from Poppy and Mother, the only people I'd ever known and loved.

The train gave a jerk. Mother rushed for the door as the conductor in a military-looking uniform stepped in. She stopped momentarily to tell him something while pointing at me. He nodded. She exited the train, and the conductor slammed the gate. Through the grimy window, Mother threw me a hasty kiss as the train gave a mighty lurch. Metal clanged and scraped together. I pressed my face to the window hoping Mother would turn back, but she was already halfway up the ramp without so much as a backward glance. There was no warm broad back of Bubby to cling to as I'd done watching Mother leave me at Nanna's house.

The first day in a new school was scary enough. But a long trip alone on a train when I'd never been on a train before? It felt like a death sentence. *Will I get off at the right stop? Will the school bus be waiting for me, as Mother said? What if the train takes me somewhere else, and nobody can find me?*

I'd never been so scared.

Another lurch followed by the grinding and gnashing of teeth. A dragon's teeth. The monster shimmied and shook as it picked up speed. Squealing and groaning, it rounded a curve, then plunged into a black subterranean labyrinth. *Will I ever see the light of day again?* The lights inside the train flickered on and off. *Oh, please, God, don't let the lights stay off.*

Faster and faster, we went through the tunnel. Dim lanterns flashed by on concrete walls. Dark caverns haunted me from my window. There was no escape. I was living my worst nightmare. The lights of the train flashed on and off again. *Oh God, please don't let the lights stay off. Please don't leave me alone in this dungeon without Poppy and Mother.*

Even with the lights on, tunnels always scared me on trips under the Hudson River in the Lincoln and Holland tunnels. Now I was being rocketed deeper and deeper into blackness. *There'll be an end,* I told myself, but this was longer than any tunnel I'd ever been in. Worse yet, I was alone.

We blasted into the light. I looked down from an elevated track. Angry graffiti filled me with fear with its bold, garish scrawls. I couldn't read what it said, but I felt its hate. For the first time ever, I saw loitering men on garbage-strewn streets. *Please don't slow down.* Danger snarled up at me from below.

But the train did slow down. *Oh God, please don't let*

this be the place where I get off!

As it came to a screeching halt, I looked down into a ghetto. I didn't see any yellow bus. *But Mother told me to get off at the first stop. Please, not here! But it is! It's the first stop.* The conductor shouted, "One Hundred Twenty-Fifth Street!"

I jumped to my feet.

In a blinding shot of fear, I snatched my school briefcase and ran for the door. As I reached the conductor, he said, "Not here. Next stop."

I went back and fell into my seat, my heart pounding as if it would jump out of my chest.

A scruffy-looking man in a crumpled beige suit stumbled in. He was talking to himself as if he were crazy. He headed for the empty seat next to me. I remembered Mother's instructions. *"Never look at strangers. If they talk to you, pretend you're deaf."* I trained my eyes on the window even though the ugliness outside scared me. The man staggered up to the seat next to me, leaned in and mumbled something close to my neck. For the first time in my life, I smelled alcohol. I held my breath, afraid to breathe. My eyes darted around for help. Everyone was reading a newspaper with a don't-bother-me expression. I was sure I was about to die. *He could grab me and drag me into those awful streets.* I remembered Poppy's warning. "Never let a man put his hand on you. Not even in a crowded bus. If a man puts his hand on you, you run like hell. You hear me? You run like hell." I looked down at the ghetto streets with laundry hanging on clotheslines stretched between the buildings. *Where will I run?*

The train lurched. The man almost fell in my lap. He then pulled himself up and shambled on, mumbling to himself.

Forty-five tormenting minutes later, the conductor pulled open the door and shouted over the clattering roar. "Stamford! Stamford! Next stop Stamford!" As he passed by, he leaned in and told me, "This is where you get off."

Afraid of missing my stop, I grabbed my school bag and scampered out the door. The shaking of the train almost made me fall. Metal plates between the cars slid back and forth beneath my feet as the tracks below flashed by. The conductor came in, opened the hatch and lowered the steps. I gripped a handlebar as the ground outside streaked by. I looked down. I was staring death in the face. The noise was deafening. Clackety clack. Clackety clack. One jerk, and it would be over. I'd be mowed under by wheels of steel. Never had I felt so frail. I held on tight to keep from being hurled out the door as the train shifted and swayed. It was all I could do to keep my balance.

We clanged to a hissing stop. I climbed down the steel steps to an open-air country platform where I'd never been before. All was quiet. Not a single person was in sight—just trees.

The train snorted and sputtered. Steel wheels started to squeal: the train jerked forward and picked up speed, leaving me behind in the creepy silence.

Don't tell me I'm lost. I don't see any yellow school bus.

I look around the station. No one in sight. Only a big wagon for hauling packages and suitcases.

Then I saw it. Waiting beside a clump of trees.

A yellow school bus.

***

It wasn't long before I made peace with the daily forty-five-minute commute on the Boston Express. Discovering the comfort of the dining car, where a smiling black waiter in a white jacket served me breakfast on a thick white tablecloth with shiny silverware, as I watched the New England scenery flash by outside.

One night, Poppy told me he wanted to buy me something nice. I thought he was rewarding me for adjusting to my new school. Eagerly, I followed him down the elevator to the store around the corner on Columbus Avenue.

As we entered the brightly lit cubby-hole of a store, my heart seized up. Luggage was stacked on one side of a narrow aisle, blankets on the other.

"What color blanket do you like?" Poppy asked, making his voice chipper. There was no fooling me this time. I was being shucked off for good like the husk on an ear of corn.

No more commuting for me. I was being sent away for good to boarding school. I don't think I ever cried as hard as I did that night—all to no avail. I would spend the next ten years of my life in boarding school.

***

I awoke to the clamber of feet galloping down the hall like a herd of wildebeests. The door of my private room burst open. Realizing I'd missed the wake-up bell, I threw off the covers and leaped out of bed. To my horror, the cold air hit my wet pajamas. I had wet the bed. "Pee-ew!" squealed Big Janet. All the girls on my dorm floor broke into derisive laughter. There I stood with my pajamas plastered to my body.

Next, I heard the thump, thump, thump of Mrs. Thompson's lace-up matronly brown shoes as she marched down the hall. Pushing past the laughing girls, she wasted no time in ripping the wet sheets off the bed. On the spot, Big Janet made up a new version of Billy Holiday's "Stormy Weather," which she belted out to the glee of everyone but me. "Don't know why there's no sun up in the sky / Dirty laundry / Life is bare, gloom and mis'ry everywhere / Dirty laundry." For the next ten years, Big Janet would chant, "Dirty laundry", every time she passed me in the hall.

As an only child, I had learned to enjoy classical music, which wafted my imagination off on its soothing refrains while I played by myself while Mother painted. I was terribly afraid of other children. I think my fear began in kindergarten when I overheard the children whispering about little Lisa, whose mother was divorced. I knew there was something wrong with me, and if anyone found out, I'd be hated just like Lisa. And who knows what they might do to me.

Having a room of my own allowed me to close the door

on the stress of trying to get along while letting the classical music on my radio carry me back to the safe and peaceful forests and verdant valleys I'd come to love in Vermont.

It was on one of these evenings that the door of my room burst open. In barged a redhead named Eunice, followed by Big Janet and a bunch of other girls. Eunice kicked the jacks I was playing with all over the floor. "Let's pull her clothes off," yelled Eunice screaming like a banshee.

It was the ultimate violation.

I let her have it with everything I had. The girls retreated, but not without Big Janet making up another mocking chant. "Modest Morris, Modest Morris."

I called Mother on the housemother's phone. Sobbing, I told her what a horrible, dangerous place I was in; how mean everyone was. I even remember telling her I feared they would jump me in a dark hallway. Maybe even kill me. There were lots of long dark halls in Adelaide Hall, which made it feel like I was living in a midlevel castle, not to mention the dungeons below where I had to wash my clothes in an old ringer-type washing machine.

In actuality, with the exception of Eunice, the kids at

Daycroft were all nice. Being a Christian Science school, none of them believed in a Devil or Evil. Consequently, there was no reason to hate. But I had no way of knowing this.

As usual, Mother told me to read Mary Baker Eddy's *Science and Health with Key to the Scriptures,* which gave me the impression she didn't care. As for Eunice, the instigator of that one and only bad experience in the entirety of my ten years at Daycroft——she disappeared. I never found out what had happened to her.

Today, I look back on Daycroft as the best place I could have been. How lucky I was to have been sent to such a wonderful school. I came to recognize the children and faculty as kind, gentle people.

I also learned how to take care of myself. At Daycroft, there was no mother to take my clothes to the laundry. I had to wash what I wore myself, mop the dust bunnies out from under my bed and set the long wooden tables in the dining hall with white lace doilies under each plate. Daycroft taught me discipline without harsh reprimands. Without Daycroft, I hate to think where I might have ended up, which goes to prove the audacity of letting children decide for themselves what's best for them.

No one must ever find out that I don't have a father. I was sure I'd be hated like little Lisa in kindergarten, whose Mother was divorced. Like Lisa, I came to think of myself as a freak of nature that would never fit in. And Mother's secret had something to do with it. Like Mother, I now had a secret too. And that secret was Poppy. I was painfully shy.

As for Big Janet, I came to live up to her epithet of "Modest Morris." I refused to get undressed or take a shower when another girl was in the bathroom. There were a couple of reasons for this. The other girls were more developed than I was, which made me feel like a freak, and some of them liked taking showers together, pretending one was a boy and the other a girl in order to practice making love.

***

At first, I got to go home every weekend, which was like letting a puppy loose in the city streets. The commute on the Boston Express had made me independent and unafraid to launch off on my own, which meant that Mother could no longer restrain me from bolting out the door. The American Museum of Natural History became my hangout. In those days, admission was free, and many of its echoing marble halls were, for the most part, empty. I would spend all day wandering the halls of the largest museum in the world. When my feet began to hurt, I would head for the Hayden Planetarium, where I could lean back in those cushy velvet seats, gaze up at the stars and contemplate the universe.

Crossing Central Park on foot, I would go to the Metropolitan Museum of Art, where I would study every painting and dream of one day being able to paint like Poppy.

***

Mother was good at carpentry——a skill she picked up from her big brother Carl. To create extra storage space, she had built two deep shelves across the ceiling of my little bedroom. The make-shift attic became a hiding place for Christmas presents before "Santa" came to visit. I don't remember ever believing in "Santa," but I liked pretending I did, which was what the Christmas spirit was all about. As Christian Scientists, we didn't celebrate birthdays, so Christmas was the one time of year when I got presents.

One weekend while at home, I decided to investigate Mother's shelf to see if "Santa" had accidentally left one of my gifts up there. I must have been about nine years old. Mother was clattering away on her typewriter when I pulled my bureau out from the wall and climbed up on top of it. Standing on tippy toes, I swiped my hand across the edge of the shelf. Touching something, I pulled it down and examined what looked like a flattened balloon with a round rubber rim. It had been lying there on the edge of the shelf as if someone had stuck it there in a hurry. Whatever it was, it had to be another one of Mother's secrets.

I stomped up to Mother, thrust out my hand with the confiscated object and demanded, "What are *you* doing with this?"

Mother froze in stunned silence. Then, her patrician cool gave way to dismay. "How do *you* know what *that* is?"

My chest swelled with pride. I had disarmed Mother's Christian Science serenity.

Mother was too shocked to realize that I was bluffing.

In haste, she proffered a speedy response. "Dr. Borow gave it to me. He invented them."

Sixty years later, I will tell Olga Steckler this story over the phone. Olga had modeled for Poppy and Rolf

Armstrong, both of whom lived at the Hotel des Artistes. Hearing a familiar name from the past, Olga's voice brightened. "Dear Dr. Borow," she crooned. "We called him the House Doctor. He took such good care of us, artists and models, at the des Artistes. We all loved him. He was well known. Had a cancer clinic in New Jersey, but..." Olga laughed, "he didn't invent the diaphragm."

***

After I discovered Mother's diaphragm, her attitude toward me changed. She stopped waking me up in the morning by kissing my feet and wiggling my toes with, "This little piggy went to market, this little piggy stayed home..." She became withdrawn, distancing herself from what she began to perceive as an adversary. In Christian Science terminology, "Error." Something to be meditated away through "proper thinking."

Gone were the days I'd seen in home movies showing Mother cooing over me as a baby, smothering me in kisses and laughing as she lifted me over her head. It made me angry, and I came to resent her for keeping her secret even more.

After the age of seven or eight, I can't remember her ever giving me a hug or a kiss. Nor did she ever tell me she loved me. I came to rationalize her aloofness as New York cool.

***

One winter night in New York, while lying awake listening to Poppy's muffled voice emanating from the studio, I overheard him tell Mother about a murder which I thought he said occurred in the Hotel des Artists. A man had shot his wife, then turned the gun on himself. The murder/suicide left their boy, Honnie, an orphan. "He had nobody," said Poppy, "and I couldn't let him end up in an orphanage. So, Nancy and I, we talked it over. We never had kids of our own, so she agreed to raise him as our own."

I was physically shaken. Was I an orphan like Honnie? Some kid Poppy took pity on?

"Honnie" did sort of sound like Holly.

Years later, the three of us drove up to Dobbs Ferry where, for the first time, I came face to face with Honnie and Poppy's granddaughter Carolyn who attended a private school in the area.

Carolyn must have been ten. One year younger than me. And by then, Honnie was a grown man who looked like a successful businessman in his overcoat and fedora. What I didn't know was that he had been interrogated by Nazis after his plane was shot down in the war. He had spent time in solitary confinement and was forced into a death march from one Stalag prison camp to another, wearing nothing but rags in winter.

Had I known this, who knows, perhaps I wouldn't have hated him for being close to "my" Poppy. Mother snapped a picture of Honnie, Carolyn, Poppy and me. There I am, arms folded across my chest, scowling at the camera as if I felt excluded from a family I coveted.

***

As Poppy's fame burgeoned, my ego shriveled.

I was ten years old when Poppy and Mother took me with them to the Parke-Bernet Gallery to see Poppy's exhibit. One of his Old Red Mill landscapes was in the window. All lit up as if on a Broadway stage. Recognizing Poppy as the great American artist she'd read about in newspaper articles, a woman on the street ran up to Poppy. Breathless with excitement, she exclaimed, "You must be Howard Chandler Christy!"

I wanted to push myself between her and Poppy and say, "Yes, and I'm his daughter!"

Instead, I smoldered inside. It was Poppy who gave me a sense of who I was, and anyone who ignored my existence as linked to him made me feel small and insignificant.

***

In 1951, I was eleven when General MacArthur returned from Korea. Poppy took me to see the ticker tape parade in MacArthur's honor. On the corner of 74th and Central Park West, Poppy bought me a little American flag from a vendor. Crowds poured in from all sides, filling the sidewalks up to the curb. When MacArthur's motorcade came into view, escorted by mounted police, Poppy yelled to me over the cheering crowd, "Wave the flag, Holly! Wave the flag!" I held up my flag and waved it at the man in a military cap passing by in the open car as cheers went up and clouds of shredded paper exploded from windows and floated down like feathers from a pillow.

The next morning, Poppy came through the front door waving a newspaper. "Hey, Kid," he called to Mother. "Look at this. Holly and I are in the paper."

"Let me see," I said, pushing my face between him and the paper. I didn't see any picture. Not having his looking glass, Poppy handed the paper to Mother, who read it aloud. "Howard Chandler Christy was in front of the crowd cheering for General MacArthur. With him was a little girl named Holly Morris, waving an American flag."

I wanted to shout, "I'm not Holly Morris! And I'm *not* just a *little girl*."

But, if I wasn't Holly Morris, who was I?

Mother's Error? Which, in Christian Science, meant Nothing more than wrong thinking?

I hadn't heard Poppy talking to the reporter. There had been too much clamor. But it had to have been Poppy who gave the reporter the name Morris I'd come to hate as standing between me and the man I loved as a father.

I felt publicly disowned by Poppy.

Now, all of New York knew the awful truth.

The newspaper confirmed the worst thing about me that increased my resentment toward Mother. I wasn't Howard Chandler Christy's special little girl. I was just a little girl named Holly Morris.

Sissela Bok, the Swedish-born philosopher, ethicist and psychologist, compared secrecy to fire. "Secrecy is as indispensable to human beings as fire and as greatly feared. Both enhance and protect life, yet both can stifle, lay waste, and spread out of all control. Both can be used to guard intimacy or to invade it, to nurture or to consume."

Mother's secret was to consume the rest of my life in a search for what I would come to call The Truth.

CHAPTER THIRTEEN

City of Orgies

Home is heaven and orgies are vile
But you need an orgy, once in a while.

- Ogden Nash

It was Christmas morning in 1950. I awoke to Poppy's voice coming from the studio. I bounded out of my room, and there, beneath the boughs of pine and glittering tinsel-draped Christmas tree, were all the things I'd said I'd wanted at F.A.O. Schwartz Fifth Avenue. The twelve-inch horse with real hair and leather saddle. Even the wind-up train I'd wanted was jerking merrily around the track—its little red caboose bringing up the rear. *Woo,*

woo, ding, ding. Surprise packages in all shapes and sizes were stacked on white cotton make-believe snow under the tree with the white angel on top. The homely warmth of roasting turkey and the scent of seasoned poultry stuffing filled the air. Best of all—Poppy was there.

Around noon, we sat down to eat roast turkey next to the Archangel Gabriel and the Virgin Mary on the tapestried wall.

"Who's going to eat the Pope's nose?" Poppy asked as he sliced into the turkey.

"Me! Me!" I said, loving the crispiness of the roast turkey tail. We laughed, and I slid onto his knee. At ten, I was almost too big, but he didn't seem to care.

"I never want you to turn out like Natalie," he said of his daughter as he gave me a bounce. "All she does is sit on her ass and knit." Poppy never kept it a secret that he had another family. I had always known that Nancy was his wife and Natalie was his daughter from his first marriage.

My Christmas cheer ended when Poppy left to spend the rest of the day with his real family at the Hotel des Artistes. Nancy, Natalie, and his granddaughter Carolyn. I didn't like sharing Poppy any day of the year, but especially on Christmas.

Shortly after he left, my wind-up train chugged to a weary stop, and glumness set in, leaving me as empty as the crumpled wrapping paper under the tree.

Then the phone rang.

Oh, Christmas joy! Peace and goodwill. Doris was inviting us over. Either she had forgotten the bad words I'd taught Wanda—or I had been forgiven. I was overjoyed that I had been accepted back into Doris's good graces.

Poppy had his family, and I did too. Doris and Wanda. It felt a whole lot better knowing that I, too, had a family to visit. Wanda was my only playmate, which made her feel like my little sister.

Mother threw on her fur coat, and I pulled on my leggings, my snow jacket, and my warm, woolly mittens, and out we went—into a cold, white blizzard.

Bowing our heads into the wind, we got off the bus at Columbus Circle. Shivering in the cold, we waited for the light at the intersection of Columbus Circle and 59th Street. Across the street, the warm glow of lights emanating from Walgreens looked inviting through the veil of falling snow. "How about a hot chocolate with whipped cream on top?" said Mother in her playful, big sister voice.

"Yes!" I cheered, and off we went through brown slush in our rubber boots.

Inside Walgreens, I could smell the radiator heat and feel its radiant warmth as we climbed onto stools at the counter. Outside a frosty window, hooded passersby clutched their coats and woolen scarves to fend off the cold. Nestles hot chocolate never tasted better.

When we came out, I had to lean into the wind to keep from being blown over. The wind cut through my coat like knives, which made me think Manhattan must be the coldest place on Earth.

Down Central Park South, we trekked. Past the Saint Moritz. The Essex House. As the awning of the Plaza Hotel came into view, we ducked into the warmth of the gleaming gold mirrored lobby of 36 Central Park South and stomped the snow off our boots. Mother smiled at the doorman, who nodded recognition as we headed for the private elevator in the back. We stepped in, and Mother pushed the button.

The elevator came to a creaking halt. Through the

ornate gate, I could see the antique tapestry, much like ours facing us from the wall of the narrow hallway. Stepping out of the elevator, I followed Mother down the tapestried hall that led into the white, carpeted, high-ceilinged, extravagant world of Tade Styka.

"You hoo!" called Mother. "Doris, we're here." No one answered.

Doris and Wanda did not live with Tade. They lived next door. Together, the two apartments took up half the floor in a building on the most expensive real estate in the world.

Tall windows facing north gave a sense of openness, with Central Park in the distance, all covered in snow. On this particular day, everything looked pristine white: Tade's wall-to-wall carpeting and the mounting snow on his balcony with New York's Fifth Avenue stretching into the distance along snow-covered Central Park. Across the street below, horses with buggies equipped with fur blankets were lined up along the park, waiting for someone to take a ride through the falling snow. It was picture-perfect.

Any noise from traffic below was absorbed by thick carpeting and a heavy tapestry that hung from two stories above our heads all the way to the floor. Unlike our religious tapestry of the same era, this one depicted an orgy in what looked like a Greek temple. Gleeful cherubs hiding behind huge columns were poised to shoot arrows into half-naked men caressing their courtesans. Everything in Tade's study was a rare antique giving the place the sedate aura of Fifth Avenue's opulent Frick Museum.

"Lee Lee" squealed Doris as she breezed in, wearing nothing but a billowing, see-through pink negligee. Giggling the way they always did, Doris and Mother swished back down the narrow hall and out the front door, leaving me behind. I stood there in the stillness. Curious, I peered into every corner. There was only one other place that enthralled me as much—the Fragonard Room at the Frick museum on Fifth Avenue a few blocks down. Fragonard's huge paintings of mystic gardens and frolicking ladies in billowing silk held me in awe and stirred my young heart with visions of romance.

Tade's studio made me feel like I was in a castle. I didn't yet know that the castles of yore were dark and dank, with no cushy white carpets, no running hot and cold water or flushing toilets, and no array of gourmet restaurants serving exotic dishes a short walk down the street.

Tade Styka didn't live like a king. He lived like a god.

I was glad Tade was gone so I could prowl around. Leaning against the tapestried wall was the life-sized portrait of Tade's father, Jan Styka, with his long white hair and beard, which is now displayed at Forest Lawn Memorial Park in Glendale, California, along with Styka's immense *Crucifixion* painting.

Propped up on an easel was a life-sized portrait of Doris in a low-cut gown as she cuddles her rosy, dimple-cheeked Wanda as a baby. Hanging on a wall was another life-sized portrait, this one of Wanda hugging her beloved collie she named Paddy after her father's best friend, Paderewski.

Perhaps it was because Poppy's studio at the Hotel des Artistes was off-limits to me that I found Tade's studio so fascinating. Upstairs was a loft overlooking the studio that served as Tade's bedroom. A gorilla skin hanging over the banister blocked the view from downstairs.

I was afraid to venture upstairs as it felt too much like the great Tadeusz's personal space. Between Tade's bedroom loft and the balcony overlooking the park was a bar. Over bottles of wine and brandy, framed photographs of Tade were clustered on the wall. All displayed his suntanned and exceptionally muscular physique. In one, he looks like Adam—naked as the day he was created, bursting out of the bushes holding a fig leaf over his privates.

"Holly, Holly," squealed Wanda bounding into her father's studio. "Come see what Daddy bought me for Christmas." She was stark naked. I wasn't surprised. Doris and Wanda were nudists. I followed Wanda back down the tapestried hallway into the apartment building hallway to the next apartment.

Into Doris's apartment, waltzed Wanda with me right behind her. The acrid smell of urine stung my nose as it wafted up from a gold shag carpet as a band of five yapping miniature, white poodles stampeded toward me. Pierre, Poupet, Jolie, Fi Fi, and the last one's name escapes me.

"Look, Holly!" screamed Wanda from behind the biggest doll I'd ever seen. Nearly as tall as Wanda. She wound it up from a lever on its back, and one of its legs kicked forward. Then another. I watched in amazement as the doll strutted toward me with a robotic whir. "And here's another one," cried Wanda. Breathless with excitement, she sent another child-sized doll my way. I stepped back as the animated mechanisms marched toward me down the soiled, yellow-carpeted hall.

"Daddy gave them to me. Daddy! Daddy!" cried Wanda gleefully, bouncing up and down behind them.

Wanda had again outdone me. Her doll would have trounced my little horse and laid him flat. What's more, she had someone she could call Daddy.

"And they talk," shrieked Wanda as she yanked a string in the doll's back. "Mommy. Mommy. Mommy," said the doll with a hollow twang before being brought down by a pack of wild dogs. The doll toppled over the poodles like King Kong and sent them yapping. I stepped over its legs as they swung in midair like mechanical scissors. The first doll kept on marching till it hit the wall––motor revving.

As I entered the dining room, Tade was sitting at the end of a long table. Facing him, above the mantel, was a life-sized nude of Doris slumped to the floor, hands manacled behind her back. Bound by a coarse rope cutting into the translucent flesh of her breasts and delicate pink nipples, she looked like a trussed turkey.

"Is that you?" I asked Doris. I wasn't sure because Tade had painted her as blond. Her identity was concealed by her head hanging in shame and her hair flopping over her face.

As usual, Doris ignored me.

Christmas presents were piled on the table and all over the floor. Doris was busy tearing them open and re-wrapping them to give to others. "This one is for Mrs. McFadden," she said. "Such a gold digger."

Bernarr McFadden was the world's first health crusader. Originally called Bernard, he changed his name to Bernarr because it sounded more like the roar of a lion. And roar he did—about the evils of female underwear, especially circulation-restricting, muscle-binding brassieres—something Doris and my mother took to heart. Bernarr MacFadden was responsible for Mother's lifelong disdain for bras and panties, a fact that worried me a lot. Especially on windy New York corners.

"Is she rich?" I asked, referring to Mrs. McFadden. I recognized the McFadden name as one bandied about as influential in New York circles.

"Augh!" cried Doris in dismay. "Never use that word!"

"What word?" I hadn't said a bad word since Mommy washed my mouth out with Ivory soap.

Doris shook her head. "Rich," she said. "It sounds too Jewish."

That was enough to convince me that Doris could never, no, never, never be Jewish. And what was wrong with being Jewish? Sensing another secret, I was afraid to ask.

A woman stepped out of a closet-sized kitchenette and headed for the door. Doris called out to her in Polish. I picked up on the only word I knew. *"Dziekuje."* Thank you.

"That's our maid," said Wanda. "We brought her here from Poland. She doesn't speak English. Did you see what big breasts she has?"

I hadn't noticed.

"She has to wear a bra," Wanda told me as if it was quite a phenomenon. "And her breasts are so heavy the straps cut into her shoulders."

I'd never heard anyone talk about breasts before.

Off in a corner, one of the poodles humped his back and strained over the shag rug as if it were a field of dandelions. Doris grabbed a Kleenex and swooped down on his deposit. Holding the poop in one hand, she scooped the offending doggy up with the other. "Poopy, poopy, Poopet," she said, nuzzling him with puckered red lips. The rest of the poodles flocked around her legs, yipping as if they were laughing.

Opposite big glass windows that looked out over a fire escape and the backs of other buildings hung a large painting of a Ming vase with the name "Doris Styka" displayed prominently on the lower left side.

I studied it closely. At the age of ten, I was already adept at recognizing individual artistic style, having prowled the halls of the Metropolitan Museum of Art for hours on end. I could tell a Corbet from a Corot, a Da Vinci from a Michelangelo, and on and on. Painting recognition was a game I played with myself at museums. And the style of this Ming vase was clearly a Styka. Tade Styka, that is. The clarity of color. The lucidity of light playing off the brilliant blue and white porcelain. How could Doris have painted that? Even the signature was the same large, square letters that Tade used. Only the first name had been changed.

Nevertheless, I held my tongue lest I be shunned as an

incorrigible brat and sent home. It was bad manners to challenge adults. No matter how wrong they might be. Don't ask questions. Just accept what they say. At the age of ten, I wasn't about to break the rules. Not if I wanted to be accepted in the Styka household, which was the only family I had.

That evening, Tade offered to take us all out to dinner. There was a sudden scramble to get dressed. "I have to go *shu-shu*," said Wanda. Polish for wee-wee. We both bolted into the bathroom. While Wanda tinkled, I examined Doris's yellow concoction of glycerin she had mixed with lanolin in a plastic jar. I stuck my finger into the goop. *No wonder Doris's face looks shiny.* Opposite the sink, the curtain rod was loaded with fur coats: silver and sable mink, chinchilla, and a gorgeous, full-length, champagne-colored sheared fur of some other animal that was softer than velvet. All those furs would never have fit in a New York closet. Naturally, they had to be hung somewhere. Why not over the bathtub?

Wanda jumped up from the toilet and bounded out. Being more modest, I shut the door. When I came out, Wanda was spinning around the mirrored bedroom like a whirling dervish, then flopped backwards onto the bed, flinging her legs apart.

"Mommy! Mommy! Powder, my woozie," she yelped. "Powder, my woozie!"

"Well, all right," cooed Doris, dipping a pink powder puff into a round flowery box.

Poof. A bouquet of perfumed talc billowed into the air.

Doris and Wanda were what I would call hedonists, but I didn't think in those terms then. To me, they were, well—entertainingly different.

That evening, Tade took us to dinner next door to the Plaza. It was the most elegant restaurant I'd ever been in. The Log Cabin Inn was more Poppy's style. Other than the Café des Artistes, of course, but I'd never been there.

Tade ordered lobster.

"What's lobster?" I asked.

"Ho, ho ho," chuckled Tade. "You have never had the pleasure of lobster? I order lobster for you," he said in his suave European accent. "That way, you will come to know what is lobster."

After dinner, we returned to Doris's place. While Mother, Doris, and Tade did whatever adults do, Wanda and I raced from one apartment to the other, screaming in the hallway and making a terrible ruckus.

Poor neighbors. Invisible as they were, the racket must have been unnerving. But for Wanda and me, we'd never seen the neighbors, so they didn't exist. New Yorkers poke their heads out only when no one is around.

Off came Wanda's dress. Flinging it onto the bed, she raced down the hall and out the door in her panties, with me chasing after her. Into Tade's studio, we dashed. Screaming, Wanda pulled off her panties and pitched them across the room. They landed on the wings of a bronze angel. This struck us so funny we doubled over and rolled on the floor with laughter.

"Take off your clothes," Wanda screamed, chest heaving.

"I don't want to," I said.

"Please," begged Wanda.

"No!"

"Catch me!" she screamed, running for the door. Down the hall, we streaked and into Doris's apartment with yipping poodles taking up the chase. We burst into the dining room. And what I saw would have shocked anyone but us. Tade—in his starched white shirt and bow tie, was sitting at the head of the table facing his painting of Doris in bondage. Merrily waltzing around the table were Doris and Mother in the nude. As for pubic hair, it was shaved. Every time one of them came close to Tade, he reached out and gave them a pinch on their behinds. It was a sight to see Doris and Mother screaming with glee. With every round, Tade would bellow a deep Santa Clause "Ho, ho, ho!"

To me, it was just boisterous fun. I'd seen this sort of thing before in a movie at the Paris theater down the street on the corner of Fifth Avenue, which was a sedate, marble building that looked more like a bank than a theater. No blinking marquees or billboard teasers. Inside, foreign films were shown in which nudity and risqué subjects were explored. A sign at the ticket window warned, "Adults only." I guess the girl at the window didn't notice me sandwiched between Doris's bulky mink and Mother's fluffy fox shawl as we got our tickets and ducked inside to see *Fernandel*—a French comedy about a heavy-jawed, leering Frenchman who went around pinching lady's butts. Doris and Mother laughed so hard that the man behind us leaned forward and asked them to be quiet. "And could you *please* remove your hat?" he added peevishly to Doris.

"Oh yes, of course. I'm so sorry," Doris had said, tugging at her hat while fumbling for the hat pins that secured it to her head. And it was so embarrassing— Mother giggling and Doris with that throaty laugh of hers tugging at her big, floppy hat—I wanted to crawl under my seat.

I hated watching Fernandel pinch bottoms as much as I hated Tallulah Bankhead in *Lifeboat*—both movies I had to sit through with Mother and Doris. Years later, I'll come to understand those jokes and double entendres, in the same way, I will come to understand many of the things I heard but couldn't understand as a child.

"Come on, Holly, take off your clothes," cried Wanda, grabbing my hand and jumping up and down with merriment. "Let's play a game. I do this..." She threw her back against the door frame and slid down till her bottom hit the floor, legs wide apart. "And you do this." She swiped my hand up between her legs.

I remember seeing something like this at the Primate House in Central Park Zoo. It never failed to draw crowds when those crazy chimps whooped it up. People would flock in to see what the disturbance was all about with all those simian shrieks. I would wriggle in through the gawking crowd, most of them men, and watch until a big male got fed up with our intrusive snooping and showed his contempt by shaking the bars in a dreadful rage. Then he'd swing across the cage, fill his cheeks with water and lope back dragging his knuckles. Spectators would shriek and try to escape as he grabbed hold of the bars. Too late. We all got sprayed with saliva mixed with water. People in front pushed back in vain. That chimp had made a monkey of us all.

"It's fun!" screamed Wanda leaping to her feet—then running and screaming back to Tade's place. It wasn't long before I, too, was streaking naked through the building and sliding down the dining room wall spread-eagle.

Then something happened that I never expected.

Wanda touched a magic spot. An electrifying lubricious pulsation made my legs go limp.

It was pure magic!

That night Mother and I stayed over. Wanda took me to Tade's brocade bed with silk pillows that looked like a room that should have been cordoned off in a Frick exhibit.

As I nestled in between the covers, naked Wanda dove in beside me and pressed her hot, moist body against mine—the flush of pleasure still on her face.

An uneasy feeling came over me. Wanda sensed my resistance and bounced out of bed, leaving me alone to absorb the seductive silence of Tade's private domain.

I got up, went downstairs, and looked out through the glass doors to the balcony. Outside the majestic windows, the city lights glistened softly through the falling snow. Although I couldn't have articulated it then, I felt something profound—a feeling I wanted to hold on to forever. There was something sacred about beauty. I had seen it in Nature, in art, and finally, in the peacefulness of this place.

When I awoke, the studio was bright in the clear morning light. I dressed and went downstairs. Tade's famous brother, Adam, was standing by the balcony almost in silhouette. Ramrod straight. He was dressed in a tweed suit, open-shirt collar, and silk cravat. I recognized him as Tade's brother, but feeling his cold, silent stare, I was afraid to speak.

Entering Doris's place, I found her stepping out of her tiny kitchen with a plate of something I'd never seen before.

"Mmm!" said Doris licking her lips. "Blueberry blintzes for breakfast."

"Goodie, goodie!" cried Wanda as we all pulled out chairs and sat down at the dining room table. And there—before that big nude of Doris, hog-tied in a crumpled heap—we ate blueberry blintzes for breakfast.

Tade was nowhere to be seen. Nor had he returned to his studio that night. I never asked where he'd gone. He had done what I now know he always did—disappeared into the dazzling New York City night. *City of orgies, walks and joys* said, Walt Whitman. *City of whom I have liv'd and sung in your midst... / O Manhattan, your frequent and swift flash of eyes offering me love...*"

For me, it was the best Christmas ever.

Lobster at the Plaza with the great Tadeusz Styka.

And—my first orgasm.

CHAPTER FOURTEEN

White Deer Mountain

Art is the beautiful way of doing things.

- Elbert Hubbard

It was like watching a painting develop. Stroke by stroke, Poppy and Mother's personalities revealed themselves in the renovation of the Old Red Mill. During our first summer in Vermont, we made frequent trips to Granville, New York, which was less than five miles away. Granville had one main street, a train station, and a large general store stocked with everything from bathing suits and dungarees (blue jeans) to bolts of fabric and gallons of paint. On one of those trips, Poppy bought me a royal blue canvas hammock, which he hung between a big maple and a hook on the side of the garage. I was delighted with the way it wrapped around me. Close to my hammock, Poppy built a ladder with a rope railing down a grassy drop-off, giving me easy access to the Mettowee below. Lying in my hammock while Poppy and Mother worked, I would let the drone of the river below lull me into what I recognize today as a transcendental state. A well-beaten path from my hammock led back to the mill through Mother's rose garden. Along the river's edge, I became acquainted with the many bullfrogs that would splash into the water and hide next to a rock when I came by. I soon learned to hunch down and approach them from the front as they could see better from the rear. Ever so gently, I'd stroke the frog's spotted greenback and round white tummy as he blinked his big eyes. He looked like a little fat man with his big stomach and skinny legs. I came to love these creatures, and I treated them all with gentle care.

One day, while swinging in my hammock, I heard the clop-clop of heavy hooves and the rumble of wheels crunching toward me on the dirt road. I sprang to my feet and bolted to the wood-and-wire fence Poppy had stretched along the road to keep me safe. Lumbering toward me on the dirt road was a team of giant workhorses hauling a load of logs.

"Whoa," croaked the rangy man with carrot-colored hair as he reined in his two Belgian draft horses. "I'm Bill McIntyre," he said. "Mr. Christy 'round? I done hear he's got work." Bill grinned, and for the first time in my young life, I saw someone with missing teeth.

Bill jumped down from the wagon. His weather-beaten face was red and furrowed like old leather. I ran and got Poppy, and the two of them went off to talk.

Poppy and Bill struck a deal. Bill would keep his horses in our stable in exchange for work. He and his wife Helen would live in the white house across the street, which was part of the mill property, and they would be our year-round caretakers of the Old Red Mill in exchange for free rent. And, being a school teacher, Helen would tutor me in reading from *McGuffy's Readers*.

The deal was sealed between Poppy and Bill with a hearty handshake. Then Bill lifted me onto one of his draft horses. Mother snapped a picture, which I still have. I look so very small sitting up there on that big Belgian draft horse.

That night, Bill's workhorses were fed from troughs in the Old Red Mill stable, and I went to bed in my sleeping, bag happy-as-could-be, reeking of "horsey."

A few days later, a crew of Bill's rugged mountain men showed up, and Poppy told them what to do. Without a blueprint, they set to work cutting out the mill's second floor, which turned the upstairs into a loft with a railing over which I could look down into the mill when I got up in the morning.

Every day brought a new addition to the Old Red Mill. Bill installed a wood-burning stove in the middle of the oak dance floor with a chimney that went clear up through the open beams of the ceiling and slate roof. A high stone wall was built on the roadside of the mill to block out dust and noise.

Next came the Old Red Mill's crowning glory: A veranda that wrapped clear around the mill from the back door where the rickety balcony had been all the way around the mill to the rock wall along the road. A right angle joined two outside walls of the mill, making a wide space the size of a large kitchen nook. "We'll put the restaurant booth here against the adjacent wall," Poppy told Bill. *So that's what Poppy meant when he told Mother, "We'll put the booth outside and eat our meals over the river."* It wasn't such a crazy idea after all. Poppy had a vision and a plan all along.

Next, the mill got a new face. Bill and his men painted the mill red and the deck floor grey. Above the wide area of the deck, a large striped awning was hung. Tucked in the right-angle corner, they installed the restaurant booth, and it was here, under the awning, that we ate all our meals. Rain or shine. This became our special place. An eagle's nest from which we could survey the glorious Mettowee valley beyond.

Talk about feng shui. We had it. The energy from the wind and the river flowed through the mountain valley straight into our open arms.

From our eagle's nest, we could see all the way to the bend in the river where the Mettowee disappeared behind the mountain. And every evening as we ate dinner, we watched the black-and-white cows a mile away wade across the upstream shallows on their way to the Smith's farm for milking. Their distant lowing was music to my ears. And when the sky darkened, the stars appeared in a show as spectacular as what I'd seen at the Hayden Planetarium. Always watchful for any new event, Poppy would alert us at first sight of a shooting star against the velvety sky.

Never had I been so in love with life and grateful to be alive.

***

The inside walls of the mill retained their rustic, bare wood appearance. Its main source of sunlight streamed in through a window in the gable between the eaves. In the big, empty space created by cutting out the middle of the second floor, Poppy hung a fifteen-foot model schooner, which he had shipped from his studio in New York for Bill to hang from the mill rafters.

The first thing I saw every morning, when I stepped out of my bedroom, was that schooner. I remember looking down one morning just in time to spot a tiny grey and white mouse skitter across the deck and disappear into the captain's cabin. I stood there waiting for the little chap to reappear. When he didn't, I ran downstairs for a bacon and eggs breakfast, allowing my imagination to picture the little mouse taking over the ship in the captain's quarters.

One afternoon when Bill and Poppy were downstairs talking, the flutter of birds up in the rafters caught Bill's attention. Swallows were flying in and out through a broken pane in a window to feed their young in mud nests they'd built along the beams.

"I can fix that thar broken pane," Bill told Poppy.

"No," said Poppy."

"Ain't you bothered by them birds?"

"Nope. Gotta wait until their babies have left the nest."

That was Poppy. As kind to animals as he was to humans.

***

I watched with amazement as a bulldozer lumbered over the embankment behind the mill. Clunking over rocks like an Army tank, it stopped midway up the river near the dam. From above the river, on the veranda, Poppy shouted orders. "Start over there. Take those logs out on the mountainside first.

Up the river climbed the bulldozer until it reached the foot of the dam on the mountainside. From my ringside seat on the veranda, I watched what turned out to be more exciting than the Barnum & Bailey Circus.

Boom! The bulldozer rammed the side of the dam. A log gave way with a thunderous roar. Water gushed through as the old log dam buckled and began its collapse like a house of cards. Roaring in protest, there went the first algae-covered log. It stood up on end, then fell with a thunderous crash. Bobbing down the river, it banged into a boulder with the crack of a cannon. Another gave way. Then another. Logs crashed this way and that, hanging up on boulders, then giving way with a groan.

But the work had just begun. Poppy waved to the driver, and the bulldozer stopped. "Those big boulders down the river!" yelled Poppy, pointing to the stone monoliths rising out of the river like monuments, "Push them up here and pile them into a line across the river below the mill."

What happened next turned our Old Red Mill into paradise.

Instead of the fierce foaming threat to the foundation of our Mill, Poppy transformed the Mettowee below the mill into a mirror of tranquility. Above the bolder dam, a gentle stream now flowed beneath the willows casting cool shadows in the quiet pools along the riverbank.

That summer, the Mettowee became a breeding ground for rainbow trout. From our veranda, we could see them darting about through the clear water, their colorful backs glinting in the sunlight as they jumped for bugs with a splash. "Watch this," Poppy said one morning as he wadded up a piece of bread from his breakfast and tossed it over the banister. Instantly a school of minnows formed a dark cloud that shot toward it through the water. They swooped in on the bread, tails thrashing the water. After that, whenever I went into the water, the minnows mistook my white flesh for a jumbo piece of bread. Converging on me, they tickled me all over as they nibbled at my body. Cutie went wild with excitement as he tried to pounce on them. He stuck his nose into the water, trying to bite them, but all he got were the bubbles he blew through his snout.

Poppy had tamed the river.

In so doing, he had made it more beautiful than ever.

***

In the Granville General Store, Poppy pulled two bolts of fabric from the pile and laid them side by side. "Holly, which one do you like?"

"The blue one," I said. It had royal blue roses and dark green leaves on a white background. A few days later, when I came in from watching Bill feed his horses in the stable, Poppy said, "Come with me. I have a surprise for you." I followed him up to my little bedroom, where he showed me what he had done. He had built a dressing table that stretched from one wall to the other. Over the top of the table, he had stretched the royal blue cloth that matched the blue roses on the fabric of its skirt. Over it, he'd hung a long mirror.

"It's beautiful!" I squealed.

Then he pointed to the matching royal blue bottle of perfume he'd placed on the dressing table. I ran over and unscrewed its silver top, and sniffed.

"Evening in Paris," he said.

Today, just a mile from where the Old Red Mill once stood, The Vermont Country Store still sells "Evening in Paris" in the same dark blue bottle.

Looking back, I think it was Poppy's way of telling me he was proud I was a girl. At the same time, it was OK for me to play like a boy, even wearing boy's bathing suits. Whatever I wanted to be or do was OK with him.

But he didn't just fix up my bedroom. He also gave Mother's room a makeover at the other end of the balcony. He made her the same dressing table with pink roses.

***

One chilly night, while Poppy and Bill were sitting by

the potbellied stove, Poppy asked Bill if he could build a cement basin to catch the spring water that tumbled from the side of the mountain across the river.

In his slow, easy drawl, Bill said, "Sure can." Tipping his chair back on two legs, he looked off into the distance as if seeing something we couldn't. "Folks 'round here say they seen two white deer up there in that thar mountain."

"Really?" I said, perking up from the floor where I was scratching Cutie's tummy in front of the fire.

"Up in that thar clearing on the top," said Bill.

That night, when I went to bed, I lay awake listening to the whirr of the river Poppy had tamed. Sitting up in my sleeping bag, I looked out my window. Across the river, looming dark and mysterious, was the mountain. At its foot, the Mettowee sparkled in the moonlight. *White Deer Mountain. That's what I'll call it.*

The next morning, I awoke to the chatter of the blue-belted kingfisher. I unzipped myself from my Army sack, scrambled up on my cot, and watched the bird flying toward me through the rising river mist. The loud rattling stopped as he landed on the rope that stretched from the mill across the river to the foot of White Deer Mountain. From his perch, over the American flag, the kingfisher kept a sharp lookout. Then down he shot like a bullet, snapped up a trout, and flew back up the river to his nest along the river bank.

I knew Poppy was up because the American flag was already flapping in the breeze outside my window. The reflection of its red, white, and blue rippled in the water below. Rolling out our big American flag every morning and pulling it in before nightfall was a ritual Poppy performed twice a day. At dusk, he pulled it back in, and together, he and Mother would fold it in strict military fashion the way I now know he had learned to do in Teddy Roosevelt's regiment of Rough Riders. First lengthwise, then inward until the red and white stripes disappeared into the starry night of a navy blue star-studded triangle.

I jumped off the cot and bounded down the stairs toward the veranda—no need to get dressed. I slept in what became my summer skin—a boy's blue-and-white striped swimsuit that had grown too tight, barely covering my butt.

Out on the veranda, I found Mother reading the weekly Christian Science lesson to Poppy, who was drinking his morning coffee. It was their daily ritual in preparation for another day of landscape painting.

Mother went inside to fix breakfast, and I slid in next to Poppy on the booth bench under the awning. Minutes later, she passed me a plate of bacon and eggs through the open kitchen window.

Standing up, Poppy went to the railing and looked off into the distance. "Isn't God good to give us all this beauty to enjoy?" he said as he surveyed the Mettowee valley. And again, he quoted his favorite verse from Elbert Hubbard, adding his own embellishments. "How much better it is to go out into the woods, lift up your heart in song and be a child than fight human inclination, trying to be proper, whatever the hell that might be."

By the end of summer, I had learned to love the way the ice-cold Mettowee made my body tingle when it flushed with warmth. It was pure magic. An energy surging up from inside. Never had I felt so alive.

I reveled in the river rippling over my body and the swarms of minnows nibbling at my toes. When I got so cold, my teeth began to chatter. There was always the big flat boulder upon which I could stretch out like a lizard and warm up in the sun. Cold, hot. Cold, hot. I never tired of the gratifying stimulation it brought. Closing my eyes, I could focus on the sounds of the Earth I'd come to love and feel so much a part of. The chorus of finches in the willows, the buzz of a bumblebee, the hum of a dragonfly overhead. Most of all, the laughing water of the Mettowee. It was music to my ears.

Nestled between Mount Haystack and White Deer Mountains, the Old Red Mill was the most perfect place on Earth.

But the sweetest sound of all was the squish, squish of waterlogged sneakers as Poppy and Mother rounded the corner of our veranda, returning from another day of painting across the river. I see them now tramping toward me, carting their paint boxes and canvases—each a window into paradise. They sit down on the bench facing White Deer Mountain, pull off their sneakers, and leave them to dry on the faded barn-red bench by the mill's back door.

Two pairs of canvas sneakers—side by side—bleached white by the sun with the scent of the sun-drenched canvas. I understand what Mark Twain meant when he said, "Wheresoever she was, there was Eden."

CHAPTER FIFTEEN

Forget-Me-Not

He who knows nothing, loves nothing.

- Paracelsus

It was the summer of 1951. I was eleven. Poppy was seventy-nine but showed no signs of slowing his pace. There was no indication that our bucolic summers at the Old Red Mill would soon end.

That summer, Poppy built a johnboat in the garage and painted it red outside and white inside. Then he and Bill McIntyre hauled it down the embankment and dropped it in the water.

"Hop in, Holly," said Poppy with a proud smile, "I'll

take you for a ride."

He sat in the back, guiding the boat with a single oar while I sat in front, taking it all in. Myriad birds chirped from the willows lining the banks with clumps of daisies, and Black-Eyed Susans leaning over the bank as if admiring their reflections in the water.

I had come to believe Poppy, and I would always be together at the Old Red Mill. Wasn't that what Christian Science taught? That there was no such thing as death? Above me, powder puff clouds floated aimlessly across the sky, casting shadows over the mossy-green pasture cropped low by grazing cows.

Looking back now, I can't conceive of anything more valuable than those rustic summers in Vermont. Through the creative impulse of two artists, I learned to rejoice in the creation and preservation of beauty.

As we approached the pasture across the river from the Mill, Poppy pulled up to the bank and let me out at the foot of White Deer Mountain. I rolled under the electric wire fence to join the cows in the pasture. Warmed by the sun, the grass felt spongy beneath my pounding bare feet. The cows jerked their heads up as they saw me approach. Unsure of my intent, the heifers swung their heads back and forth, the whites of their eyes big as golf balls as they tried to decide whether to stampede or not. As I got closer, they reeled and galumphed off, kicking their rumps in the air. "Scaredy-cats," I told them. As usual, Bessy stayed right where she was, placidly chewing her cud as she lay in the shade of the willows along the river bank.

"Nice, Bessy," I told her as I drew close. She swallowed her cud and swung her head around. I stopped and waited until the serene look in her big brown eyes returned. Kneeling, I curled up beside her, nestling my head in the hollow between her shoulder and her bulging black-and-white belly, which was pushed up by the ground beneath her. Stroking behind her ears, I rubbed my cheek against her warm moist neck and breathed in her scent. Above me, sunlight streamed down through the leaves, turning them into a stained-glass window in Nature's cathedral. Below, dappled patterns of light danced across the grass. Beyond the trees, blue sky reflected in the mountain stream. Closing my eyes, I meditated on the rustle of leaves in the breeze, the burble of the river, the croak of a nearby frog, and the hum of a bumblebee lazily alighting on a wildflower. A Monarch butterfly hovered above, then fluttered silently off. I took a deep breath, inhaling the cool mint that grew in the same shady place along the river bank every summer. The air was perfumed with mint and wildflowers and rich, dark earth. Above me, in the arching limbs of the willows, a chorus of finches sang like a hundred canaries. It was moments like these that filled me with awe and gratitude for life and a sense of love and oneness with the Earth. Something I will never forget.

Bessy's belly lurched with a low rumble. Up came her cud, and she resumed chewing. I rolled over, propping myself up on her belly as I sucked on the sweetness of a long reed of grass. A buzzing horsefly landing on Bessy's back provoked a smack across my face with her manure-crusted tail. Ouch!

After visiting Bessy, I headed for the blackberry bushes at the foot of White Deer Mountain. Loaded with plump, ripe berries, they readily fell into my hands at the touch. I gobbled them up by the handfuls, staining my hands and face purple as I smooshed them into my mouth. When I had eaten my fill, I mounted my imaginary white stallion and galloped toward the Smith's farm on the other side of the river.

I took off at a gallop, slapping my thighs to make the sound of two extra pounding hooves. "Hi Yo, Silver!" I was The Lone Ranger as I galloped across the pasture, hurdling a rotting log where a clump of wild rhubarb sprouted in the same place every summer. Such familiar sights gave me a sense of continuity. Surely life would always be this way. Close to the river, the pasture was splattered with cow flops where the cows congregated before crossing. I played hopscotch with their droppings, my feet splatting into their midst. Hot from the sun, the brown liquid oozed up between my toes. I didn't care.

Wading across the river, my feet ached from the cold as they slipped and slid over the rocky bed, as the swiftness of the current almost swept me away. Up the gravel barnyard road, I galloped past the Smith's barn, which had faded to a variegated red and grey. As I passed through the shade of a gnarly oak, I heard the squeal of a screen door as Mrs. Smith leaned out and tossed a bowl of table scraps to the chickens. A cacophony of clucking hens broke out as red and brown chickens descended on the scrapings in a frenzy of hammering heads.

"Well, if it ain't Miss Holly," she said as I passed under the clothesline between the bleached-out dungarees and billowing sheets warmed by the sun and scented with sunshine as they batted about in the mountain breeze.

"I was just fix'n to frost the cake," Mrs. Smith said. A hardy women of Italian descent, her features were coarse. She wore no make-up and always wore sturdy work shoes and a printed cotton house dress. She had no interest in style or glamor, but to me, she was beautiful. Even the wart on her nose did not detract from the warmth and kindness on her face.

I bounded up the steps and followed Mrs. Smith into the kitchen of her hundred-year-old brick house, which was hot from the wood burning in the big, black stove by the door. All the meals for their family and farmhands were cooked on that stove.

In winter, Mrs. Smith taught school, but in summer, she worked alongside the men in the field and prepared their meals. In spite of all that hard work, the inside of the Smith's house was always neat and sparkling clean with floral wallpaper and bright white painted moldings.

A fresh, yellow cake made with eggs from Mrs. Smith's free-range barnyard hens was cooling on a vintage hutch. Mrs. Smith had just finished mixing a bowl of fudge icing made with cream from the morning's milking and churned into butter right there in her kitchen.

The warm scent of buttery vanilla cake made my

mouth water.

"Fudge icing's your favorite, ain't that so, Miss Holly?" Mrs. Smith scraped the last glob of thick chocolate out of the bowl and slathered it over the cake. I will never forget the aromas that filled that kitchen, nor the taste of that cake.

The screen door squealed open as Nate came in. His brawny tan back was covered with hayseed sprinkled over glistening sweat. Nate was only ten. A year younger than I, but to me, he looked and acted like a grownup. He drove tractors and baled hay. To me, he was all man.

"Someday, can I help you bale hay?" I asked, wanting to be like him.

"If ya want," he said as he strode past, clunking across the kitchen floor in heavy work boots. He leaned over the kitchen sink and began lathering his hands with soap. "You been riding them cows again, ain't yuh?" he said without looking back.

I felt my face turn red. Nate and his sister, Anne, were my best friends. I didn't want to do anything that might make them mad. Nate and I sometimes played farm with toy trucks in the dirt. All three of us played hide-and-go-seek in the mounds of hay in the barn.

"How'd you know?" I asked.

"They ain't been given as much milk."

"I won't do it again," I said. "Besides, last time I did it, Bessy rubbed me off on a low-hanging branch."

Nate grinned as he grabbed a towel from the rack.

That made me feel better.

Many years have passed since then. But Nate, Anne, and I are still friends. Nate has a degree in agriculture from the University of Vermont, and he no longer says "ain't"—a word I secretly admired as a kind of tribal identity. Anne has a degree in history and is married to a Commander in the Navy. She lives in San Diego, where she works as a real estate agent.

They still own the farm, but they tell me the river is low, and because the temperature of the water has warmed, there are no more trout. They also tell me that sleeping with the windows open is no longer possible. The roar of traffic echoing through the mountains keeps them awake.

***

"Hi, Anne," I said as Nate's sister came in. Her wide smile always made me feel good. "I like your top," I said, observing the red halter top she was wearing. I was wearing nothing but a boy's swimsuit. Although my breasts were just beginning to bud, no one seemed to notice or, for that matter, care. I certainly didn't feel embarrassed.

Like her brother, Anne was dark brown from haying long hours in the sun. I wanted to be brown from the sun like Anne and Nate. But I had skin like Poppy's. No matter how much time he spent in the sun, all he got for his effort were quarter-sized, scaly black patches on his back. I didn't get the black patches, but I did get freckles and blisters.

I held my arm up to Anne's arm. Mine was pale by comparison. Fifty years later, my freckled competition with Anne's Italian heritage will show up as spotted, sun-damaged skin.

"Have a seat, Miss Holly," said Mrs. Smith as she cut into the cake.

I pulled out a chair and plopped down at the oilcloth-covered table. A fresh mountain breeze from the open window fluttered through the country curtains, fanning them out over the table as Mrs. Smith slid a square slice of cake in front of me.

"Ol' Man Crawford's got lambs," she said as she poured me a glass of frothy milk straight from the cow. "Seen 'em yet?"

"Where?" I asked after a big gulp of milk.

"Up at Butternut Bend. Maybe your Poppy will get you one."

I liked the way she said, "Your Poppy."

Just then, I heard Poppy whistle for me from the mill. A shrill *Whippoorwill! Whippoorwill!* Echoing through the mountains. It was how he always called me home. It was a skill I had never mastered, no matter how many times he showed me how to hold my thumb and forefinger flat on my tongue and blow.

"Gotta go," I said, scarfing down the rest of my cake and gulping down the milk.

"Anne," said Mrs. Smith, "I'll bet Miss Holly could use that top you outgrew. Why don't you run to get it."

Anne ran upstairs and clambered back down, waving a ruffled white halter top.

"Thank you," I said, pulling it over my head. The elastic around my rib cage made the eyelet embroidery puff out, making it look like I actually had something to hide. It made me feel grown up.

Poppy's "Whippoorwill! Whippoorwill!" echoed through the valley.

Thanking Mrs. Smith for the cake, I bolted out the screen door, scattering the chickens, which clucked noisily in protest.

Instead of crossing the river, I followed its bend along the bank. Sprinting through weeds and tall grass, I slid down an embankment to the stony riverbed, hopping from rock to rock. Beyond the limbs of the elm reaching over the Mettowee, I could see the Old Red Mill high on its granite foundation with the red, white, and blue of the American flag flapping over the river. How I loved the sight of those stars and stripes against the rich green of the mountains. It came to mean happiness, freedom, and safety. Above me, Poppy waved from the veranda railing. Behind him hung the striped canopy under which we sat, rain or shine, to watch Nature's continuous show.

Scrambling up the rope ladder, I bounded past my hammock and down the dirt path past Mother's rose garden. Next to the steps that led to the veranda stood a young, blue spruce Mother and Poppy had planted. Forty years later, I will look up at that spruce. Taller than I ever imagined it might grow. Alas, it will become the only marker that can identify where the Old Red Mill once stood.

Racing past the two smaller striped awnings over Poppy's bedroom windows, I bounce up to Poppy, who was standing by the railing playing a happy tune on his harmonica.

"You've been gone for hours," he said with a smile as warm as the sun on my back. "I was beginning to wonder what happened to you."

His eyes dropped to the puckered white ruffled band across my chest. And it gave me the strangest feeling. For the first time, I became aware that I was hiding a part of my body I used to leave bare, never thinking about it.

Poppy must have noticed my embarrassment because he said, "Holly, never let anyone make you ashamed you're a woman," Then he turned toward White Deer Mountain across the river. "I want you to run wild and free in that mountains. Naked if you like. The way God intended it."

***

"Lambkins," I cried. The name came to me the minute

I saw the woolly bundle frolicking around his mother on Crawford's farm. Black teardrop markings under his eyes set him apart from other lambs in the flock. Lambkins was a word in a Christian Science hymn written by Mary Baker Eddy. *Shepherd show me how to go / Lead my Lambkins to the Fold.*

"He looks as if he's wearing black stockings," I told Poppy as we watched Mr. Crawford chase Lambkins down amidst the scampering sheep."

"Oooh," I mewled as Mr. Crawford handed me the bleating lamb. My heart filled with such love. It felt like it would break as I scooped his woolly body into my arms and gazed into his adorable face. And right there, I made a silent promise to myself. *I will be his shepherd, his protector, all the rugged way.*

The black bar on Lambkin's nose made me giggle. I hugged him tight and buried my head into his wool, breathing in his sheepy, warm lanolin smell. Mother handed me a bottle of milk. I stuck the nipple into his mouth, and he sucked with all his might.

After that, everywhere I went, Lambkins was sure to go, just like in the nursery rhyme, *Mary Had a Little Lamb.* Lambkins and I were inseparable. He pushed me in the swing by butting my bare feet with his head. We played hide and go seek. I loved Lambkins so much it hurt. This worried Poppy. "You know we can't take him back with us to New York. I told you that when you first asked me to buy you a lamb."

That summer was the best summer ever. I'd carry Lambkins across the river, and we'd play all day on White Deer Mountain. In him, I found a friend that would never leave me. He wasn't happy unless I was within his sight.

I'd never felt so loved.

Toward the end of summer, a storm began to gather. I could smell the rain and feel the electricity in the air as its angry gusts blew toward Lambkins and me. I could hear the distant rumble of thunder. Poppy was worried. I could tell by the urgency of his whistle. *Whippoorwill! Whippoorwill!* I gathered Lambkins up in my arms and scrambled down the side of the mountain. As I waded across the river carrying Lambkins, I saw Poppy at the back of the mill, reeling in the American flag from the veranda as big drops of rain spattered before me on the surface of the water.

I joined Poppy in our eagle's nest beneath the canopy and pulled Lambkins up on my lap. "It's gonna be a big one," warned Poppy. Up the river, dark clouds were roiling toward us through the valley. The wind picked up, howling through the trees spinning the flypaper over the table and flapping the awning above our heads.

For Poppy, a thunderstorm was a show he never wanted to miss. But this time was different. There was concern on his face—gravity in his voice.

Upstream, the clouds burst. Gusts of wind sent sheets of rain blowing over the river. The sky darkened. The rain came down hard, riling the river with silt washed from its banks. The river turned brown as it rose. Bolts of lightning lit up the sky with massive claps of thunder.

The chill in the air made me shiver. I hugged Lambkins close, snuggling up to his warm woolly body. How good he felt. With every clap of thunder, I could feel his little heart beating faster. The awning over our heads rattled as if the wind would tear it from its hinges. The slamming rain beat down on our canopy like a drum. The saplings across the river bent low as if praying for mercy as their leaves turned inside out—the backs of their leaves turning silver in the wind—an ear-splitting crack. The sky lit up in a florescent glow as flashing daggers stabbed down on White Deer Mountain. I felt a warm trickle down my leg as Lambkins trembled with fear. I slipped my hand under his belly. It was wet. I didn't care.

"Poor Lambkins," I said as I tried to kiss away the fear on his face.

The sky seemed to open up, dumping bucket-loads of water down on our canopy. It swelled and grew heavy under the strain. Water sloshed over its edges, splashing down on the deck.

The river rose fast, turning angry and brown.

"Damnation!" shouted Poppy, leaping to his feet as the rain whipped his face and plastered his hair to his head.

I saw it too. An uprooted tree from upstream was hurling toward the dam.

"It's gonna bust the dam!" shouted Poppy as he gripped the railing as if he were a captain on a pitching ship.

The tree hit the dam and lodged against the boulders. Water built up behind it. The dam cracked and groaned, then gave way with a roar. One by one, the boulders that had held the dam broke loose and rolled away. With nothing to hold it back, the tree reeled and plunged into the rapids, which drove it into the foundation of the mill. It spun, then sailed on down the river.

Peering over the railing, I saw what at first appeared to be a large rock traveling toward us under cover of the muddy water.

"Snapping turtle!" I screamed, visualizing its sharp beak separating me from my big toe.

Poppy saw it too. "Hey, Kid!" he yelled to Mother, who was inside cooking dinner. "Get your gun!"

Mother readied her .22 rifle and aimed, holding the snapping turtle in her sights as soon as the menacing creature lumbered into shallow water; BAM! Blood belched up through the murky water. Mother had calculated the refraction of water and hit her mark.

Gone was my tranquil swimming hole. The storm had left a scattering of rocks and boulders with rapids swirling around them, no more mirrored pools along the bank reflecting the willows and wildflowers above it—only raw severed banks. The morning after the storm, I went out on the veranda. All I saw was an angry river frothing at the mouth as it flung itself violently against the foundation of the mill below.

Poppy reeled the American flag back out over the Mettowee, but its reflection no longer danced in the merry ripples below. Nor could we hear the splash of rainbow trout leaping for bugs. The river had returned to the wild.

I left Lambkins bleating for me on the shore and waded into the rapids swirling around the rocks. Try as I would, I could not push the boulders back in place. I hated what the storm had done to the river, but I was no match for the bulldozer Poppy had hired many summers ago.

Unable to restore the tranquillity of the river, I felt helpless and depressed.

It was the end of summer. The crickets had begun chirping at night, and the goldenrod had grown tall. Soon we would drive back to New York. Poppy would return to his wife and friends at the Hotel des Artistes, and I'd be banished to my New England boarding school.

I staggered up on shore. I could barely see Lambkins across the river as he grazed amidst the goldenrod. *"Poor Lambkins. What will happen to him when we leave?"* Poppy had warned me that there was no taking him back to New York. Would he end up as lamb chops on Ol' Man Crawford's table? The thought made me grimace.

Seeing me, Lambkins bounded out of the goldenrod

and leaped onto the jagged slate ledge where he could keep an eye on me from across the river. BAAAA, he bleated pitifully as he scampered up and down along the rocky ledge.

"Lambkins must learn to be brave," I thought as I watched him bleating for me. Wasn't that why Poppy taught me to ride the waves in the Atlantic?

Then another thought came to me. *"How much does Lambkins love me? Enough to jump into the river and swim to me?"*

It was a crazy idea, but *Doesn't God test those He loves?* I decided to test Lambkin's love for me.

"Come on. Lambkins. Come on."

He looked down at the swirling river and bleated helplessly.

Wading toward him, I sunk deeper into the cold, swirling rapids. My body turned red from the mountain-spring-fed river. My skin tingled, then turned warm and limp with pleasure reminding me how hard it was for Poppy to convince me of the river's icy delight.

"Baaa, Baaa, Baaa," bleated Lampkins as he frantically ran down to the river's edge. "BAAA, BAAA."

His little black hooves touched the water. He jumped back.

"Lambkins," I called. He hopped back up on the jagged ledge and looked down into the dark undulating current, then back at me, terror in his teardrop eyes. But then, wasn't I scared when Poppy first coaxed me to dive into the ice-cold river?

"Come on, Lambkins," I called as I stood waist-deep in the swirling river.

All animals can swim, can't they? I had once ridden a neighbor's pony across the river in that same place.

Lambkins trotted back and forth along the ledge, bleating as if to beg me not to make him do it. "Come on, Lambkins! If you love me, you will jump."

Lambkins gave one last bleat, then plunged into the swirling water, his dainty hooves flailing helplessly against the current.

He went under.

"Lambkins!" I screamed as I fought my way through the water to reach him. His black nose bobbed up, gasping for air, then went down again as the current pulled him under, sweeping him out of my reach.

"Lambkins!" The weight of his waterlogged wool kept pulling him under in the ferocity of the current. The rapids dashed him against a boulder, spun him around, and sucked him under. Screaming, I thrashed my way toward him, my toes bashing into rocks. I grabbed for his collar but missed. Lunging again, I reached over a rock and grabbed the wool on his back. Together we went down into the swirling vortex.

Leaning against a rock, I braced myself against the current's fury and pulled Lambkins up into my arms, gripping him tight. Waterlogged and heavy, it took all my strength to haul him back to shore.

***

I told no one what I had done and spent the whole day trying to undo it. I made a bed of dry hay in Lambkins' stall. Brought him a bowl of warm milk. But he just stood there dazed and shivering. I could barely hear him breathe. I prayed all the Christian Science prayers I could remember.

The next morning, I was up bright and early before the chatter of the kingfisher. I ran to the stable, where I found Lambkins lying in the hay. I fell down beside him and hugged his woolly body. It was stiff and cold.

"Lambkins," I wailed, but his cold, dead eyes no longer saw me.

***

Poppy never asked me what happened to Lambkins. He probably figured it out by feeling his woolly wet body. By now, the storm was in the past, and the water had gone shallow. Silently, Poppy carried Lambkins across the river, where somewhere at the foot of White Deer Mountain, Poppy buried my beloved Lambkins.

That summer marked the end of innocence. Not only had I witnessed death, but I had also been the cause of it.

After the burial, Poppy and I slogged our way to the spring, where the runoff from the mountain kept the ground perpetually cold and wet. He took the tin cup that hung on a nail under the spring's roof and filled it with water from the spout. He then sat down on a big moss-covered rock. I sat down opposite him on another mossy rock.

Silently, we sat in sad and shadowy seclusion beneath the translucent leaves of the forest. Aside from the shrill warble of an occasional bird, the only sound was that of water babbling down the mountainside. Blades of sunlight cut through the surrounding foliage of birch and pine and glinted off the emerald-green moss.

Knowing I was responsible for Lambkins' death, I lowered my eyes to the ground. Between Poppy and me, sunlight danced in shimmering brilliance over a thick bed of tiny blue delicate flowers at our feet.

As I choked back tears of remorse, Poppy reached down and picked one of the tiny blue flowers and held it out to me.

I took the flower from his hand. Tiny, delicate petals. At its center was a dot of sunny bright yellow. How tiny and insignificant it looked between my fingers. Smaller than the tip of my pinky. Yet amassed together at our feet, these delicate flowers turned darkness into light, spreading beauty over what would otherwise have been cold, dark mud.

As I lifted my eyes from the flower, Poppy's eyes met mine.

"Do you know the name of this flower?" he asked

I shook my head.

"Forget-me-not," he said.

CHAPTER SIXTEEN

Terror in Eden

Time does not bring relief; you all have lied.
Who told me time would ease me of my pain!
I miss him in the weeping of the rain;
I want him at the shrinking of the tide.

- Edna St. Vincent Millay

On March 2, 1952, I awoke to the clanging of the Daycroft morning wake-up bell. Reluctant to get up, I lay in bed wishing I were back at the Old Red Mill.

The second bell rang. I rolled out of bed, grabbed the white blouse I'd laundered the night before, and hauled my languid body down the hallway to the ironing room.

I'd have to hurry. It was my turn to set the dining room tables in what looked like the hall at Hogwart's in *Harry Potter*, only smaller. After putting on my freshly ironed white blouse, I pulled on my navy blue blazer with the Daycroft emblem and was about to leave when Mrs. Starr, the third-floor housemother, came to my door. "Holly, your mother is on the phone."

Mother never called unless it was serious. I seized up inside. I knew Poppy had been ill for weeks. For the first time in my life—I feared the inevitable. That he would leave me—not just to return to his family at the Hotel des Artistes—but for good. I had been writing him letters with healing quotes from Mary Baker Eddy. "Man *is*, not *shall be*, perfect and immortal."

"Holly, dear." Mother's voice was faint, as if speaking to me from another world. "Poppy asked me to call you. He wants you to come to the des Artistes. Come right now, dear."

A chill ran through me worse than any blizzard on a New York corner. Poppy was summoning me to that forbidden place.

It could mean only one thing.

Death was waiting at the door.

Panic gripped me as the New York Express clattered over the tracks. Outside my window, patches of snow clung to the hard, frozen ground as twisted, bare grey tree limbs whipped by. It would soon be Easter, and yellow sprays of forsythia heralding spring would be spilling over the stone walls that bordered Central Park—after which summer would be around the corner. Was this the end of my happy days at the Old Red Mill in Vermont?

I stepped out of a yellow cab in front of the Hotel des Artistes, where Poppy had lived since 1915, right after it was built. Grim-faced gargoyles monitored my approach from gothic ledges. A doorman guarded the entrance. Decked out in military attire, he looked very stern in his visored hat and gold braided epaulets. I brushed past him feeling as if I were entering the realm of the gods.

The click of my patent leather shoes echoed off the marble floor as I scuttled down the steps into its gothic lobby. Following Mother's instructions, I went to the reception window and told the switchboard operator I was Holly Morris. "I'm Holly Morris here to see Howard Chandler Christy," I said, recoiling at the sound of my name in connection with the man I always wanted to be, my father. It made me feel all the more like an outsider who didn't belong in this building which looked like a medieval castle. Why would a girl named Holly Morris be inserting herself into Poppy's world?

Was this really happening? I was entering what felt like a parallel universe. One from which I had been alienated all my life.

"Take the elevator to the seventh floor," said the woman at the switchboard. "Mrs. Christy will be waiting for you."

"Mrs. Christy? How would she feel about me inserting myself into her life?"

The elevator lurched, then slowly groaned its way up. Reaching the seventh floor, it clunked to a stop. I stepped out. Nancy Christy was waiting in the doorway of Apartment 710. She was a heavy woman with a Gibson-like bosom, minus the tiny waist. Her doughy face was framed by short, yellow, tightly permed hair. Other than that, I didn't take much notice as to how she looked. Many years later, I will be told by those who knew her that Nancy didn't take to being restrained by underwear or tight clothing. Nor did she care about her appearance. She wore striped kaftans from Roaman's Department Store, under which she wore no bra. Those who knew her said she caked on her makeup and then left it on for days. But I have no recollection of anything that specific. My interests lay elsewhere.

Reserved but polite, Nancy ushered me in. Silently, she led me down a hall and out into Poppy's high-ceilinged, open studio. Twenty-two-foot-high wall-to-wall windows flooded the room with a northern light, which made it feel like an outside atrium. Tapestries and life-sized paintings were everywhere. To my right was a grand piano covered with a fringed red floral Spanish shawl. I recognized it as where Poppy said Nancy fed Winky the cat. Even Mussolini's bust was there, just as Poppy had described it. These familiar sights made me feel as if I'd been there before.

Nudes of Mother filled every space. Next to Poppy's easel, a polar bear rug was stretched out before an ornate limestone fireplace. As I passed it on the way to the stairs, I remembered the story Mother had told me about the day she brought my cousin Tommy to pose for a little boy in one of Poppy's posters. "Tommy looked at that rug and said, 'Whoever stepped on that bear, why didn't he step on his head?'" It always brought a laugh.

As I followed Nancy up the stairs, Mother's smiling

face, youthful nude body, and playful gestures leaped out at me from Poppy's workspace below. On an easel was an unfinished self-portrait of Poppy painting a nude of Mother.

Dominating the studio high above us was a long, life-sized painting of a regal woman in a long satin gown standing between two afghan hounds. I did not recognize her elegant visage as the woman now leading me up the stairs.

Where's Mother? I dared not ask. Not with all those nudes of her occupying so much space below. Reaching the top of the stairs, I followed Nancy along the balcony to the room on the end. Nancy opened the door and then stepped aside. I stepped in, and she closed the door behind me.

I stiffened with fright. Poppy was lying motionless beneath a burgundy comforter. Eyes closed, he appeared as one resting in state, his head on a stark white pillow below a massive headboard of chiseled mahogany. On the opposite side of his bed sat Mother in a wingback chair. She glanced up from her bedside vigil and stared into space, not really seeing me.

My eyes darted back to Poppy's expressionless face.

"How long has he been like this?" I asked.

Mother appeared drained. "Several days," she replied as if under a spell. "I have not left his side the whole time."

"Poppy!" I called as if to summon him back from the dead. He had called me here for a reason. What was it he wanted to say? "Poppy, I'm here. Please. Talk to me!"

I felt the corners of my mouth pull down as I stared at his listless once-animated face. Didn't Christian Science teach there was no such thing as death? I choked up as I remembered Lambkins. He had died. Was Poppy going to die too? I desperately wanted to believe there was no death. But in my gut, I knew Mary Baker Eddy had lied.

Was there nothing in which I could trust?

Nothing in this world I could cling to?

"Poppy," I sobbed, burying my head in his comforter. "Pl-e-e-e-ase..."

I felt him move. I jerked my head up. His eyelids fluttered.

"Poppy!" I cried.

He gave me a feeble smile. "Holly. I'm so glad you're here." His voice was weak.

I leaped on top of him and gave him a big hug. Sliding

back off the bed, I accidentally dragged the bottom of the comforter with me. As I reached down to pull it back over his feet, I saw his ankles, red and swollen with peeling sores. I knew nothing of phlebitis—a condition caused by poor circulation and a weak heart—nor did I know he had refused medical treatment, preferring to trust God for his healing.

Fifty years later, Jocelyn Green, his next-door neighbor, will tell me that Nancy had been secretly slipping sleeping pills into his glass of milk. This was probably why he was sleeping so soundly when I arrived.

Mother's head drooped heavily over her big leather *Science & Health With Key to the Scriptures* that was flopped open in her lap, and began to read aloud Mary Baker Eddy's words. "Divine Love is my shepherd, I shall not want. Love maketh me to lie down in green pastures; Love leadeth me beside the still waters..." Meanwhile, Poppy drifted back to sleep.

Dejected, I slunk out of his room onto the light-flooded balcony overlooking his studio and closed the door behind me. Mother's voice faded as I ambled along the balcony. Stopping, I stared down into what looked like a castle filled with treasures. Heavy velvet drapes were drawn off to the side, tapestries and paintings hung on every available space, and statues and antiques occupied every corner. In one corner stood a full suit of armor that had once been worn into battle by a European knight. I remembered Poppy telling me that it was in this open space over the studio that the twelve-foot model schooner had hung before he had had it taken down and shipped to the Old Red Mill in Vermont, where it now hung from the rafters.

Poppy's spirit was everywhere—in his art, in the richly textured decor. His vibrancy. His interest in life filled every space. His studio was a reflection of his belief in creativity as the most fulfilling purpose on Earth. He did not believe in endings. Only beginnings. A new, more beautiful vista ahead. To him, Eden was ours for the creating.

Moseying along the balcony, I passed a partially open door and peeked in. Nancy was sitting on the edge of her bed. It was shaped like a gondola with golden carved flowers. On either side of the headboard were two white swans.

"Come in," she said, beckoning.

Warily, I stepped inside.

"It's Italian," she said, noticing me eying the swans on her gondola bed. "We brought it back with us from Europe when Poppy painted Mussolini's portrait." Something about her and Poppy made me feel out of place. I started to leave.

"Holly, I have something for you." She held out a large picture book. "Poppy has told me how much you love horses. I was about to wrap it up, but I don't suppose you'd mind if I give it to you like this."

"Oh, thank you," I said, taking the book from her hand. It featured a drawing of a horse on the cover.

"Do you like doggies?" She hoisted her hefty body from the bed and trudged over to a mirrored dressing table. "I have lots of them. Come see." I stepped further into her cloistered abode. The dressing table was cluttered with a dusty collection of porcelain pups. "Here," she said, offering me a yellow dog with big eyes and long ears. I shook my head. I didn't like the way it looked. Cartoonish and unreal. Politely, I excused myself, thanking her again for the book, and scampered down the stairs into Poppy's studio.

At the bottom of the stairs, I came face to face with something I hadn't noticed when I first came in. Poppy's painting of Christ bathed in light—arms outstretched—ascending into Heaven. Below was another carved Giovanni Bologna table with lion paw feet like ours. The only others like it that I have ever seen were in our studio and the Frick Museum. Pulled up to the table was a crimson throne like the one Poppy always sat on when he came to Mother's studio. Poppy was all about color, workmanship, line, and texture.

I stared up at the barrel-chested Christ, remembering what Poppy had told Mother as she posed for another picture of Christ in our 74th Street studio. "I'm fed up with all those goddam pictures of a Christ with no balls." I knew what balls were. I'd seen them on Johnny the Bull back on the Smith's farm. I also knew that without Johnny, the cows didn't bear calves, nor would they give milk. That was all I knew, but it was enough.

The phone rang. Nancy answered it from her room. Moments later, she came clambering down the stairs. "Fred Waring's on his way up from the lobby," she said. "You know who that is, don't you? He's the man who taught America how to sing."

I knew who he was. Mother listened to his show on the radio every Sunday night, and it was Mother's dream to one day sing with his *Pennsylvanians.*

When Fred Waring walked in, he was carrying a big package wrapped in brown paper. "I know how much you like to cook," he told Nancy. "So I brought you a turkey."

Years later, I will come to doubt this memory. *"Why would Fred Waring bring Nancy a turkey for a present? And in March?"* I will tell Olga Steckler this story. She knew Poppy and Fred Waring well. She will answer my question by telling me, "Oh, darling, it makes perfect sense. Fred Waring had a farm."

Nancy introduced me to Waring as "Holly Morris, the daughter of one of Poppy's models." Waring was a distinguished grey-haired man, but what interested me most was his handsome dark-haired son. I searched for an indication that the young man thought I was pretty, but he never even looked my way. Later, I worried that it was because I'd outgrown the velvet dress I was wearing that Poppy bought me at Wanamaker's. I had lost one of its gold buttons in front. Looking back, I wonder how I could have worried about something so trivial at a time like that.

A few minutes later, the Warings left, and Nancy returned to her room and shut the door.

Alone in the silence, I kept vigil. Twilight settled over the studio, casting eerie shadows. The standing suit of armor seemed to glare at me through menacing black slits in his helmet while the ticking of the grandfather clock tormented me with the ominous passing of time. Feeling tired, I curled up on the cushioned monk's bench and waited for the inevitable. Any minute, Mother might step out of Poppy's room. Knowing Mother, she wouldn't speak, but I'd know the awful truth.

Grasping for relief from my fear, I forced myself to believe what I'd learned in Christian Science. *Life is eternal. There is no such thing as death.* I chanted the magic words over and over in my head in an effort to drive away the worries that tormented me. Darkness fell like a heavy cloak. *Life is eternal. Life is eternal. There is no such thing as death.* More than anything, I wanted to believe Mary Baker Eddy's words could heal Poppy.

I dozed off briefly, only to bolt upright at the sound of Poppy's door opening upstairs.

I was prepared for the worst, but what I saw was even more of a shock.

At first, I thought I was dreaming. Or perhaps it was a ghost. There was Poppy, all dressed up in a three-piece suit and tie. He leaned over the banister and gave me one of his impish grins. "Holly, I'm taking you out to dinner tonight."

"Poppy!" I yelped. Leaping to my feet, I ran to meet him coming down the stairs. He folded me in his arms, and I was so happy I hardly noticed Mother rushing down the stairs behind him. There was a look of dread in her eyes as she swept past us. Then she was gone.

My heart swelled with pride. Poppy was taking me out to dinner. Alone without Mother.

Never had I felt so special.

***

The foyer of the Café des Artistes was packed with elegantly dressed people waiting to be seated. "Good evening, Mr. Christy," said the maître d', a dignified man in a black suit and bow tie. The calmness in his voice belied the surprise on his face. "Glad to see you're feeling better."

"This is Holly," Poppy announced with a proud grin.

"Welcome to the Café des Artistes," said a woman with a French accent as she held me in her gaze. Poppy introduced her as Marie Turner, wife of the Café's manager.

I felt like Cinderella at the ball. All eyes were on Poppy with me by his side.

"I'm taking Holly to dinner," Poppy told Marie.

"I'll get you a table," Marie said and hurried over to the maître d'. He came right away and made a path for us through the gaggle of waiting guests. As we stepped from the crowded foyer into the Café des Artistes, we were surrounded by Poppy's murals of life-sized nudes romping in the woods. It was like stepping into Eden before the Fall made us ashamed, "afraid" of our nakedness, as it says in Genesis. Mother's laughing face was everywhere. In the mural closest to the entrance, Doris and Mother were playing ring-around-the-oak-tree with other laughing nymphs. At that time, I didn't recognize Doris. Only Mother.

Poppy and I followed the maître d' to a table in a corner beneath a life-sized image of Mother, up to her thighs in water. The maître d' pulled the table away from the wall. Poppy slid in first on a red leather seat adjacent to Mother's image. I slid in next to him. Directly across from us was another mural of a woman with alabaster skin and long, flowing blond hair. She, too, was wading in a pool of crystal-clear water amidst two white swans.

I felt as if I'd stepped into a sacred place, as innocent and free as a deer leaping through the forest at my White Deer Mountain. It reminded me of what Poppy had told me as we stood on the veranda of the Old Red Mill with a view of the mountain across the Mettowee. "I want you to run wild and free in the mountains. Naked if you like, the way God intended it." I understood what he meant, and it wasn't that he wanted me to run around naked. What he wanted was for me to live in harmony with Nature, unashamed of being me.

The laughter of the guests reflected the laughter in the paintings as the scent of fresh flowers filled the room— fronds of palms blended in with Poppy's murals on the wall. I had entered what felt like Poppy's domain. Here in the Café des Artistes, I felt as happy and carefree as I'd been at the Old Red Mill. The happiness on Mother's face in the pictures brought back memories of their laughter and their joy as Poppy and she went off to paint the natural beauty around them.

Wherever he went, Poppy created Eden. And here it was again at the Café des Artistes. The Eden of Poppy's creation. An Eden made beautiful by his human devotion. A place where Creation is revered and Life is symbolized in the water he included in almost every scene.

I scanned the menu for something that looked familiar, but most dishes had French names. Puzzled, I looked up at Poppy for help. Directly behind him was his painting of Mother knee-deep in water. Unlike the other murals, this one was different. Cast in a grotto-like jungle shadow, there was fear in Mother's eyes as she tried to cover her nakedness with her hands. It stood out in sharp contrast to what Poppy had always told me "Never let anyone make you ashamed you're a woman."

"I usually get the half-broiled chicken," Poppy said, scanning his menu. "I think you'd like that."

Still staring at the picture next to us, I noticed a blue-and-orange macaw above Mother's head. Its beak was open as if screeching a warning as it spread its wings to take flight into a golden sunset. "Why did you make Mother look scared?" I asked Poppy.

"Conquistadores," he said. Although I couldn't see them coming around the corner from where I sat, I would eventually see the full mural, with these men in armor coming out of the bushes.

"Remember Sargent?" said Poppy referring to the Great Dane he'd named after his favorite artist, John

Singer Sargent. I'd never met Sargent any more than I'd met Winky the cat, but I remembered him from the stories Poppy had told me about him. "Well," said Poppy, "Sargent was sleeping while I painted the model for the Conquistadors. I had to leave the studio for a few minutes, and damned if that model didn't try to scare Sargent out of his sleep. Must've kicked him or something 'cause Sargent leaped for the only part of that man's body that wasn't covered by armor. His head. Knocked him to the floor. I had to pull 'im off."

"Served him right," I said, turning to the deserts on the menu. "Look, Poppy, they have something called Christy's Palette. What's that?"

"Scoops of different-colored ice cream on a cookie shaped like a palette. If you like, you can have that for dessert."

With dinner ordered, my eyes wandered around the room, taking in the murals. On a back wall, there was Mother again, this time lolling in the grass with an open book.

I was thinking how wonderful everything was and how happy I felt when I noticed the scornful look of an elderly couple sitting across from us beneath the painting of the nymph wading with the swans. She leaned in and said something to her husband, who looked my way. I knew she was gossiping about us by the sneering look on her face. Perhaps she was outraged that an old man like Poppy would bring an innocent little girl into a restaurant filled with pictures of nudes. Or perhaps she wondered where my mother was and why this old man had brought me there alone. Who knows what vile thoughts she had conjured up, but her looks of disapproval were making me uncomfortable.

I looked away and then glanced back. The woman frowned and shook her head as if I'd done something awful. It reminded me of the woman who scolded me for using my left hand.

Looking up at Mother and the parrot, I felt that same fear I saw in her eyes.

I looked at Poppy for reassurance. "Holly," he said— his voice heavy with concern—"There's something I want to tell you."

Just then, our dinner arrived. Not having eaten all day, I dove into the crispy char-broiled chicken and tried to ignore the disapproving glances of the couple across from us.

"Those people—I don't think they like us," I said, lowering my head and speaking under my breath as if letting Poppy in on a secret.

Finally, I told Poppy about them, and he tried to jolly me up as he had always done. "Holly, remember the Yankee Doodle song? Let's sing it." I shook my head in the negative. "Come on, Holly, be a sport." He started to sing. "Oh, Yankee Doodle went to town, Upon a load of lumber. He let a poop behind the car and blowed it all to thunder!"

As if to give it a grand finale, Poppy leaned over and let one fly. The sound rumbled over the red leather seat like a cannonball, and he threw his head back and laughed one of his great belly laughs as if nothing else mattered. There was power in Poppy's laughter. It slew monsters. I couldn't help laughing too.

When it came time to go, I slid out first, but Poppy had become weak. Clumsily, he struggled to get out, pulling the tablecloth with the dishes and silver with it. A waiter rushed to his assistance and helped him walk out to the lobby. Poppy was slumped. Clutching his chest, his breathing was labored. Marie and the maître d' both rushed to his side, straining to hold him up.

"Call Mrs. Christy. Call Mrs. Christy!" shouted Marie to the switchboard operator.

"Please, Poppy, be well," I prayed out loud.

With the maître d's help, Poppy slowly made his way to the elevator. Poppy then waved him away and motioned for me to get into the elevator with him. Alone. I stepped in, and the maître d' closed the gate behind us.

Poppy pushed the button for the seventh floor. With a lurch, the ancient pulley elevator started its laborious climb, with Poppy leaning against the wood-paneled wall for support.

"Holly, there's something I want to tell you," he said for the second time. Only this time, his voice was labored as he tried to catch his breath.

My legs went weak. *Please, Poppy! Don't leave me! Oh, God! Please don't let Poppy tell me goodbye.* The lump in my throat was so big I couldn't speak.

The elevator clunked upward. One floor after another. Three. Four. Five. Six.

"Holly," he said, gasping for breath as he leaned against the wall.

"I want you... to know..."

The elevator groaned to a stop. I could see Nancy waiting on the other side of the gate.

He paused to catch his breath again. "You've meant more to me than anything in this world."

I burst into tears. He was telling me goodbye.

Nancy flung open the iron gate, pushed past me, and took Poppy by the arm to help him out. Without a word, she thrust a finger on the "L" button and slammed the gate.

The elevator lurched and began its descent. Through the bars, I watched Nancy hold Poppy's arm as they hobbled toward number 710 together.

I knew I'd never see him again. I descended into hell that night as the elevator groaned downward.

My life as I had known it was over. Poppy had told me goodbye. He had also told me something I would cling to for the rest of my life.

Mother was waiting by the gate as I reached the lobby. Poppy had been my life's happiness. And now it was over. I was gripped by choking pain, the likes of which I'd never known in my life. Mother helped me on with my coat, and we hurried out into the cold, dark night.

Sobbing, I managed to blurt the most painful words I had ever had to say.

"He's leaving us. I know because he told me goodbye."

Mother gasped.

Sobbing, I told her, "He... he told me he wanted me to know..."Through agonizing gasps, I managed to blurt out his last words.

"...that I meant more to him than anything in this world."

And, for the first time—I saw Mother cry.

CHAPTER SEVENTEEN

Dust Thou Art

Dust thou art, and unto dust shalt thou return.

- Genesis 3:19

The morning after my dinner with Poppy, Mother took me to the Dakota Building on 72nd Street to stay with the Finks while she returned to the Hotel des Artistes. The Finks were elderly members of the Christian Science Church on West 68th Street, where Mother was the soloist.

Mother moved quickly past uniformed doormen along Central Park West without saying a word to me. Reaching the Dakota building, menacing iron demons clung to the railing around its dry moat.

We ducked into the building and took the elevator up to the Finks' apartment. Whatever was going on in Mother's head, she wasn't sharing with me.

The Finks' spacious apartment had a balcony overlooking Central Park. I fell into an overstuffed chair while Mother talked in a hushed voice to Mrs. Fink. A suffocating sense of doom lay heavy in the air and on my chest. Without explanation, Mother left. I didn't need to hear where she was going. Instinctively I knew she was returning to Poppy. I didn't ask to go with her. Poppy had already told me goodbye. I knew this was the end.

Mrs. Fink offered me some cereal for breakfast. I refused. I just wanted to be left alone. Less than four months ago, I had stood on the Finks' balcony and watched the Macy's Thanksgiving parade of marching bands and giant inflated balloon characters. At the end of the parade, Santa Claus waved a jolly "Ho, ho, ho to you all" from his fake reindeer-drawn sled. *Jingle Bells, Jingle Bells / Oh— what— fun— it— is...* The memory made me feel like a record winding down.

Mrs. Fink padded down the hall in her slippers and disrobed in front of a hallway closet. Until then, I'd been blind to the aging of the human body. Never once had I thought of Poppy as an old man. Now—as I watched Mrs. Fink jiggle into her corset—I became aware of the dreadful reality that death is the end of all flesh. What kind of God would create death and decay? Poppy had taught me to embrace life as if it would go on forever. To dive into the pounding surf and ride the waves.

I felt betrayed.

The world of Poppy's creation was an illusion.

Death was more powerful than Life.

The jangle of the telephone felt like a dagger in my heart—a death knell.

I didn't need to hear Mrs. Finks' words spoken in somber tones. I already knew.

Poppy was dead.

***

The day of the funeral, Mother remained mute—her face pale and waxen as if in a daze.

It was as if the gates of Eden had closed with Poppy's death. The beautiful world of his creation had ended. We were now being forced into another world. One neither one of us was prepared for.

***

The Walter B. Cooke Funeral Home at 117 West 72nd Street was packed with hundreds of mourners. No sooner had we wormed our way into their midst than Mother disappeared. I don't remember her telling me it was Poppy's funeral. Nor do I remember knowing that he was somewhere there in his casket, or I would have gone to see him. I never saw his body, and I have since learned it was an open casket ceremony.

What I do remember is feeling lost and confused. I knew no one. I felt unwelcomed as if I was a stranger that had drifted in off the street.

And this is where my memory of Poppy's funeral conflates with an incident that happened when I was ten or eleven years old.

***

After Mother's fox terrier, Cutie, died, she and Poppy pored over library books on dogs, looking for a breed that would be good with children. They settled on two: a wire-haired fox terrier or a Dalmatian. I picked the Dalmatian. I named her Brunhilde after the fearless heroine who stands up to the uppity Norse gods by singing of a spiritual light that will bring love and put an end to war.

Something like Spotty might have been a better name.

Still, neither Poppy nor Mother made any effort to change my mind, knowing that Brunhilde was my favorite heroin in Richard Wagner's opera series, *Der Ring des Nibelungen.*

It turned out to be the worst possible name for the wiggly, soft white puppy with black spots that soon arrived in a crate.

Brunhilda, as I called her, was so traumatized from being banged around in transit that she yelped in terror when I tried to coax her out. Mother and I offered her tasty morsels of hamburger and doggie treats, but she merely cringed in a back corner with her tail between her legs. Finally, she exploded from her crate, slipping and sliding across the hardwood floor, and scrambled under the divan to hide.

Brunhilda finally got used to us, and there were times when she even looked happy, like when she blew bubbles through her nose in the Mettowee and tried to snap up the minnows nibbling at her nose. She also loved snowy days when Mother pulled her red sweater over her head and hitched her up to my sled. Other than that, it was such a shame. A thoroughbred Dalmatian with papers, she remained timid and would go crazy with fear at the blare of a horn or the screech of brakes. My brave Brunhilda, that vanquisher of warring gods, soon became Bruny for short. The sound of Bruny reminded me of Cinderella's broom.

Like my own name of Morris, it was nothing to be proud of.

One day—months before Poppy's death—Mother and I were walking back from the Chinese laundry. Mother was carrying a bundle of freshly pressed sheets wrapped in brown paper while I held Bruny's leash. We were almost home when a passing truck slammed on its brakes. There was an ear-shattering squeal. Bruny reared up. Twisting and turning, she jerked her head this way and that, straining against her collar until she slipped it off. She bolted down the street with me after her. The first open door she came to was the Walter B. Cooke Funeral Home, the same funeral parlor where Poppy's funeral would be conducted. A solemn ceremony was in process.

Bruny burst into the midst of the mourning guests. I dashed in after her, trying desperately to grab the scruff of her neck, but she darted in and out, dodging my lunges between the legs of mourners. I fell to my knees and scrambled after her. I remember looking up into the stern face of a man in a dark suit. Never had I felt so wretched and despised.

And this is where my memory of Poppy's funeral and that unfortunate incident get fused as one. I see myself as an unwelcome guest. An abomination at the feet of strangers towering above me in a place I did not belong.

Condolences were offered, but not to me. No one even said hello or asked who I was.

Mother never told me Poppy was there, so I never saw him in his coffin for the crowds of people milling about. Nor did I hear the eulogy because we arrived late.

I looked for Mother. She was nowhere to be found.

Then, I saw her off by herself in a corner.

Her face covered by a black veil.

***

Half a century after Poppy's death, I will meet someone who will tell me what Mother never told me. The inside story surrounding Poppy's death.

Jocelyn Green was in her late 60s when I met her. She had been Poppy's next-door neighbor on the seventh floor of the Hotel des Artistes where she lived with her parents. I first met Jocelyn in the summer of 2003 after Helen

Copley (author of *The Christy Quest*) gave me her name and phone number. Jocelyn and her husband, Ray, stopped by to visit me in Lafayette, Indiana, on their way back from a lecture tour on China and the Yangtze River. Jocelyn and Ray had made travelogues of distant lands their vocation. Together they had trekked the dusty plains of Afghanistan and filmed the flowing, ghostly shapes of women in their burkas.

As soon as I saw their Ford Crown Victoria pull up in front of our house, I ran out to meet them.

The door on the driver's side swung open, and out came a cane, followed by Jocelyn's legs. Planting her feet firmly on the brick street, she gave a heave-ho and hauled herself up tall and straight. She was a big woman with a beaming smile that reminded me of Poppy's happy disposition. She even had his familiar sparkle in her eyes and his down-to-earth manner.

Ray came around from the driver's side. He was a quiet, slight man with a kind face. To look at them, you'd never think they were adventurers.

"Here," said Jocelyn handing me a package. "I thought you should have this."

I opened it on the spot. It was an old, cracked leather

Bible.

"Poppy's Bible," she said.

On top was a lovely card. A picture of a river winding past a tree with a clump of purple wildflowers in the foreground. The inscription read, "A Special Gift for a Very Special Person."

"Oh, Jocelyn, thank you," I said as I opened the card and read her personal message inside. "With fondest wishes from the caretaker of The Book."

As I examined the old, crumbling book, it fell open to *Philippians 2*. Poppy had bookmarked it with a Southern Vermont Art Center postcard. In soft, artist's pencil, he had underscored this passage.

Let nothing be done through strife or vainglory; but in lowliness of mind let each esteem the other better than himself. ...Let this mind be in you, which was also in Christ Jesus: Who, being in the form of God, thought it not robbery to be equal with God.

It was just like Poppy to pick that particular verse. He never vaunted himself above others, nor was he a braggart. But he also believed that all races were created in God's image.

My husband Jim and I took the Greens to lunch at a French restaurant called Bistro 501. There I had the opportunity to catch up on the many things I didn't know about the man I always wanted to call my father.

Jocelyn first met Poppy in 1941 when her mother and stepfather moved into an apartment on the same floor in the Hotel des Artistes. Jocelyn's stepfather had been an executive with Pocket Books, Inc., and was launching a career as publisher of his magazine, *The Smart Traveler*. Jocelyn's mother wrote radio and television commercials. As Jocelyn talked, I couldn't help thinking how we could have been friends during all those fifty years she was now telling me about. To my disappointment, Poppy's granddaughter, Carolyn, had been living with Jocelyn only a hundred miles from Lafayette before her untimely death from cancer. How I wish I could have met Carolyn. Too late. But then—if it hadn't been for Helen Copley's research for her *Christy Quest*, I never would have met Jocelyn either, and oh, the stories I would have missed out on.

Secrets Mother never told me.

"I met Poppy in the elevator," Jocelyn said as she scanned her menu over lunch. "He introduced me to Gene

Autry. When we got down to the lobby, Autry told me he was in town for a rodeo. If I would give him a call, I could come over to his hotel for drinks before the show. I took my college roommate to the rodeo—she was a fan of Gene Autry's—but I did not avail myself of his invitation."

I looked up from my menu. "Drinks? Before the rodeo?"

Here I was, after all these years, catching up on some des Artistes gossip. That mysterious place where Poppy and his friends would meet. That place where I could not go.

"Yes," said Jocelyn, "I thought it was a bit weird myself. I didn't get the impression his wife would be there. We saw a lot of Poppy and Nancy after that. We called him 'Poppy' because Nancy called him that, and it was just easier to refer to him that way."

Over lunch, Jocelyn filled me in on the gossip surrounding the people she and Poppy knew at the Hotel des Artistes. "Fannie Hurst lived at the des Artistes," she said.

"Yes," I said. "I remember her. Poppy talked a lot about her. I always pictured her as blond with soft curls and lovely blue eyes sitting by a sunny window in her studio with statues all around."

Jocelyn set me straight. "No, no. Fannie Hurst was known for her dyed, jet-black hair slicked back in a chignon. She had thin, red lips and always wore a calla lily broach that had a six-inch stem that reached across her chest and curved up to her neck."

Mother used to say, "You're known by the company you keep," and "birds of a feather flock together." Now, after all these years, I was finding out about the company Poppy kept.

Fannie Hurst was a best-selling novelist and the highest-paid writer in America. Many of her books about immigrants, shop girls, and slum dwellers have been made into movies. Like Clare Booth Luce, she was an outspoken feminist and anti-segregationist. Having obtained a degree from Columbia University, she waged a one-woman battle against sexism and racism in America. It was no wonder Poppy—a feminist himself—talked so much about her.

As I listened to Jocelyn's description of Fannie Hurst, Poppy's admonishment that I never let anyone make me ashamed that I was a woman began to sink in—as did his emphasis on the importance of education. He admired strong, intelligent women.

As Jocelyn talked, my mind flashed back to the Old Red Mill when I was seven. After I flunked reading at Daycroft that summer, Poppy hired a tutor to drill me from *McGuffy's Reader*, which was the same book from which he had learned to read. Closed up inside the mill for what seemed like hours, glimpses of sunshine glistening off the river through the window made me want to run outside. Instead, I had to read the words I would never forget. "If at first, you don't succeed, try, try again."

"No wonder Poppy liked Fanny Hurst," I told Jocelyn. "He hated any kind of discrimination. Sexism or racism. In fact, he believed in the "apotheosis" of women irrespective of color or race. He used that word, "apotheosis" in one of the books he wrote, *The American Girl.*"

It was obvious that Jocelyn enjoyed bringing me up-to-date with what should have been my past as well as hers.

"Fannie had these two little dogs," said Jocelyn. "She carried them in a rather large purse and wouldn't let anyone touch them. In the elevator, she'd clasp them to her breast. We had a Saint Bernard named Rowdy. One day in the lobby, Fannie threw her arms around Rowdy. As he shook her off, he slobbered on her face. Fanny sued us for Rowdy's bad behavior. Her lawyer said she wanted $10,000—or a facelift. He said, 'Granted, Miss Hurst needs a facelift, but it isn't because of the dog.' In the end, Fannie settled for a face lick instead of a facelift." We all laughed. It was all such fun, like eavesdropping on Poppy and Mother again.

By 1958, all had been forgiven between Jocelyn and Fannie because the two of them resumed their walks together at what was called the Sheep's Pasture in Central Park, the exact spot where Poppy sometimes took me to rollerskate. It's a wonder we never ran into them.

"Ray had given me a small carved St. Bernard for Christmas," Jocelyn said. "After one of our walks, Fannie came up to the apartment and saw it. She picked it up and looked at it carefully and said, 'I never should have sued. Rowdy was *such* a sweet dog.'"

Jocelyn told me that Fannie's remorse was so touching that Jocelyn's mother's eyes welled up with tears when she heard it.

The conversation switched to another des Artistes resident of a different stripe.

General "Jimmy" Doolittle—a colleague and best friend of General Patton. When I heard Jocelyn mention his name, I said, "I remember him! Poppy talked a lot about him also."

"Oh yes," Jocelyn assured me. "He was a frequent visitor at Poppy's studio."

"Yes, I know. Poppy always referred to him as Doolittle," I said. "'Saw Doolittle today.' You know, like that."

Doolittle was a stunt flyer and bomber who—on July 6, 1989—was awarded the Medal of Freedom, the highest honor bestowed on anyone by the President. But there was more to Doolittle than his daredevil World War II feats. In fact, contrary to his name, Doolittle did a lot. He was the quintessential Renaissance Man, a presidential advisor, and a scientist with a Ph.D. from MIT (Massachusetts Institute of Technology). Because of Doolittle's research, flying is safer. As an aeronautical engineer, he was offered the position of NASA Administrator but turned it down.

Hearing this, Poppy and General Doolittle didn't seem to have a whole lot in common. So what made them such good friends? Maybe Poppy's interest in boxing. Doolittle had been a professional boxer in Los Angeles. But, more likely, it was their shared love of the great out-of-doors. Both made it their life mission to preserve the natural beauty of the Earth and leave it better off than they had found it.

As Jocelyn talked, I thought how wonderful it would be to live in a building where you could share ideas with so many interesting, creative people. To me, that would have been Heaven on Earth. Artists need a refuge—and this is what the architects had in mind at the turn of the 19th century when they built the row of buildings on 67th Street, the most romantic of which was the Hotel des Artistes—designed for the world's creative elite.

Soon after the des Artistes was built in 1907, the sidewalk along short 67th Street began filling up with recognizable faces: Isadora Duncan, Noel Coward, Rudolph Valentino, Zasu Pitts, Jo Davidson, Alla Nazimova, Lawrence Tibbett, Marcel Duchamp, Al Jolson, Philippe Halsman, Mae Murray, Childe Hassam, Edna Ferber, Norman Rockwell, Maurice Maeterlinck. The Hotel des Artistes was second only to the Algonquin Hotel when it came to the rich and famous who passed through its gates.

"If I could make a wish, I would wish to live in a place just like that," I told Jocelyn. "All that creativity. How wonderful it must have been."

Ray didn't say much at lunch but didn't seem to mind that Jocelyn and I were doing all the talking. I loved hearing Jocelyn talk about Poppy's friends. She made me feel like I was right there with him in the gothic lobby of the Hotel des Artistes or carrying on a conversation with all those interesting people in its Café.

The conversation then switched to Poppy's personal life with his family.

And the inside story of what led up to his death.

"One summer when I was home from college," Jocelyn told me, "Poppy introduced me to his granddaughter, Carolyn Chandler. Carolyn was..."

"Yes, I know," I said, "She was Natalie's daughter. Natalie was Poppy's only legitimate child. The daughter of his first wife, Maebelle."

"That's right," said Jocelyn. "Carolyn lived with her mother, Natalie, and her grandmother, Maebelle. They lived only a few blocks from the Hotel des Artistes. One day, Poppy decided it would be good for Carolyn to get out of the house and go to a movie with me. Carolyn was eight years younger than I, and Natalie was very protective. She quizzed Poppy at length about me. Who was I? Who were my parents? Where did I live? Finally, in exasperation, Poppy called out, 'My God, Nat, it's only a movie. You don't have to see the girl's pedigree.' Natalie still wanted to meet me before she would entrust her daughter's safety to my care.

"That next Sunday afternoon, Carolyn and I went to a movie. I had instructions to walk her home and wait until she waved to me out of the window to let me know she was safely in her apartment."

"Didn't Carolyn go to a private school in Dobbs Ferry on the Hudson river?" I asked. "I remember meeting her there with Poppy and Mother. She was about my same age, I recall. I hated her right off the bat for having one of Poppy's names."

"Actually, Ira Chandler was Natalie's husband's name. No relation to Poppy. Oh, you would have loved Carolyn."

"I wish I could have known her," I said, realizing my childish envy was for lack of knowledge.

"After Carolyn got out of school," Jocelyn told me,

"she took some courses in New York and eventually went to work for *McCall's Magazine* and later for *Time/Life*.

"What did she do there?"

"I don't know."

"Didn't you ask?"

"No. Never did."

I sighed. "Guess my family wasn't the only one that didn't ask questions. Why is that?"

"The culture," said Jocelyn. "They didn't ask questions back then. Anyway, Carolyn was a delightful writer with a wonderful sense of humor. But very quiet."

Sadness swept over me as I listened to Jocelyn talk about Poppy's family. Here was a family from which I had been excluded. All because of a secret.

"Do you know if Nancy knew about me?" I asked.

"Yes. She knew."

"But did she know I was Poppy's daughter?"

"Yes, she knew that too."

I was stunned by this disclosure.

"One day, she confided in me that Elise had a daughter. I remember her exact words. 'I'm pretty sure she's Poppy's child, but I can't prove it.'"

This was a stunning confession. "Are you sure?"

"Oh, yes. We all knew."

I leaned back in my seat and took a deep breath. What I had just heard was confirmation that Poppy was, indeed, my father. I shook my head in amazement. "And everybody knew it but me."

It was dumbfounding. My whole life, I had longed to know if Poppy was my father. I had gone through such anguish to uncover the secret that almost wrecked my life.

What if I hadn't found out? The "what if" gave me a chill.

I stared blindly at my *creme brulee*. "Do you know anything about Poppy's death?" I asked, remembering the devastation I suffered that day.

Jocelyn took a sip of her tea, then placed it back in the saucer.

"Well, when Poppy passed away, I had just finished a year at the University of Vermont and was honing my secretarial skills at a small business school during the day. In those days, that's about all a girl could aspire to. I knew Poppy had been ill, and Nancy had told my mother she was afraid he might start drinking again. Years ago,

Poppy had been a heavy drinker, you know. Personally, I never saw him drink anything stronger than coffee. But he had been sick for nine weeks, and I overheard my stepfather tell my mother that a doctor friend had given Nancy a prescription for some liquid to slip into his glass of milk at night. I knew Poppy was against taking drugs."

"You mean Nancy was drugging Poppy without him knowing it?"

"I'm afraid so."

"It was Dr. Borow, wasn't it?"

Jocelyn avoided saying his name. "He was a friend of my stepfather's."

She paused. "And he probably broke a code of ethics in telling my stepfather about it. Or maybe a couple of codes of ethics, for that matter. Well, Nancy was dropping this liquid into Poppy's glass of milk every evening. She said it was 'to help him sleep.'"

As Jocelyn talked, I remembered the partially empty glass of milk that had been on the nightstand by Poppy's bed. *Was that why he drifted off to sleep so quickly after I arrived?* The thought sent me into moiling over what-ifs: *Had he not drunk that milk, might he have told me the truth?*

Why did Mother run past us on the stairs and out the door without speaking? Was she afraid he was going to tell me the truth? Was that what he planned to do that night when he took me to dinner at the Café des Artistes—without Mother?

Jocelyn continued to describe the intrigue surrounding Poppy's death. "I had heard that his legs were swollen, and it had something to do with a heart condition. But two days later, Poppy had improved enough to be in his usual place by the front door of the Hotel des Artistes."

"That must have been the morning after he took me to dinner," I said.

I pictured Poppy greeting Fannie Hurst, Jimmy Doolittle, and all his friends as they went in and out of that lobby. I pictured him smiling at them, one and all—the doorman and the garbage collector too. He knew every garbage collector by name, even the ones at our place on 74th Street. Poppy loved people. All people. Regardless of race, creed, color, or vocation.

"It was warm for March," Jocelyn said. "I said good morning to him as I rushed by on my way to school.

He said, 'Wait a minute. I want to tell you something.'

I said, 'Poppy, I'm late. I'll see you later.' I turned and

blew him a kiss. He reached out as if he wanted to pull me back, but I had to run.

"The next morning at school, the teacher had a copy of the *New York Times* lying on her desk. Poppy's picture was on the front page. 'Oh, that's a friend of mine,' I said, peering over her shoulder. 'I wonder what he's done to get his picture in the paper.' Then I read the article and learned that he had passed away the day before."

"Wait," I broke in. "How can that be? The night before he died, he took me to dinner. It was the night he told me...." I wanted to tell Jocelyn I thought he would have been too sick to get up in the morning, but I was unable to speak. After all those years, I was reliving the pain I'd felt that night in the elevator of the Hotel des Artistes.

I covered my face and took a deep breath. After regaining my composure, I said, "He told me..." I took a deep breath. They were the words into which I had placed so much meaning, words I had to believe meant more than he could say, words that would one day turn knowing the truth into an obsession that would alienate me from everyone in my family.

I heaved and took a deep breath, and repeated his last

words to Jocelyn. "'I want you to know—you've meant more to me than anything in this world.'"

I dug a Kleenex out of my purse and wiped the tears from my eyes, then continued telling Jocelyn about my last moments with Poppy. "Nancy met us at the elevator," I said, feeling like I was reliving the whole ordeal. "She had to help him out." Tears ran down my cheeks as I remembered the iron gate of the elevator slamming shut between Poppy and me and the horrible ordeal of knowing I was being cut off from him forever.

Jocelyn's voice grew heavy. "Over the years, I've often wondered what it was he wanted to tell me that day. I regret it now that I was in too much of a hurry to hear it. "I skipped school for the next several days so I could help Nancy with the funeral. My teacher was very understanding.

"My stepfather was so upset over Poppy's death that he wasn't able to handle going to see Nancy, so he asked me to express his condolences for him. You see, about twice a year, my stepfather would drink heavily. On one of those mornings after, he got up to go to the bathroom. He made a wrong turn and fell down the stairs of our duplex. Mother picked him up and guided him to the couch, where he promptly wet the couch. He thought he was on the toilet. Mother called Nancy. She came over, and between the two of them, they got him back upstairs and into bed. Mother had an appointment she couldn't cancel, so she left me in charge and told me to call Nancy if I needed help. Later my father had to get up to go to the bathroom. I called Nancy, but she had gone out. Poppy answered the phone. He came right over. He was very gentle and caring. My stepfather never forgot it."

"Where was Poppy when he died?" I asked. "Was Nancy with him? Or was it Mother?"

Jocelyn began re-counting the last climactic scene as if it were a movie set with cameras rolling. Then, momentarily, she'd digress into telling me something else I'd never known about Poppy.

"As you enter the studio, Poppy's *Resurrection* painting was directly in front of you, just to the right of the big studio windows. It hung over Poppy's desk." Jocelyn called it a desk. I remember it as an antique table with a single drawer in front.

"The painting was huge. It reached up, I'd say, six to eight feet above the table. Poppy had a huge Italian chair in front of the table that was usually turned so that it faced the center of the studio with the painting at his back. It was a picture of two angels guarding an empty sepulcher. The angels are reaching up toward a glowing light. The picture was commissioned by the Salvation Army. But when the commissioners saw it, they got really upset. 'Why aren't the angels women?' they wanted to know. So, Poppy told them. 'All the angels I know of in the Bible are men. Gabriel and Michael. There are no female angels in the Bible.'"

I laughed. "He's right. It never fails to amuse me how people profess to know the Bible when they've never even read it."

Jocelyn agreed. Then she began describing the unfolding of the scene of his death. "On the far wall was a painting of Nancy with the Afghan hounds."

"That was Nancy? That beautiful woman with the two Afghans was Nancy?" I had not recognized the elegant lady in that painting as the same frumpy, bleached blond who had met me at the door.

"Yes, that was Nancy," Jocelyn said. "That painting must have been done in the *Roaring '20s*. It was a time of great opulence *and* decadence. Those hounds were huge, and they needed exercise daily."

"You mean those big white hounds actually belonged to Poppy and Nancy? I thought he might have put them in the painting just because they looked nice."

"Yes. Nancy told me that by some arrangement Poppy had with City Management, part of Central Park would be closed off at a certain time each day. Poppy and Nancy would get into their limousine with the dogs outside on either side. Poppy would hold a leash out one window, and Nancy would hold the other leash out the other one. The driver would then proceed through Central Park with the dogs running alongside.

"During those heydays, artists entertained frequently and lavishly. Nancy had been written up in the papers as a famous hostess. Kitchens in the Hotel des Artistes were all small. They would order food from DiPalma's around the corner. They had the best steaks. When it was delivered, Nancy would put them on the dumbwaiter with a note telling the cook how many she was entertaining that night and at what time she expected the prepared meals to be ready. The meals would all arrive on time by the dumbwaiter. Most of Nancy's meals were prepared this way by the Café downstairs. That's one way their bills skyrocketed."

"I heard that—for painting the murals—Poppy was promised free meals for the rest of his life by the Hotel Board of Directors. Is that true?"

Jocelyn hadn't heard about that, but she did hear that painting the murals was the way Poppy paid off his debt to the Café.

Switching back to Poppy's death, Jocelyn said, "Poppy was sitting in his big Italian chair below the *Resurrection* painting. Your mother was sitting next to him reading from *Science & Health with Key to the Scriptures*. Nancy had gone out to buy Poppy his favorite flower. I'm not sure. It might have been a rose."

"A rose was in his coat of arms from Normandy," I said. "A picture of a swan picking the meat from her chest to feed her young with the inscription 'Faithful unto death.'"

Jocelyn paid no heed. She was too deep into her memories of that fateful morn. "The colored maid was there. She saw it all. I mean, what happened after Nancy left, and she told Nancy about it later. Poppy asked Elise to stop reading. Suddenly, he pushed his chair back from the table and stood up. He thrust his left hand in the air as if reaching for something in the ceiling. Then fell back into his chair."

I was speechless.

In my mind, I was witnessing Poppy's death, seeing every detail. As if I were there. It was the strangest feeling. I even saw what he was reaching for. A glowing light. Just like he had painted it in his *Resurrection*.

The next day was Tuesday, March 4, 1952. *The New York Times* published his obituary. "HOWARD C. CHRISTY, NOTED ARTIST, DIES — Magazine Illustrator, Creator of the Christy Girl, Victim of Heart Attack at 79. COVERED WAR WITH SPAIN — Sketches of Troops in Action Widely Printed — Painted Portraits of Celebrities."

The article was wrong about one thing. Poppy's age. He was eighty. Something I learned only recently when his birth certificate was discovered amid his papers. Apparently, he had granted himself an extra year. A fib repeated over and over again for years by *Webster's Dictionary* and the *Encyclopedia Americana*.

The newspaper article expounded the wide range of Poppy's art, from illustration to the *Signing of the United Nations Charter*. It went on to say he "died yesterday after an illness of nine weeks at his residence in the des Artistes

Hotel, 1 West Sixty-Seventh Street... Death was attributed to a heart attack."

The article gave a synopsis of his illustrious life, listing President and Mrs. Harding, President Coolidge, Vice President Barkley, Amelia Earhart, Benito Mussolini, Will Rogers, and other people whose portraits he had painted. It also mentioned that he had many models. "The last to pose," stated the article, "was the blond Miss Nancy Palmer, whom he married in 1919."

They sure got that wrong.

The last model to pose for Poppy was Mother in his World War II *I Am An American* poster. Just goes to prove you can't believe everything you read in the paper, not even when it's in *The New York Times*.

The article ended with these words: "His painting, *Signing of the Constitution*, hangs in the Capitol Building in Washington."

Just as I was beginning to think this was the end of the story. Jocelyn said, "After Poppy's death, that's when the trouble started."

"Trouble? What kind of trouble?"

"Well, this may sound crude, but when I got to

Poppy's studio, I was surprised to find Nancy holding court with some friends who had come to console her. She kept saying it was that 'damned Christian Science' that killed Poppy. She was angry with Elise for reading to him from *Science and Health*. She didn't know I knew she had been slipping Poppy drugs without his knowledge; she didn't mention that at all."

Jocelyn told me that on the morning of the funeral, Nancy gave Jocelyn a fresh gardenia to replace the one in Poppy's buttonhole. When Jocelyn looked down at Poppy lying there in his coffin, she suddenly felt ill at ease and asked one of the attendants to replace it for her.

At Nancy's behest, Jocelyn stayed at the funeral parlor in case someone arrived early.

"Mrs. Babe Ruth showed up drunk," said Jocelyn. "She said she couldn't attend the funeral but wanted to pay her respects... When I mentioned this to Nancy, she told me that Babe and his wife were both heavy drinkers.

"My stepfather sent a blanket of mimosa for Poppy's casket. It was a Christian Science funeral service. Afterwards, I rode with the Turners, who were the managers of the Café des Artistes to the Fernwood gravesite. Mrs. Turner mentioned how uplifting the service was. She and Charlie were Catholics. She said that Catholic services were usually depressing."

I listened intently as Jocelyn filled me in on what happened after Poppy's death.

"Carolyn and I became traveling companions across the U.S. and to Europe. Carolyn's mother, Natalie, didn't want anything more to do with Nancy, so she relinquished all rights to anything that might be due to her from Poppy's estate. Then Nancy started drinking heavily. She withdrew from her old friends and got in with a crowd of alcoholics like herself. One of those people was Robert Coneen. Nancy called him Bobby. Everyone else called him 'the gentleman jockey' because he always wore riding breeches and worked in the stable across the street before it was bought by ABC and turned into a television studio. Nancy married Bobby, and he moved into Poppy's studio with Nancy.

"One day, Natalie asked Carolyn to go over to Nancy's apartment and 'retrieve' Poppy's sword and a medal he had received during the Spanish-American War.

"When she got there, Carolyn was shocked by what she saw. The whole studio was crawling with cockroaches. The walls had been whitewashed up as high as one could reach, bringing sharp contrast to the cockroaches skittering over them. Nancy and Bobby had been drinking heavily for quite some time and had done nothing about cleaning the apartment. Dirty dishes were piled in the sink. Garbage was dumped in the corners. The place stunk of rotten food and filth.

"Carolyn told me she had to 'buy back' items she wanted because Nancy and Bobby had to sell everything to pay the upkeep. The apartments in the des Artistes were co-ops. Owned, not rented. I imagine there were condo upkeep fees, not to mention taxes which were getting higher and higher in New York."

I remembered Poppy's studio as I had seen it that one time he called me to join him there. All that creative energy that filled every space. All that celebration of Life.

And in the end—cockroaches swarmed in.

***

The day after Poppy's funeral, I was back in boarding school.

There had been no time to mourn.

"Hey, Dirty Laundry. Where have *you* been?" sneered Big Janet as if I had been playing hooky.

For six years, calling attention to my flaws had been her pleasure. "Modest Morris," "Holly's got a mustache," and "Dirty laundry" were her favorite taunts.

"I went to a funeral," I muttered, not wanting to talk.

"Oh? Whose funeral?"

"Howard Chandler Christy's."

"So? Who's he to you?"

"He was..." A wave of staggering grief slammed into me full force.

"He was... just like my father," I wailed.

CHAPTER EIGHTEEN

Forbidden Fruit

And when the woman saw that the tree was good for food, and that it was pleasant to the eyes, and a tree to be desired to make one wise, she took of the fruit thereof, and did eat...

- Genesis 3:6

Mother never mentioned Poppy again. Like Morris—my putative father—it was as if Poppy never existed. Her silence made me afraid to mention him. The feeling was palpable. Something was shameful and must be hidden. It was as if talking about Poppy would be like tasting the forbidden fruit of the knowledge of good and evil, which, of course, made me more determined to know what I shouldn't.

Seeing things as they really are is hard enough, but a world immersed in secrets is like driving through a thick fog. It's scary and dangerous.

As I was to find out, Mother wasn't the only one keeping secrets. One whole side of Mother's family had secrets that would alienate me from both sides of my family. With Poppy gone, I found myself suffering from the kind of secrets that philosopher and ethicist Sissela Bok compared to a fire that stifles, lays waste, and spreads out of control.

***

After Poppy's death, Mother fell silent. No more whistling or bursts of song issued from her lips. Who was I? I could never be sure, and uncertainty about my identity left me unprepared for life as an adult. Mother's secret spread like a bottomless pit between us. Needing love and a sense of belonging, I married the wrong man. When he turned out to be abusive, I turned to religion and joined a fundamentalist Christian church, which eventually sent my husband and me, and our two children to Mexico City on private jets. Six years of living in a Mexican villa a thousand feet above Mexico City could not quell the yearning to know the truth. I could stand it no longer. Was Poppy my father? I had to know.

In 1974, I took my two children with me on a pilgrimage back to New York City to claim my identity. By then, Mother had died of cancer, and there were only two members of my family left whom I thought could tell me the truth. By then, I was thirty-four years old.

Five hours after takeoff from *Aeropuerto Internacional de la Ciudad de Mexico*, the plane banked and began its descent over New York City. With me were my two children: Ricky, fourteen, and Christina, ten. Excitedly, I pointed to the Statue of Liberty as the New York skyline rose up to meet us like jagged spikes. I felt a foreboding chill. It had been sixteen years since I'd left, and no one I knew was left in this inhospitable-looking place. Mother's sister Doris had moved from New York to her Massachusetts estate when Leona Helmsley tore down the building that had been their home on 36 Central Park South and built what is today Park Lane. Mother's big brother Uncle Forsberg lived in Montauk Point, Long Island. I wasn't sure if either one of these people were still alive, nor had I announced that we were coming.

The plane bumped down and taxied toward the

terminal, at which there would be no friendly faces to greet us.

I no longer remember the details of the trip to Montauk. All I know is I took a train to Long Island with the intent to visit my Uncle Carl first. Nordic daredevil that he was—surely he wouldn't shrink from revealing long-held family secrets.

I breathed in the briny air as my children stepped off the commuter train at Montauk Point, Long Island. As we walked toward the dock, a bleached-out sign over a diner squealed on rusty hinges. Hungry after the long trip, I took my children inside and climbed up on the barstools the way Poppy and I had done at the Log Cabin Inn. Before me, a framed newspaper clipping hung on the wall. "That's Carl," I said, pointing to the man in aviator glasses and a white captain's hat—his broad shoulders jutted from his tank shirt like iron scaffoldings on a high-rise building. Beside him hung a huge marlin from the day's catch. As with Mother's other siblings, I called him by his first name, something I had to explain to my children, who addressed their Mexican aunts and uncle's as *tia* or *tio*. Culturally my children were now Mexicans. They spoke Spanish, went to a private Mexican school, and participated in Sunday *cenas* with their father's family.

As the waiter slid our food onto the counter, I asked him if he knew where I might find Captain Carl Forsberg. "Just up the road," he said, "The Viking Fleet. Can't miss it. He should be coming in soon." The bristle-faced man looked at his watch. "It's about that time."

I breathed a sigh of relief. I hadn't called. I had counted on Carl's history of not missing a day of fishing since he and my grandfather built their first boat.

The Viking Fleet groaned against the ropes that tethered them to the dock as my children scampered ahead, eager to peer into the dark swells at the end of the dock. The pungent smell of a salt-water marsh and the hypnotic sloshing of the waves against the dock swept me back to Captain Allen's Clam House, where Poppy first introduced me to the pleasures of the Earth he loved with the warmth of the sun on rough-hewn boards beneath my bare feet; the cry of seagulls; the creaking of boats moored to barnacled posts; the chafing of old wood, and the squealing of oars that heralded Captain Allen's return with a boatload of clams.

Instead of joy, I found myself filled with remorse. *I*

wish I could have been a Poppy to my children. Instead, I had married a man who filled our lives with shouting and turmoil. It didn't matter that we lived in a villa with seven peacocks strutting across our courtyard. All the *joie de vive* I'd had known was not to be found.

As we waited for Carl's boat to come in, the waves heaved up and down like a mother's breast. It was hypnotic. More memories flooded in, sweeping me back to Captain Allen's and the nearby channel Poppy had taken me to swim at in the channel below its rocky ledge. I remember shivering as I looked down into its dark, swift current. Poppy wanted me to jump, but I was too scared. I wanted to cry as I stared into the cold, choppy water. Behind me, I heard Poppy brag to Mother, "Look at Holly. She stands straight as an arrow, and she can swim like a fish."

I couldn't disappoint him. I had to be brave. Like Hiawatha and Minnehaha.

Mother snapped a picture as I leaped out over the dark swells. My belly smacked into the waves. I was scared as the numbing coldness of the current swept me away from Poppy. I flailed against its surge. "Don't fight the current," yelled Poppy from the ledge. "Swim with it.

Ease your way to shore!" It was the same advice he would later give me in the more threatening waves in the Atlantic. I was scared as the current swept me past the rocks. Then I saw Mother—her white bathing cap bobbing like a buoy downstream. I couldn't fail. I had to make Poppy happy. I dog-paddled toward the wall. As the current scraped me along the rocks, I grabbed hold of a cleft and hauled myself out.

I emerged triumphant as Poppy wrapped a towel around my stiff, shivering body. "Never fight the current," he reminded me as if he was giving me an important lesson in life. "Remember, always ease your way out."

The screeching of seagulls roused me from my reverie. "That must be him," I called to my children as the sound of a beating motor came into range. Gulls screamed overhead as they dove for scraps of fish being thrown overboard. "Move back," I told my children. "We need to leave room for the fishing party to disembark."

A rangy man in a white captain's hat jumped onto the dock and looped a thick rope around a post. I barely recognized him. Last I saw him, Carl was young and handsome. Mother always said he looked like Randolph

Scott—a film star of old black-and-white Westerns.

After all the men were safely off the boat, the man in the white captain's hat ambled toward me. Wind and sea had wizened his face, and his tall frame was now gaunt.

"Carl," I called out to him. He stopped short and looked up.

"Well, I'll be..." He strode toward me and took my hand into his rough palm, and I could feel the gap where he had lost a finger working on the Lincoln Tunnel. He threw a lanky arm around me. "So, where've you been all these years?"

I told him Mexico City. "Papa left me some money in his will, so I'm using it to acquaint my children with my family."

"Yeah," said Carl. "Dad remembered everyone in his family that was still alive. Even left something to my kids."

I introduced Carl to my children and asked him about his kids, now grown. I had met my cousins only once. Our families were always distant. Life in the US was so different. There were no family get-togethers so common in Mexico.

"So, what are you doing in Mexico?" he asked as we strolled down the dock.

"Oh, my husband is the head of an American-based organization," I said, then quickly changed the subject. Being close to the open sea makes me want to forget my reason for being there was a religion that believed we were on the brink of the End of the World. "Oh, Carl, remember the time you took us on a fishing trip, and we got caught in a storm?"

"Sure do. Gosh, by then, you were in your teens."

I conjured up memories of a terrible storm. A pitching boat. Waves washing over the bow. Spray blowing in my face and that awful sensation in my stomach heaving with the ship.

"Yeah," said Carl. "That was one hell of a storm. All sixty men got seasick and went downstairs."

I laughed. "And you called out, 'Anyone down there want a baNanna? All those groans. A couple of them came running up the stairs and threw up over the railing."

Carl gave me a crooked smile. "You've got a good memory."

"How can I forget? I was so sick. I thought I'd die."

Carl laughed and shook his head. "Yeah, that was one hell of a storm. We didn't have radar to predict the weather back then."

As we reached the road, I felt my heart begin to pound. *Why am I so afraid? For heaven's sake, we're both adults. Get to the point.* "Carl, I've come all the way from Mexico to ask you a question."

"Yeah?" He swept off his cap and wiped the strands of steel grey hair off his furrowed brow, then pulled it back on. "What's up?"

Gripped by fear, my throat tightened. I was about to broach a long-held taboo. I took a deep breath. "Carl, I have to know the truth. Was Poppy my father? Carl, please tell me."

I felt like Eve reaching for that damned fruit—every fiber in my body yearned to know what the adults in my life had always made me feel was a sin to know.

"What makes you think I know?"

He's putting me off. Anxiety mounted.

"Carl, please! I've come all this way to find out. Was Poppy my father?"

"If I knew, I'd tell you."

"But you are my mother's brother. You and she were hunting companions. How could you *not* know?"

He tugged at his captain's hat as if feeling the squeeze, then peered down at me from under the shadow of its visor. "Holly, your mother and I, we stopped talking after she moved into that place on 74th Street. I never saw her after that. There was a war. There were blackouts. Gasoline was rationed. People were afraid to go anywhere."

I felt my stomach lurch. What else could I say? Either he was telling me the truth, or he wasn't. It was true that he and Mother didn't get together. I could only remember meeting him twice when I was a child.

"How 'bout coming up to the house?" Carl nodded in the direction of swaying grass leading up to a large, white-frame house on a hill. "Adel can fix us some dinner. We've got plenty of extra beds. You can spend the night."

"Thanks, but I don't have time. I need to get back to New York before dark."

"Look, Holly. I'm sorry. I wish I could help. Why don't you ask Doris? She'd know for sure. She and Elise were always close. Heck, they were practically next-door neighbors.

"Doris would never tell me the truth. That's why I came to you first."

"Times change. Maybe now she will."

Sobs of disappointment bubble up inside. "I have to run," I said, not wanting him to see me cry. I had just started down the road with my children when he called out to me. "Holly! Wait!"

I turned, tears streaming down my face.

"There's something you should know."

I took a deep breath, preparing myself for something bad as he trudged toward me, head bowed. "One day, I went into the city. Musta been 1940. Maybe 41. We were still at war. Thought I'd pop in, you know, surprise your mother. I thought she'd be happy to see me. By then, she was living on West 74th Street. I knocked. She came to the door. I'll never forget the look on her face. She gave me some excuse for why she couldn't let me in. I thought it was strange. Here we were at war. And there we were, together after so long apart. It was strange. All I know is, just before she closed the door, I looked past her and caught a glimpse of a baby in a highchair."

Goosebumps rose on my arms. I felt my hair follicles

stand on end.

"Musta been you," he said. "She sure hadn't told me anything about a baby.'

Of course not. I was Mother's dirty little secret.

I thanked him and ran back down the road.

"Sure, you don't want to stay the night?" He called after me.

"Gotta go see Doris," I called back.

CHAPTER NINETEEN

Cursed is the Ground

Thorns also and thistles shall it bring forth to thee.

\- Genesis

"Three tickets to Ashley Falls," I told the ticket agent at Grand Central as throngs of hustling bodies bustled past me in the colossal marble rotunda.

"Never heard of it."

"It's in Massachusetts."

He thumbed through his book. I gazed up at the domed ceiling. Through the high arched windows, the darkness of night was descending.

"Look, Mommy." Christina pointed to a glowing Kodak Colorama of a sunny pastoral scene on the largest transparency in the world, stretching across the far end of the station.

"Reminds me of the Old Red Mill," I said, forgetting that I'd never told her about the Eden of Poppy's creation.

"Gate 3," said the ticket agent as he slid my tickets through the window. "If you hurry, you can make it. The Boston Express. You've got five minutes."

I seized my children's hands. "Get off at Hartford! From there, you'll have to take a bus." As we started to run, he yelled something about a "detour," but there was no time to wait.

"Run," I yelled, dodging throngs of people as we raced toward the gate beneath the huge Kodak sign. A male voice resounded through the rotunda. "Boston Express. Now departing. Gate 3. Stamford, New Haven, Hartford, Boston." *It's the same train I commuted to school on!*

Christina's fingers dug into my hand. "It's okay, Pumpkin," I told her as I pulled her along through the crowd. My effort to ease her fear was lost in our mad dash, but I knew how she felt. I'd felt her fear before, when I was seven years old, being pulled by Mother through the horde of strangers.

Gate 3 was just ahead. As we passed under the Eastman Kodak transparency, past and present merged. I braced myself for impact as I was catapulted back in time to my first day alone on the Boston Express. As we hurried through the gate and down the ramp, it wasn't Christina's hand I was holding. It was Mother's.

Almost thirty years had passed since I first felt abandoned in a perilous world of helplessness and fear as I was being sent away from my happy world with Poppy.

Now here I was again. This time with my children. My goal? To uncover Mother's secret.

Once in the train, the roar of steel was deafening as the train pulled out of the station. Seeing no seats, I rolled back the door to pass between the cars. Clackety clack. Clackety clack. I grasped Christina's hand and pulled her over the moving plates between the shaking cars. Two cars later, we entered a smoker car with a meager assortment of pre-wrapped sandwiches, candy, and chips.

"Where's the dining car?" I ask a man in a plaid shirt, sipping coffee in a paper cup.

"You're in it," he quipped.

"You're kidding! I used to commute to school on this train. I clearly remember eating breakfast in a dining car with white tablecloths."

The man laughed. "Not anymore. Those days are over. Where'd you go to school?"

"Daycroft in Stamford, Connecticut."

"So you're one of those snobs on the hill."

"How'd you know we were called that?"

"I used to live in Stamford. We'd hide in the woods and watch the stretch limos drive under the stone arch."

I'd forgotten about the stretch limos that took us to the Metropolitan Opera and the Philharmonic on weekends. It reminded me of the cozy feel of the red velvet seats in the box reserved for us kids, but I kept that part to myself lest I confirm my reputation as a snob. "Is Daycroft still there?" I was saddened to hear it had been torn down and replaced by Clairol. Gone was the Tudor mansion on the hill and the girl's dorm we called Adelaide Hall.

Our train pulled into Stamford, and the man in the plaid shirt got off. I looked for the shady lot where my school bus used to wait. Instead of trees, I saw skyscrapers.

As we settled in for the long ride to Hartford, I thought about change and how it's not always for the good. Like skyscrapers in place of grass and rolling hills and the cooling shade of forests. And I wondered about Doris. Gorgeous Doris. Mother's sister. What will she look like after all these years? I hadn't called to tell her I was coming. There wasn't time. Besides, long-distance calls were too expensive. I was sure she'd be there. Where else would Doris go since Leona Helmsley, "The Queen of Mean," forced them out of their 36 Central Park South building, tore it down and built the Park Lane in its place? Ever since then, Doris and Wanda had lived at their summer estate in Ashley Falls.

As the train shimmied and shook, it brought back a yearning for Poppy and the Old Red Mill. *Take me back. Take me back,* clackety-clack.

Three hours later, I heard the conductor cry, "HARTFORD, HARTFORD!" as he entered our car. It woke me up. "Our stop," I told the two nodding heads on the seat facing me

Entering a nearby bus terminal, I went straight for the

phone booth and dug into my backpack for change. By now, it was late at night. From my little phone book, I dialed the number out of my past.

The phone rang and rang. I looked around me. The station was empty. An ominous awareness of isolation crept over me. What if they don't live there anymore? In my mind, everything had to be just as I'd left it. I clung to this belief as I huddled my children around me in the phone booth.

"Hello!" Doris's breathy champagne-and-diamonds voice was a soothing melody to my ears.

"Doris! This is Holly. I'm in Hartford."

"Holly, dear! I can't believe it!"

"My children and I are in a pay phone at the bus depot. The bus leaves in ten minutes. I'm coming to see you. I'm sorry it's so late. I hope it's okay. I couldn't make it sooner."

"Oh, Holly dear, that's wonderful! No, of course, it's alright. Now, Holly. Listen to me. The bus doesn't go through Ashley Falls. But they will make an exception if you ask."

"That's what I was told at Grand Central. Something

about a detour."

"Yes, dear. A detour. The driver must take a detour. Be sure to remind him that you want to go to Ashley Falls. Now dear, listen carefully. The bus will stop on top of a hill. Our driveway is..."

An operator cut in, telling me to deposit more change. I dug furiously into my backpack and plunked in two more quarters. It was all the change I had left.

"Oh, Holly dear. I thought we'd been cut off. Wanda and I will walk up to meet you. Oh, Holly," crooned Doris in the same gushy bedroom voice I remembered as a child. "So good to hear your voice. It will be wonderful to see you."

And to think I thought I didn't have a family. I was overcome with joy.

"Bye, for now, dear," Doris breathed into the phone. "Mwah!" And I could just see her red lips throwing me a kiss.

***

Shadowy forests whipped by outside as the Greyhound bus trundled over lonely country roads. Here and there, I glimpse farmhouse lights with long stretches in between.

My children stretched out on an empty back seat as I fought to stay awake. *What if the driver forgets to take the detour?*

My thoughts turned to Wanda. *We were like sisters. We had so much in common. Our mothers were models. We grew up in art studios. Both of us had world-famous...* I caught myself as I realized that that was what I had come here to find out. Was Poppy my father? *Surely now that Wanda and I are adults, Doris will have no excuse not to tell me the truth.*

A foreboding chill ran through me. *What if Poppy wasn't my father? What if I was like Honnie—an orphan Poppy took in? Then who would my father be? A rapist? A one-night stand? Is that why nobody ever talked about him?* There were so many worrisome what-ifs.

Doubt was too disorientating to contemplate.

It threatened the integrity of my deepest instincts.

Whatever the truth was, I had to know.

The bus slowed and came to a stop. "Ma'am, this is your stop," the bus driver called out over the rumble of an idling motor. I grabbed my backpack and rousted my sleepyheads. "We're here. We're going to see Doris." Still half asleep, my children and I stumbled down the aisle. The door swooshed open, and we got off.

I looked around. Nothing but dense forest. Not a house in sight.

"Wait!" I yelled as the door swung shut. "There must be a mistake."

Too late. The bus roared off with a blast of fumes. I followed its lights and the rumble of its wheels until it was swallowed up by the night. The open stretch of rural road was painfully silent as the hum of the bus faded into the distance.

And there we stood in the darkness of night beneath the menacing cover of murmuring trees.

What did Doris say about a hill? Wait where? Did I miss something when I got cut off?

"Mommy... where are we?" Christina said as she squeezed my arm.

"If this was a town, wouldn't there be some street lights?" asked Ricky.

What have I done?

"Everything will be fine," I lied, trying to sound confident. There we stood. Alone in the dark. Not so much as the lights of a car in sight. I took the children's hands and started down the hill, growing more fearful with every crunching step on the gravel shoulder. Had the driver made some awful mistake? Taken the wrong detour?

Could Doris have misled me? She was always a bit scatterbrained. Walking faster, my heart pounded with the fear of having put my children in danger. Fear of being left alone in the dark. Fear of never seeing Doris and Wanda again. Fear of losing the only family I had.

I stopped. "We mustn't go any further," I said. "Doris told me to stay put when I got off the bus." The moon slid in and out from behind baleful clouds, casting eerie shadows on the road. Not a sign of human life. Only the shaking of leaves and the haunting hoot of an owl.

"Holly, dear!" Doris's voice rang out in the night like an angel of light. She was waving at me in the moonlight by the side of the road. We ran to greet her. She looked the same as I remembered her—complete with turban and big red, over-the-top, Lucille Ball lips.

"Oh, Holly! You poor dear. The bus was early. I'm so sorry to keep you waiting."

We hugged, and her lusty laugh filled me with gladness.

"Poor dear," she said. "You must have been terribly worried!" And the foreboding forest lit up with our laughter.

"And the children!" gushed Doris leaning over to plant a big, red lipstick mark on their cheeks. "Aren't they, darling? Amazing! Just amazing! And Ricky! How he's grown!"

"That's right," I said, following her into the forest. "You haven't seen Ricky since..." I hesitated, remembering Mother's death... "When he was four."

"Oh, Holly dear, it's so good to see you."

"You look just the same!" I said. "Beautiful as ever."

"Aren't you sweet."

We turned down a long gravel driveway. I wondered where Wanda was but was too tired to ask. Huge trees formed an arch over our heads, cutting off the light from the moon. It was eerie, like entering a foreboding dark tunnel.

The next day I awoke to the song of birds outside my window as I climbed out of bed. *How will Wanda look? Tall and glamorous like her mother?* I opened the door, crept down the hallway, and peeked into the room where I'd left my children. They were still sleeping, so I moseyed down to the next bedroom door.

Hearing movement inside, I stopped outside the door and held my breath. *What if it's Doris? If I hope to ever get a straight answer about Poppy, I must ask her when she's alone. Not with Wanda.* Old fears began to haunt me. At thirty-four, I still felt like the child I was when I first toddled up to the white-haired man on his crimson throne to ask, "Why can't I call you Father?"

Doris and Wanda had not attended Poppy's funeral. Yet, I never thought to ask why. The last time I saw Wanda, she was twelve. I tried to imagine how she might have changed now that she had a degree from Brown University. How different our lives had turned out. Me— married with children. Wanda—an Egyptologist.

I opened the door a crack and peeked in. Doris was sitting alone on the edge of her bed. Her dark hair—still long and thick–framed her lovely square face. She looked up. "Oh, hello, dear," she said, sounding trancelike. "I hope you slept well."

As I stepped in, she gathered up a pile of photographs scattered over her bed and dumped them into a grocery carton on the floor beside the bed. There was a faraway look in her eyes. I didn't know what to make of it. I'd never seen her like that. The box was filled with black-and-white photographs. I caught a glimpse of one as it fell into the box. Tade and Doris sitting on the couch in Tade's studio—the tapestry soaring above.

"Can I see your pictures?" I asked.

"Of course, dear."

I delved into the box, feeling like a pirate who had fallen upon buried treasure. I pawed through scores of pictures, all rich with scenes of a past more opulent than I had imagined. Sitting down beside Doris, I pulled out a photograph that I remembered hanging over the bar of Tade's studio. In it, Tade looks like a sultan in loincloth and turban. Flanked by Grecian pillars and fronds of palm, he is descending what looks like temple steps with an oriental rug laid out to cushion his kingly feet.

"Where was this taken?"

"Oh, that was at our villa on the Isle of Capri," said Doris in a slow matter-of-fact voice. Almost zombie-like. It was the first I'd heard of a villa. *And why is he wearing that turban? And is that lipstick? Is he wearing lipstick?* I dared not ask.

I pulled out another photo. Tade in a tight bathing suit, flexing his muscles. I snatched up another one. Tade, charging out of the bushes stark naked, holding a fig leaf over his privates.

"I remember this," I said. "It used to hang over the bar in Tade's studio."

I rifled through more pictures, many of them large eight-by-twelves, and pulled out another one of Tade on the beach. This time he was God in the act of creation as he molded Doris's naked form out of wet sand.

I want these pictures. But Doris would never let me have them. Stacking the ones I wanted in my lap, I said, "Is there any way I can make copies of these before I leave?"

"Take them, dear. Take whatever you want."

I stared at Doris in disbelief. She still had a faraway look in her eyes—as if in another world. And perhaps she was, as the pictures revealed a life she no longer lived.

"Are you sure?" I felt like a thief stealing from the blind.

"You may have them. Really, dear."

I snapped up one picture after another. Tade was in his top hat, his face powdered ghostly white with a thin line of lipstick on his lips. I never asked why Tade powdered his face white, afraid too many questions might give her cause to reconsider.

Doris had given me a part of her past. I pressed the pictures to my chest. *Does this mean she is now willing to tell me the truth about mine?*

"Doris," I said. "There's something I must ask."

My throat tightened. Voices in my head warned *You can't just ask her straight out. Appeal to her sympathy first.* "Doris. You wouldn't want Wanda to grow up not knowing Tade Styka was her father, would you?" Voices in my head warned me to keep my place. I was a child: she, the adult. I had no right.

"Doris. I've come all this way from Mexico City to ask you to tell me the truth. Was Poppy my father? I need to know."

I waited for the answer that would, at last, make me equal to those adults who had always towered over my life.

Doris's eyes brightened as if coming to life.

My heart quickened.

She grinned haughtily. Then looked away. "We'll see,

dear. We'll see."

It was the same old trick Mother had used to stop me from whining. I searched Doris's eyes. It was as if Doris was gazing into the magic mirror of her past. Mirror, mirror on the wall. Who's the most wonderful man of them all? Tade or Christy? *Damn her all to hell! She knows. But she's not telling.*

I couldn't beg. It would only have given her more power over me and made me look foolish. I felt like I was under the curse of the wicked witch.

Even adopted children come to a point where they want to know—if only for genetic health reasons. It's quite another to adore the man who raised you as I did, yet never be told the truth. Before my eyes, gushy, kiss-throwing Doris had turned into the Wicked Queen, determined to keep me from getting the glass slipper.

Knowledge is power. I was no match for Doris. She alone held the key to the mystery that was me. I was helpless. Nothing I could do or say would convince her to give me what I wanted. Somehow, I had to outsmart her. Break her code of silence.

Fearing Doris would change her mind about the pictures, I scuttled back to my room and tucked the photographs into my backpack. My only hope now was to catch Wanda alone while Doris was still in her room

I ran downstairs. No one was there. I ran outside.

All I remember next is Wanda's chalk-white face. Those dimpled cheeks. Her plain cotton dress hung on her rail-thin body. We stood for a moment, sizing one another up. Her powdered face was the same ghostly white as her father's in the photograph I'd just squirreled away. There were no hugs. Her dark hair was parted in the middle, pulled severely back and wrapped around her head in thick dark braids. No makeup, other than that pasty white mask. Barely discernable was what could have been an exotic beauty underneath. I felt like I was looking at a ghost rising out of an Egyptian crypt. *Why does Wanda powder her face so white? Does she fancy herself the reincarnation of her father—the great Tadeusz Styka? Is she reliving the past as a member of a mystic Egyptian cult?* I dared not ask. Indeed, Wanda was the image of her father. That Polish face. Nostrils slightly flared. Lips drawn thin with determination. Like him, Wanda had become one of the initiates. A priestess of sorts. Keeper of the temple secrets.

Then came the second shock.

A sense of disorientation overtook me. I had been here before, but this was not the way I remember the Styka's retreat. The sunny yellow house on the hill had turned ramshackle grey. Gone was the view of the whooshing falls that blew in the wind like a horse's tail. Gone was the sweeping lawn that had sloped down the hill to the river. In its stead, spindly trees blocked off the view of the falls. Crowded together, they blocked out all light. Poison ivy twisted up their trunks and around their limbs.

I looked back at Wanda standing in the shadows, her face plastered like a Halloween mask. "Where's the waterfall?" There wasn't so much as a hint of its drone beyond the encroaching trees.

"Oh, Holly dear, I know..." she said in her mother's same Park Avenue accent. She giggled. "It's a jungle out here."

Except for the giggle, Wanda's voice was the same as her mother's. It was as if she had reincarnated herself into both Tade and Doris. "I used to mow this whole property myself," she said as she wandered up the driveway. Wearily, I traipsed after her. "Then the mower broke. Oh, well." She sighed. "It took us a while to get it fixed. By then, the saplings had sprouted. Oh, Holly!" Wanda turned around and faced me. Her smile radiant, her expression playful—the way I remembered her. "Have you ever tried to mow down trees?"

We broke into laughter, and for a brief moment, we were children again.

"I remember Pah..." I breathed the rest of Poppy's name into the wind. I was about to tell her how Poppy liked to let things grow wild and free. But stopped, realizing the mere mention of his name was taboo. Something I knew by the code of silence surrounding any mention of Poppy when Mother and I were with Doris.

Wanda's Ivy League education had not changed her at all.

To lighten the mood, I said, "Remember Fire Island? The time we thought we heard ghosts? How we pretended they had set fire to the waves and how scared we got?"

"Yes, I do," said Wanda as she picked a spade out of a wheelbarrow. I watched as she stepped into the freshly tilled soil of a tiny garden carved out of the hillside behind the house. The only sunny spot on the property. Was she trying to avoid having a meaningful conversation? I kept talking. "Remember the time we ate lunch in the Museum of Natural History cafeteria?"

Wanda's brows knit together as if trying to recall something memorable.

"You stood up on your chair and yelled, 'I have to go shushu!' I was so embarrassed."

"Oh, Holly. Yes! I do remember that!"

"And the times we ran around naked in your father's studio?"

Wanda feigned a bashful face. "Naughty, naughty. We mustn't talk about that."

And, for a few minutes, it was such fun reliving our childhood that I forgot about Poppy and my mission to get to the truth. Being with Wanda transported me into the past. A comfort zone where I could bask in the innocence of childhood. A time without responsibility. A time when all I had to do was believe what the adults in my life told me.

I was enjoying these moments of mirth too much to risk dredging up skeletons. I wanted to keep on laughing. I hadn't laughed like this in a long time. I kept on talking. "Remember the time Doris took off her clothes and went swimming in the nude down by the falls?"

"Yes, yes!" cried Wanda, loosening up. "I was

climbing down a big boulder and stubbed my toe." Her voice had changed from stuffy aristocrat to innocent child. She sounded carefree again. In my memory, I could see her, that sturdy little girl climbing naked down the rocks toward the falls while calling out to me to take off my clothes and go naked too. Remembering the sound of the falls and the splashing of water made me think of Poppy and me swimming in the Mettowee, and I couldn't help but blurt out the forbidden word. "Poppy always said..."

Now, I'd done it.

Communication stopped. Wanda became highly focused on digging up a stubborn weed. The only sound was the jabbing of her spade and the churning of dirt.

Not knowing what to say, I headed back toward the narrow trail that led into the forest. "The guesthouse was somewhere over there," I called back to Wanda.

"My father's studio," Wanda corrected me as she lay down her spade and came up behind me.

"Let's go see it," I said, forging into the thicket of weeds and clinging vines.

"No!" said Wanda. "You can't go there."

"Why not?"

"It's where we store his paintings."

"Great. I'd love to see his paintings. I'll be taking my children to see Poppy's murals in the Café des Artistes. I'd said the forbidden name. A name that had loomed so big and wonderful in my past was now a faux pas. It made no sense. Wanda was denying me my story. Damn it.

My identity.

"Holly dear..." This time it was Doris. She had come out of the house and was standing behind me. "It is a shrine to him now," she said, referring to Tade's studio. "Surely you understand."

I didn't, but I turned back, stopping at the open door of their garage, now crooked and sagging.

"Where's your Cadillac convertible?" I asked, peering into the shadows of the dilapidated shack. "I remember you taking Wanda and me for rides with the top down. Remember that, Wanda? How we used to scream Wheee! as we flew over the bumps?"

It was Doris who answered. "Amazing, dear, how much you remember."

"Do you still have it?" I asked, thinking it would be fun to take it for a spin.

"No, dear," said Doris. "Last winter, the motor froze. It had something to do with..."

"The manifold," said Wanda.

"Yes. Yes, the manifold. That's what it was. It just stopped running. I sold it to this sweet little boy for fifty dollars."

"Fifty dollars?!" To me, Doris's white Cadillac with the snow-white top and white leather upholstery was a symbol of her worriless past. Spotting a rusty old pickup parked in the bushes, I asked, "Does Wanda drive?" It was a question only someone my age who didn't drive would ask.

"No," said Doris. "I drive her everywhere she needs to go."

"I see." *Doris would never allow her "treasure" to get behind a wheel.*

"Holly dear," said Doris. "The children are up now. I know they must be hungry. Let's go have breakfast."

Wanda went in ahead to tend to the children, leaving me with Doris beside the crumbling garage. The wind shifted. Limbs creaked. A flash of sunlight cut through a gaping hole in the roof and lit up the back of the garage. I poked my head into the gloom. It smelled like a grave. Another flash of light illuminated something that looked familiar amid vigorous vines that had snaked through holes in the walls and up through the eaves, threatening to ravage the building.

"Squirrels," said Doris gazing up at the gaping hole in the ceiling. "They're so adorable. But very destructive."

I marveled to myself at how quickly the Styka's opulent world had crumbled into decay and ruin.

Another flash of light, and there it was. Mother's grey tin file box in a corner beneath a tangle of vines and a pile of debris.

I lunged for it, tearing away the tangle of vines. Grabbing hold of its metal handle, I dragged it from the grip of the vines, scraping it across the cement floor.

My life is in this box. The truth was finally within my grasp.

"Mother's file box," I shouted as I picked it up in my arms and lugged it outside, where I put it down on the driveway. I tried to open it, but it was locked.

"Oh, Lee Lee's box," said Doris with blasé indifference. "I forgot it was there. Poor, dear Lee Lee. She died so early. And she loved life so."

I picked up the box and hugged its rusty sharp edges as I remembered the photograph of Poppy and me—cheek to cheek—at Purdy's Apple Orchard. The way life used to be. Would I find all those memories in that box?

"You may have it, dear," said Doris as she strolled back to the house.

My children were already sitting at the dining room table when we came in, and Wanda was passing around a bowl of fruit. It was the same table Mother and Doris had once cavorted around naked in front of Tade.

"Where are the poodles?" I asked, forgetting all the years that had passed.

"We just have one cat now," said Wanda.

That's when I noticed the smell. The dank odor of mold from a black stain on the wall. *Another squirrel?* I looked at the painting over the mantel. Doris in bondage. *Deja vu. Apparently, Doris couldn't part with it.* The picture of the Ming Dynasty vase was there too—the one Doris claimed to have painted, yet it was in Tade Styka's style.

As a child, I always got the impression that Doris was in competition with Mother, who excelled in everything from sports to song and dance. To top things off, Mother became an artist—a respected member of the Grand Central Art Gallery in New York, an honor in itself. It takes years of dedication to rise to such heights of achievement. In contrast, Doris had never shown the slightest commitment to anything but pleasure.

"We've become health nuts," Wanda said, passing a carton of yogurt around the table. "We're trying to maintain our beauty." She batted her eyelashes demurely.

I put a dollop of yogurt on my children's plates. "We don't have yogurt in Mexico," I said, trying to explain the grossed-out looks on their faces. "It's good," I assured them as I bit into my apple.

Any real communication was doomed from the start. It wasn't long before we ran out of insignificant trivialities to alleviate our discomfort. I looked up at the painting on the wall—Doris in Bondage—and wondered what Doris would say if I used that as a topic of discussion over breakfast. Would Wanda call that naughty too? My children didn't seem the least bit interested in it—much less bothered by it.

"Oh, aren't they good," crooned Doris, referring to the children. "Look, Wanda, aren't they well-behaved? And so adorable. Amazing how time flies. And your husband, dear? Eric. Wasn't his name Eric?"

"Enrique," I said, wishing she hadn't brought him up.

"Enrique. That's right!" Doris clasped her hands together as if pleased to get it right. "How is he?"

"Fine," I said, not wanting to get into it.

"Beautiful day, isn't it?" said, Wanda.

Now that's a safe topic. I wonder how long we'll be able to keep this up?

Doris chimed in. "Wanda used to mow the lawn. Imagine that! What a task! She is such a hard worker."

"Holly, dear," said Wanda, "You are so lucky to be living in a warm climate. The winters here are very cold. I prefer a Mediterranean climate. I think that's why the ancient Greeks accomplished so much. They didn't have to waste time keeping warm. Mexico is like the Mediterranean. Isn't it?"

We haven't seen one another for twenty years. And this is all we can talk about?

"Holly, dear," said Doris, "Do you ever listen to Jerry Falwell?"

"No." I wondered if she was trying to make me think

she had espoused a religious life.

"Such a nice man," she mused.

A wall of secrets stood between us.

The small talk went on and on. About the weather, Wanda's garden, the squirrel that ate the hole in the roof that let the water in, the cat that keeps the population of mice down and discourages forays of squirrels in the house. All told in good humored-laughter. But Wanda's attitude had changed. Much cooler. More reserved. Sharing nothing personal. The way you might pass the time talking to a stranger in a bus terminal.

Doris was my last chance to get at the truth. *I didn't come here to fritter away the hours with small talk. If I leave here without finding out if Poppy was my father, I will never know who I am.* I looked at my watch. *I need to leave if I'm going to get to New York before dark.*

"Oh, Holly, dear. It must be beautiful in Mexico," Doris said.

"Uh-huh."

When we finished eating, the children asked to be excused. I gave them permission to go out to play, warning them to stay away from the poison ivy, and they romped off, leaving the three of us alone.

"It's bitter cold in winter," Wanda said as if this were the topic she'd been waiting to broach. "Last year, our water pipes froze. We had to..."

"Wanda," I interrupted. "Poppy was my father. You know that. Don't you?"

Dead silence.

Doris spoke first. "Holly dear! Your belief is so far from the truth that I do not even like to address it. But I see that I must set the record straight. It is one thing to love someone as a father and quite another to *claim* him as your father. Holly, you never knew your father."

"That's a lie!" I shouted, jumping up from the table, remembering Poppy's love for me. "Poppy was *too*, my father."

"Nonsense!" exclaimed Doris. "Lee Lee left your real father before you were born."

"That's not what she told me!" I shouted. "She said he was a correspondent in the war."

My head began to spin as if I'd had too much to drink. Adrenaline coursed through my veins. Cortisol shut down my brain. My heart started to race. I thought I'd pass out.

I couldn't think. I felt like I was going crazy.

Wanda tried to console me. "Holly, dear, I know you loved Poppy. And it's only natural that you would want him to be your father, but Holly! You are fantasizing."

"Fantasizing! Poppy was, *too*, my father. I know it. And so do you. If he wasn't, then where are the photographs of this man you say was my father?"

Doris clasped her hands to her breast as if in prayer. "Holly dear. Listen to me. Your mother never spoke of your father. Doing so brought back much unhappiness."

Wanda chimed in. "Holly, it was a mistake that Lee Lee didn't tell you about your father because now your imagination, your emotions and wishful thinking have filled the void."

"What would you know about it?" I shouted. "I was already four years old when you were born. I don't recall seeing you around until you were six."

"Holly. Holly. You're fantasizing," Wanda insisted, her voice firm as if trying to calm a raving maniac.

That's when I felt myself blow like a cork.

"You are the one who is fantasizing," I screamed. "You think Tade Styka was the greatest man on Earth.

How would you like it if I told you he wasn't your father? That your *real* father was someone else. How would you like that?"

"Oh, Holly," said Doris, moaning as if it pained her to see me in such a state of delusion. "You are terribly misled. You have deceived yourself into believing something that is untrue."

My head was spinning. My world was collapsing. They spoke with such conviction. *Could I be wrong?* I fought to regain my equilibrium. I honed in on Doris. "You and my mother were Poppy's models. You posed for the Café des Artistes murals. You know damn well that my mother was very young when she met Poppy. There were no other men in her life—not unless you want me to believe she was a floozy."

"Holly!" says Doris, shaking her head as if in shock. "This is becoming absurd. I never even met Christy."

"Never met him?" I shouted. "You and Wanda visited us at the Old Red Mill."

"Holly, he wasn't there when we came," Doris shouted.

I ignored her and turned to Wanda, "Remember,

Wanda? You came dancing in, bragging about the hair on your woozie. You were singing, 'I've got a hair on my woozie. I've got a hair on my...'"

Wanda's Grace Kelly cool burst into red-hot rage. "You're lying!" she shouted as she leaped out of her chair.

"Lying? You even wanted me to go with you to the john so you could show me. You thought you were so grown up. You wanted to know if I had one too."

"All right!" Doris said as she pushed her chair back from the table and stood up. She leaned on the table like a judge in a courtroom calling for order. "That's enough. This conversation has gone far enough. We're not going to talk about this anymore. You understand?"

I ignored her and turned back to Wanda.

"Wanda, how do you explain that Poppy and my mother spent the summers together in Vermont?"

"Holly!" Doris was livid. I'd never seen her so angry. "Lee Lee was Christy's Boswell. Nothing more."

"Oh really? I don't remember her taking shorthand at the Old Red Mill."

I turned back to Wanda. "How can you be an Egyptologist and not see the writing on the wall?"

"Holly, in those days, they didn't have sex," said Wanda with Ivy League conviction.

"What?" I was stunned.

Suddenly Wanda lost her erudite manner, leaped to her feet and shouted, "Holly, you were never born."

A Freudian slip?

"That's it, isn't it? You wish I'd never been born. I guess I always knew it. You never did accept me as part of your family." I was Mother's Error. Her Nothing.

Doris was wringing her hands. "Oh, Holly. Dear. Please... Let's just put all this away."

Just then, I heard the rumble of a car rolling down the gravel driveway and pulling up in front of the house.

"That must be Jim," said Doris breathing a sigh of relief. "I called him this morning and told him you were here. He said he wanted to see you."

Jim was my uncle through marriage to Mother's oldest sister, Audrey. He had been the Fire Chief of the City of Greenwich, Connecticut, for as long as I could remember. I hadn't seen him since I was thirteen. He had always been a master at deflecting questions, and I was always put off by his teasing Long Island twang. Over six feet tall, broad-shouldered with a don't-give-me-any-bullshit attitude. He had always intimidated me. Now I saw him as my savior. I rushed out to meet him. He was swinging his long legs out of the car. I bounded toward him as if running from a fire. He stood up and threw open his arms, and I crashed up against his rock-solid chest.

"How are you, Jim?" I whimpered.

"So far, so good. You staying out of mischief?" There was vigor in his voice. The way I remembered it. Chipper but brusque. I forced out a smile. "I'm trying."

"Well, that's quite a problem. How's everything otherwise?"

I could tell right away he still thought of me as a child. I didn't care. Just getting away from Wanda and Doris was a relief.

He threw an arm over my shoulder and pulled me along with him as we strode toward the house. "So, what are you doing for excitement? That's what bothers me now." His voice crackled with humor.

I stopped. Tears streaming down my face, I turned and looked him straight in the eye. "Jim. Do you know anything about Poppy?"

"How could I forget?" He said with a sarcastic laugh.

"Jim," I sobbed, "I've come all the way from Mexico City. Please... please tell me the truth! Was Poppy my father?"

"Of course he was."

I felt as if my knees were going to buckle. *Is this possible?* In a startling moment, my uncle Jim had given me the answer to the first big question in my life. I could hardly believe my ears.

"How do you know?"

"I know. I was in the middle of the whole thing. Your grandmother was behind the whole set-up."

I staggered backwards, feeling as if I was teetering on the brink of emotional collapse.

His sharp blue eyes turned dead serious.

"Now, don't you tell Doris. She'll crucify me."

CHAPTER TWENTY

Cardinal Sins

Behold, the man is become as one of us, to know good and evil!

- Genesis

Uncle Jim shifted into reverse, and the car lurched backward, kicking up gravel as he backed up the hill. I was in the front seat; my children were in the back. On my lap was Mother's rusting, grey metal file box. Inside, I had not yet had the time to look inside, but I felt sure I'd find the many photographs Mother had taken of our lives before Poppy died. Without pictures, memory fades. I remember thinking; *The real me is in this box.* As for Doris and Wanda, my uncle's presence had lightened the mood with idle jesting.

I was leaving with what I had come for: the truth. But Mother's secret lived on. This time inside me. I wanted to call Doris and Wanda liars, but Jim had sealed my lips.

They were standing in the driveway as we crunched gravel backing up the hill. I waved to them, knowing I would probably never see them again. Our goodbye waves were mere empty customs. The real stuff of love and empathy had perished. Casualties of the tormenting fear of sin.

My heart heaved; I was leaving a part of myself behind. My family. The one I grew up with. The only one I'd ever known. I would miss my childhood playmate. But I had committed the unpardonable sin: attacked their devotion to a lie. In so doing, They would banish me from their lives.

An afternoon storm was brewing. The sky grew dark. Droplets of rain splattered on the windshield. Doris had already taken cover inside. Only Wanda remained, her arms wrapped around her to ward off the mustering wind. Beneath the darkening sky, her face looked white as a ghost.

"So where are you going when you get to New York?"

asked Jim as he pulled onto the open road.

"The Hotel des Artistes."

He shot me a discerning scowl. "Never could stay out of trouble, could you?"

"I'll take you to the Hartford station," he said, picking up speed. I turned to look at my children sitting quietly in the back seat. I had hoped for a happy family reunion. The stuff of fairy tales. I now knew better. I'd gained the truth but lost my family's love.

"So, what are you doing for excitement these days?" asked Jim with a wily grin.

"Oh, nothing," I said, not wanting to admit I was waiting for the End of the world when Jesus Christ would take His revenge.

Jim shook his head and said, "Doris and Wanda. They're a peculiar couple."

His frankness took me by surprise. "They are, aren't they?" I wasn't used to thinking out loud, but it felt liberating.

Jim, now a widower, lived alone in his farm house on a hill in Armonk, New York. I hadn't seen him since I was about ten. He'd always had a mouth like a steel vault, so

I was surprised when he opened up and spilled the truth about Poppy. I figured it was a spur-of-the-moment thing. That I'd lucked out. But—as we cruised down the road— he opened up again and again, telling family secrets as he'd never done before.

"They are strange!" he reiterated in his tough guy Long Island twang. "You know—like mother, like daughter. They're a pair of old maids. If a man got close to them, it would scare them to death. That white-faced Polack. Never uses rouge or anything. Just powder. Why she puts that powder on her face, I'll never know."

"Maybe it's because her father powdered his face."

"Well, he's another lunatic. Artists were a wild bunch. Had orgies and things. I know how they were; I was a fireman. A lot of rich folks in Greenwich."

How does he know about orgies?

"What do you mean— 'because you were a fireman?'"

"Fires start when you don't expect it. Firemen get there fast. No time to cover up. They see it all. Catch 'em with their pants down.'"

We both fell silent after that. I'd never thought about Poppy and Mother as a "wild bunch."

"Wanda was a screamer," said Jim, breaking into my thoughts.

"What do you mean?"

"You asking me? You oughta know. You both used to stay with Audrey and me on the farm while your mothers were off doing their thing. Foxy, that Wanda. A slick Polack Princess. Put ideas in your head, and you'd carry them out and get in trouble."

"Wait a minute," I said, remembering the time I coaxed Wanda to get out of bed, knowing she'd get spanked by Papa at my grandparents' house. "I got her in trouble too."

"Yeah, I know about that," he said. "You were another prissy little princess. Used your feet as if they were hands. Could grab on to things with your toes. You were a handful. Had to have four eyes and six legs to keep up with you."

Jim was bringing up details I'd forgotten. It was true. I was almost as agile with my toes as I was with my fingers, probably because I ran around barefoot all summer.

"Such a lady, that Wanda," he said. "Never did a

damn thing. She'd sit back like a Polack Princess and watch you get in trouble. You were always the goat."

"You mean scapegoat?"

"Oh—! I'll say. Doris and Audrey blamed you. Said you taught Wanda swear words." Jim shook his head. "Great old days."

I kept quiet on that one.

"Your mother was working with Tade for one year in the Sistine Chapel."

"What?" I was shocked. I'd never heard anything about the Sistine Chapel. But Jim was on a roll and kept right on going. "On the run all the time, your mother. Someone else had to be looking out for you. I'd be left with the brat. I'd turn my back, and you'd be into something. I was always chasing you around."

"What did you just say about the Sistine Chapel?"

Jim rambled on in his brusque but chipper way. He said something else about that "Proud Polack," but all I could think of was the Sistine Chapel. What on earth was Mother doing at the Sistine Chapel? I didn't know she'd ever been to Europe. Let alone worked on the Sistine Chapel. In those days, travel wasn't easy. They called it going abroad, and it took a week to get there by ship and another week to get back. Expensive too.

"What did you say— "

"Remember the old Manor House? You were always begging me to take you to see it."

"You mean the haunted house?" It always reminded me of Dracula's castle in the mist.

"Rosenstiel's manor. He threw parties there for the rich and famous. Five or six hundred people at a party. I worked for the Jew. I knew all the theatrical people in New York. I dealt with all of them. I took care of everything from soup to nuts. Even security. There were people there wearing million-dollar diamonds."

During and after the war, Jim had worked two jobs to support his wife and five boys. Caretaker of the Rosenstiel estate was his second job. There was a pig farm on the property. What a racket those pigs made when we entered their pen. All that grunting and squealing. I was scared when they bumped up against me. Their wide backs came up to my waist as we slogged through the muck—Jim in his big fire boots and me in my snow boots—huge pigs rubbed up against me with their hard pink skin and bristly white hair. The Manor House was far off by itself. A solitary stone mansion with a naked grey forest behind it. I only saw it in the bleakness of winter because every summer, I went away with Poppy and Mother to the Old Red Mill in Vermont.

"The Old Manor House. It was haunted as hell," said Jim.

"It was?" *Is he teasing me?* He and his boys—all five of them—loved to scare me when I was little.

"It was haunted, I tell you. It was empty when I saw it. I know. I was the last one to see it. Took care of the farm. The chandelier used to swing. You could hear the footsteps of some guy dragging chains around. And a woman up on the third floor singing. What a beautiful voice she had."

"Really?" I said. *What if it's true? If there are ghosts, maybe there are angels and demons too. Maybe the Bible is true?*

"Yeah. Really. Really! I'm not kiddin' ya."

"Gosh!" I felt like a little girl again. I didn't know what to think.

"Well, how could anybody live there with all that going on?" he said. "They didn't stay long."

"Who didn't stay long?"

"Seventy-six women in there, and they had a cook. I didn't know how long they were going to stay. Had a colored cook."

"You mean servants?" I asked, picturing my servant, Florencia, in her coral-striped dress and starched white apron.

"Yeah."

"And they all moved out?"

"They all woke up one morning at 2 o'clock. The dog was barking at something on the spiral staircase. Then they come to find out—Calbert was a great guy for women."

"Who's Calbert?"

Jim didn't answer. Just kept right on talking. "Reminded me of Poppy. Come to find out, one of the girls was stabbed to death. Years later, if anybody slept in that room, they'd wake up, and there she'd be, sitting on the edge of the bed, combing her hair.

Jim's ghost story worried me. Surely a fire chief wouldn't lie, would he?

"The help got spooked. I gave them their paychecks,

and they got the hell outta there. After that, Rosenstiel only used the mansion for parties."

Jim glanced at me to see if I was listening. "Only for parties," he repeated as he went back to his story.

I looked back at my children. They were all ears.

"It was empty the rest of the time," said Jim returning to his Manor House tale of horror. "Then somebody tried to burn it down. Vandals. Hippies tried to live there. Then I moved in and took over. I was the guard. Worked for Rosenstiel as a spy. He was worried about the Nazis during the war. They used to row into town from their submarines and mix with the people. You didn't even know they were there. Rosenstiel, he had a bunch of offices in the Empire State Building. I worked for him for forty-two years. Had to watch over his daughters, too."

Jim pulled into a gas station and hopped out. "I'll be just a minute."

While Jim was gone, I told my children that Jim had told me the truth that Poppy was my father, but they were more interested in the ghosts at Rosenstiel's manor.

Jim came back, and we hit the road.

"What happened in the Sistine Chapel?" I asked.

"An earthquake or something. There was a crack in Michelangelo's *Creation*."

"No, I mean about Tade and my mother. Why did they go there together?"

"Tade and the Pope, they were in cahoots. So, the first guy the Pope thought about coming and fixing it was Tade. But Tade was getting old. He was too scared to climb up there on that scaffold, so he took your mother along. She was a tomboy. Scared a' nothin'."

"Oh my god!" I could just see Mother stretched out on a scaffold beneath God's belly on the celestial ceiling.

"You mean—my mother went off to Rome with Tade Styka? For a whole year? Are you telling me..." I found it hard to complete my sentence. "You mean they had an affair?"

"I don't know. I don't think so." Jim seemed to be battling the same quandary. "No. I don't think so!"

That's when I remembered the painting of the Ming vase with Doris's name on it. Had Doris demanded that Tade put her name on it to show Mother up? To prove she was a better artist than "Lee Lee"? Was that Doris's way of getting even with Mother for going to Rome with her husband? What could be loftier than rising to touch the face of God?

"There was always rivalry between Doris and my mother. Wasn't there? "

"Oh yeah," said Jim. "It was always going on. I didn't want any part of it."

"What was my mother like?" I asked, thinking maybe I never really knew her. What I really wanted to know was what was going on between her and Tade in Rome.

"Well, both your mother and Doris had a lot of respect for me because I demanded it. I call a spade a spade. And when they needed a chewing out, I chewed the hell outta them. And when either one of them got in trouble... who'd they come to?"

"You," I said, remembering how much Jim was a part of my life too.

"You bet they did," Jim said.

"What kind of trouble are you talking about? They always seemed happy to me. I mean, I never saw them angry or upset or anything."

"They had problems," Jim said.

"They did?" I was still struggling with the notion that

Mother's life might have been different than the one I saw through the eyes of a child.

"They did!" said Jim in his terse way.

I was curious. "What kind of problems?"

"Well, in later years, they... they always swore they... they felt bad for what they did. Running around naked like they did. After they got older, they felt bad about it."

I'm surprised that Jim knows about their orgiastic frolics with Tade. "They shouldn't have felt bad about it," I said, coming to their defense.

"In those days, you better feel bad about it! Or you get put down, and you're no longer considered in the richer echelon."

"Didn't you just tell me about those wild parties in Greenwich and all the stuff you found out when the rich people's houses caught fire?

"But in the old days, they didn't. The only ones who had wild parties were the artists and the hustlers. Now, they all do."

"I see," I said, wondering if Wanda and Doris were still living in "the old days."

"How old was I when my mother worked on the Sistine

Chapel?" I was trying to remember being abandoned for a whole year.

"Damned if I know. You were old enough to know better, I know that."

I was still reeling from the news that Mother fixed the crack in Creation. "And I suppose Tade got all the credit," I said.

"Of course. You don't think the Pope would acknowledge a...?"

"And where was I while Mother was in Rome?"

"With Audrey and me on the farm."

"For a year?" I asked.

"Actually, I think it was more like three months?"

"Three months?" Even that seemed like a long time. I remembered the little room I slept in, eating dinner with Aunt Audrey, Jim, and their boys. I remembered there was no other house in sight. Nothing but snow. I watched Dracula movies at night with the boys—something my mother would have never allowed. "I'm surprised that Mother would leave me for so long."

Jim gave a sarcastic laugh. "Listen, Doris and Tade left Wanda longer than that."

"Where'd they go?"

"Off to their villa in Capri. When they came back, Tade couldn't even be bothered to get out of the car to greet his own daughter. He just sat there and waited till Wanda came out to the car with her mother."

"What did you say?"

"I said, Tade couldn't be bothered to come in to get Wanda."

"Before, you said Tade was gone a year. Could that have been how long he was gone without Wanda?" All this time, I had assumed—judging by the way Wanda worshiped her father—that their relationship was like mine with Poppy. But Poppy never would have ignored me.

"Did you know Poppy?" I asked.

"Didn't like him much. Never cared for him. In the first place, he was a braggart. A womanizer. After all the young girls."

"He was?" I resisted seeing Poppy as flawed. It was okay to find fault with Tade, but *Don't you dare say bad things about Poppy.*

"Sure he was," said Jim, oblivious to my feelings.

"Howard Chandler Christy. He walked around like he thought he was some damned king. Howard Chandler Christy. The great ar-teest! Cocky old son-of-a-bitch. Wanted to be in the front all the time."

Son-of-a-bitch? Jim had just taken the name of Christy in vain. I could hardly bear to hear any more. Still, I couldn't stop myself from asking, "Front of what?"

"Front of all the excitement! You knew that, didn't you? When he was in a room, he'd sit down in that chair of his that looked like a throne. And there he'd sit like Mussolini. In the middle of the room. He took over."

"I remember that chair," I said numbly. "It was red velvet. Something like the Pope would sit in."

"Allah to him, you know. He was an old sex nut. That's all he was. He thought of himself as Christ, and you were supposed to be the Pope. He was God, and you were his little princess. He loved having you run around him. He was proud as hell. You were his spoiled little brat."

"Are you kidding?" I said.

"Oh, Christ. Listen to you. Your mother was supposed to be the Virgin Mary. And you come along. The wrong gender. So that knocked that out. If you had come along the other gender, he'd a been happy, you know, you'd be the new Messiah. He was a nut!'" He laughed

I felt myself caught between parallel universes. Child on one side. Adult, on the other, afraid of falling into the void. Jim was attacking my view of reality. I fought to reject his verbal assaults. *He's jealous,* I told myself. *That's why he's talking like this.* Anything to defend Poppy and keep on believing. I couldn't wait to get out of the car.

"Do you think he had other children? I mean, besides me and Natalie?" I asked, feeling like a glutton for punishment. But I had to know.

"You're damn tootin'!"

"Did he raise those kids too?"

"He had to've. Or how'd he get out of it? He didn't go to jail."

"What do you mean?" My head was whirling.

"Lots of paternity suits out of Ohio."

This was something else I'd never heard. What a shock. To think I had half-brothers and half-sisters out there. I'd always thought of Doris and Wanda as my only blood relatives.

"Did his wife, Nancy, have any children?"

"No. She was an alcoholic. He was living high on the hog. He took care of her as his cover. Nobody could touch him. He was a married man. His first wife wanted to divorce him. She wanted to commit suicide too."

"She did?"

"Yeah. Because of a cult religion."

"Was it Christian Science?"

"Well, I don't know that. Anything that would give him an excuse for an out, he'd take. Let's put it that way."

"He had a lot of women in Ohio. A place called the Barracks. Sure bamboozled your mother. But I don't blame your mother. I blame your grandmother. I don't blame your mother for anything. Or Doris, either."

I wanted to say, "What did Nanna have to do with it?" but everything was coming at me so fast. "What did Doris do wrong?" I said, wondering if Wanda was illegitimate too or maybe conceived out of wedlock.

"She married Tade. I mean for going into that type of life. It would've been better if they had gotten themselves a decent man and had a saner life. Wanda certainly didn't turn out very sane. No, she's an aristocrat. Doris and Wanda both. As far as the Styka family is concerned.

Babushka, the whole bunch of 'em. And what a pain in the ass they were. They thought they was the greatest Polack muckety mucks in the world."

"Muckety mucks! You mean the Stykas?"

"Adam Styka and his wife Vanja. They were highfalutin."

"Are Adam and Vanja still living?"

"I don't know. Lost track of 'em. But Tade, he was the most humble guy I ever met."

"I thought you just said..."

"I mean when you got to know him. He wanted somebody that he could talk to and confide in about the Catholic Church."

"What happened with the Catholic Church?"

"The Vatican took his villa in Capri."

"What?" I asked, remembering the photographs of Bacchanalian splendor stashed in my backpack.

"They got everything," said Jim referring to the Catholic Church. "I saw pictures of his estate on the island. Five or six million dollars it was worth back then."

"I saw them too," I said, looking to make sure my backpack was still in the back seat with my children.

"The Vatican took it." There was anger in Jim's voice.

"How could the Catholic Church take Tade's property away from him?"

"Tade was traveling all the time. He went to South America and South Africa. He went all over painting, you know. And ah... these Vatican priests, they said, if he wasn't going to use the villa in the summer, they would like to use it. I think for vacation or something. Anyway, they had some use for it. He was away, and when he came back, he didn't know that the Church had it. Beautiful place. Cardinal so-and-so came along. He wanted it. So Cardinal so-and-so showed up with only ten percent of what it was worth. And that's what they paid for it."

"Wait a minute. How could Cardinal whatever-his-name-was force Tade to sell his property to the Church?"

"Ever try to evict a Cardinal from your house? He was already living there. Then, when Tade died, it cost seventy-five thousand dollars to bury him."

"Is he buried at Forest Lawn?"

"I don't know. He was in a vault for over a year. There was a big fight over where he would be buried. The Church wanted him buried in one place—maybe Rome and the family wanted him buried in Forest Lawn."

"How can the Church get away with something like that?"

"The Church gets away with it. Cardinal Spellman comes to mind. I knew him personally. Yeah. Met him at Tade's place. With the white carpets and all those paintings."

"So Doris and Wanda were left with nothing after Tade died? All because Cardinal Spellman took their villa in Capri?"

Jim shook his head. "Doris should have moved out of that place next to the Plaza long ago, but she hung on to it. Then some European Count asked her to marry him."

"I remember something about a Count. She laughed about it. Said he bounced her around on his tummy when they danced."

"Yeah, well, Wanda put the kibosh on that. She's the boss, you know. Someone offered them a lot of money for that estate in Ashley Falls. Wanda said, 'No.' And you see what a shambles it's in now."

I was surprised to hear Wanda was "the boss." Guess I should have known. *Could it have been Wanda who*

prevented Doris from telling me the truth? I always thought it
was the other way around.

Jim was feeding me information so fast I could hardly digest it. "Your mother was an award-winning actress on Broadway. A student at the best school in New York. Alviene School of Drama. Why she threw her life away on the old goat, I'll never know. She was a fine arts painter. Then she became a commercial artist. A wallpaper and drapery designer on Fifth Avenue. She was very successful. Why she talked about Poppy as if he was God, I'll never know. But he gave her that impression. And that's the way she wrote his biography. As if he was some damned god."

So that's why Doris called Mother Poppy's Boswell. She
was writing his biography. "She and Christy went on trips," said Jim. "Left you alone at school. All you was worrying about was why you couldn't go with your mother when your mother took trips. It used to burn you up."

"Well, I didn't like being left in boarding school."

"Your mother put you in that school to get you the hell out of the way," Jim's words cut through my heart.

"You think so?"

"Yeah. They wanted to get rid of you."

"Well, maybe so," I said, feeling exhausted. Jim had turned my whole memory of childhood upside down. Then I thought again. "No!" I said, remembering how it was I ended up in boarding school. "It was over modern art. A teacher at my school in New York embarrassed me in class by..."

"They wanted to get rid of you," Jim insisted. "Sent you off to school alone on that train. Couldn't get away with that these days."

"Yes," I said, remembering how scared I was my first day on the Boston Express. "Can you imagine? My mother left me alone on that train. I was only seven."

"They sent you there to get rid of you, kid." Jim laughed derisively. "Out of sight, out of mind."

"You had to come and rescue me. Remember that?"

"You bet. You were into mischief all the time. One day, the school called me at the fire station. You'd been gone three hours. I caught up with you on the way to the Stamford railroad station. You were going somewhere."

I was shocked by this disclosure. "How'd you find me? I mean, how did you know where I was going?"

"I figured you always wanted to go, go, go. So, I knew the first place you'd head for was the railroad station."

"I figured if I got to the railroad station before you got there, I'd have you. You wanted to get the hell outta there, come hell or high water. And that's how come I was standing there waiting for you to walk up. And you walked up with a sailor."

"Sailor?!" I said, straining to remember. "How old was he?"

"Much older than you."

"Scary," I said, still drawing a blank.

"You met him in the drug store."

Drugstore! Sudden recall. It was as if Jim had pushed a button in my memory bank. I knew immediately where I'd met that sailor and how it all happened. It was in the drugstore down a lonely road from the Adelaide Hall dorm. I remembered standing at the counter paying for my *True Confessions* magazine and pack of gum when a man in a white sailor suit and cap standing behind me said, "You must be one of those snobs on the hill."

"They're snobs, all right," I said. Then I launched into a sob story about how awful it was in boarding school, how lonely I felt and how much I missed Poppy, "Who was a world-famous artist." I told him the girls I'd come to the drugstore with had gone off by themselves and left me behind. He told me if I came with him, he'd be my friend. "We'll walk to the station and take the train to New Haven." New Haven. It sounded heavenly. A brand new chance at happiness.

At this point, I was thinking, Oh, my god! *What if…*" when Jim broke into my thoughts. "And you were crying on his shoulder."

"Crying?"

"Yeah… about how you was neglected, and your mother put you in this school, and your mother was off someplace else."

"You heard that? You mean, I told you all that?"

"It's the truth. I know that. That's what made me mad. Why the hell didn't she take care of you?"

"My God!" I exclaimed. "You mean I was going to get on the train with that sailor?"

I felt as if I was talking about someone else's child. Not me. No. It couldn't have been me? But it was. And I knew it.

"You really rescued me that time, didn't you? Who knows what could have happened? If it had been today, I'd a been gone with the wind."

"Yeah. Well, if it was today, who'd go looking for you? Who today would put themselves out to go running all over the country looking for you?"

"You say I was gone three hours?" I was drawing another blank. "Did he have a car?" I asked, horrified at my own gullibility while wondering if something might have happened that I'd blotted out of memory.

"You were both walking. I stood there and waited for you to walk up to me. I grabbed you so damned quick and beat your ass for running away. And that guy stood there dumbfounded. He didn't know who the hell..."

"How old was I?"

"Christ, you were young. I'd say twelve or fourteen... something like that."

That's when I realized it was after Poppy's death. I had lost all will to live, and "New Haven" had a promising ring to it. "And what was he going to do—" I asked still, dumbfounded, "Take me with him on the train? Take me to New Haven?"

"I didn't ask him," quipped Jim. "I just grabbed you by the arm, and your feet never touched the ground. Your mother and Audrey were in Boston. That's why the school called me. I don't know what the hell they were doing there."

"Probably, they were visiting the Christian Science Church."

Jim had offered me the Forbidden Fruit, and I'd taken it. I'd bitten right into it. The Eden of Poppy's creation lay smashed like a rotten apple on the floor of Jim's car. *Is there nothing in life I can cling to?*

We arrived at the Hartford railroad station just in time to catch the New York Express.

"All aboard for New York City," cried the conductor from the station platform as I helped my children scramble up the steps. Jim gave me a one-armed hug, then handed me Mother's grey metal file box.

For a split moment, I was a child again, boarding the New York Express on my way home from boarding school. The hissing of the train. The smell of steam. The cry of the conductor. All was the same, yet changed. Knowing Mother's secret had already begun to change me too into someone I hardly recognized.

The train lurched. I waved one last time at Uncle Jim as he watched from the platform. He gave me a wry smile. "You stay out of mischief," he shouted over the chug-a-lug of the train. There was relentless churn of steel on rails as the train of life rolled away, picking up speed.

CHAPTER TWENTY-ONE

Gargoyles at the Gate

And he placed at the east of the Garden of Eden. . . a flaming sword which turned every way, to keep the way of the tree of life."

- Genesis

The yellow cab pulls up to the gothic edifice that looks like a castle. I step out of a yellow cab and into the past. White letters on a burgundy awning read: *One West Sixty-Seventh Street*. My children and I enter the sedate lobby, and everything is just as I remember it. The painting of a disembarking ship still hangs above the elevator gate behind which Poppy told me goodbye. Through its gate, he'd walked out of my life on Nancy's arm. I feel as if I'm entering a dream state, one from which I never will escape. It was here in this place, twenty-three years ago, that life——as I'd known it—came to an end. Yet something remains unfinished, something yet unsaid.

I feel Poppy's presence. As if he is waiting for me. I yearn to step inside the elevator and push the button for the seventh floor. Ricky jumps in ahead of me. "Wait," I say, "We need to ask permission."

I go to the receptionist's window. Nobody's there. The doorman hauls himself out of the chair and saunters over. "Are you looking for someone?"

"I'm here to see Mrs. Christy."

"May I tell her who's calling?" he asks as he ambles into the reception room.

"Holly..." I hesitate. I can't say, Ruiz. Nancy won't know who I am. "Holly Morris." A name from my distant past. A name Mother made up. A name I could never accept. A name I now know was never mine to begin with. "Elise Ford's daughter," I tell him—not that Nancy will welcome the illegitimate daughter of her husband's mistress—but I can try.

The doorman strolls out of the reception room and

heads back toward his post at the door. Without looking back, he says the words I should have expected. "Mrs. Christy does not wish to see you."

"She probably doesn't know who I am." I trot after him, my breath in short gasps. "I'm Howard Chandler Christy's daughter!"

I've just said the words I've longed to say all my life. To my ears, they sound like a thunderbolt. A long-desired proclamation. Yet they bring no consolation. Nor do they quell the mounting turmoil I feel inside.

My words echo off the marble in the empty lobby as the doorman plops into his chair. "Ma'am—" His response is drawn out in a disdainful yawn. "She knows who you are."

More than ever, I feel shut out of Poppy's des Artistes life. I remembered overhearing him tell Mother about all the friends he hobnobbed within its café. All world-famous people with exciting creative lives. How I would have loved to have known them. As yet, I do not know that Nancy is married to what those friends of Poppy's called the "Gentleman Jockey" she used to see while Poppy was off in Vermont with Mother and me. Nor do I know that she and Mr. Coneen are probably both upstairs drowning in booze in a room filled with pale ghostly spaces where paintings and tapestries once hung. Where beauty had once dwelled, cockroaches now skitter, leaving trails of filth.

I dash across the lobby into the dimly lit foyer of the Café des Artistes. It's silence wraps around me like a tomb. I grab hold of its doorknob. It's locked. Frantic, I bang on the door as if finding myself locked out of Eden. The truth has not set me free. It has unhinged me. I feel myself suspended between two worlds, fast drifting apart like clouds in the sky. The world of Christ and Christy. It is becoming clear that I love Poppy more. His world is what I yearn to return to. Not some New Jerusalem with streets of gold and jewel-studded walls coming down from the sky. If only I could see his smile, that twinkle in his eyes.

I can't shake the feeling that Poppy is still here where I left him. His spirit of playfulness and joy. Furor mounts inside as I yearn to see his brush strokes once more.

I call to the doorman lounging in his chair. "Why is the Café closed?"

"Closed for the summer, ma'am."

Frustration and confusion spiral out of control. I turn my face toward the wall and sob. My children watch in stunned silence. When I look up, I find myself looking at a photograph of Poppy on the wall. He is smiling at me. A shudder runs through me. I gasp as if I'd seen a ghost. It's so like him. That "What-me-worry?" expression, an attitude for which Norman Vincent Peale praised him in his best-selling book, *Power of Positive Thinking*.

First the shock of seeing him. I haven't seen so much as a picture of him since I was twelve. Then staggering joy. Then, rage. "Damn you, Poppy!" I tell him. "Why couldn't you have told me the truth? Instead, you left me with nothing. Not even your name."

I whirl toward my children. Ricky is wearing a worried frown. Christina looks as if she's about to cry. They have never seen me so out of control. So much for introducing my children to a better life.

Furious, I snap my head toward Poppy. "You took me with you when you died." I slam my fist against the wall beside his grinning face. "Well, I'll show you."

Poppy smiles back.

I rest my forehead against his picture and sob. I am so distraught I don't hear the Café door open.

"May I help you?" says a woman with a French accent.

The presence of a stranger shocks me back to reality. I spin around, eyes burning, face flushed. I recognize her as Marie Turner, the woman Poppy introduced me to at our last supper. Unlike that night when I felt so proud to be standing by Poppy's side, I am ashamed.

I was only twelve when she met me. *She won't remember. Just as well. I'm too upset to speak.*

"I... I just wanted to see the murals," I say as I wipe the tears from my face.

Marie eyes me carefully. "But of course," she says. "Come in. I show them to you."

We follow her inside.

The murals are more beautiful than I remembered them.

Amidst plumes and foliage, Mother's laughing face beams out at me. Doris, too, dancing around the oak. Why hadn't I seen Doris in that picture before? They look so in love with life. But was it for real? Or was it just an act? Uncle Jim's words come back. "They had problems."

"The murals were painted by Howard Chandler Christy," Marie tells me. There's hesitancy in her voice as she studies me.

The sound of Poppy's name plays in my head like a Hallelujah chorus. How absurd that I should be moved to religious fervor by pictures of Mother romping naked in the woods.

I can't help myself. The scene brings on another gush of tears.

"But, of course," says Marie. "That face. I know that face." She glances at the murals and then back at me. "It is the same face. I knew it the moment I saw you. But it has been many years since I see you. You are Elise Ford's daughter. No?"

I nod a weary yes. Marie throws her arms around me and kisses me on both cheeks. "I'm Marie Turner. You probably don't remember..."

"Yes, I met you the night Poppy brought..." my words strangle on a lump in my throat.

"You were only a little girl." Marie turns to Ricky and Christina. "Like them. And these are your children?"

I nod. Ricky offers her his hand, "I'm Ricky Ruiz, and this is my little sister, Christina."

Marie is delighted. She invites us in and pulls a table away from the wall. It is the same table where Poppy and

I sat out last night together. "Sit down. Sit down," Marie coaxes.

My children and I slide in on the red leather seat where Poppy and I last sat. I look up again at the painting of Mother, her eyes wide with fright. I think of the words in Genesis. "I was afraid because I was naked...."

"How is your lovely mother?" Marie asks as we sit down at the table.

I shake my head in remorse.

Marie's voice lowers to a reverent whisper. "No-o-o. She was so young."

"It was cancer."

Marie shakes her head and moans. "I'm so sorry." She lowers her eyes in sad resignation. "So beautiful. And such a talented artist."

"You knew she was an artist?"

"But of course. Everyone knew. She had that exhibit on Park Avenue. All her paintings sold out on the very first day. And I did so want one of her lovely Vermont scenes." Marie clasps her hands together in disappointment. "They were every bit as good as Christy's."

She lays a reassuring hand on my arm. "My dear, how long has it been? I mean, since her passing?"

"1963. She was 51. I got the call right after Christina was born."

"O-o-oh," moans Marie shaking her head again. "What a tragedy."

We fall silent.

A young woman bursts in and hastens toward the kitchen. Marie calls out to her, "Julie, look. This is the daughter of the model you see in the murals."

"I don't happen to like those paintings," says the girl without stopping.

I take her comment to mean she sees Poppy as having exploited women for his own purpose rather than freeing them from Puritan "shamefacedness."

Marie ignores the comment and asks me where I live. I tell her Mexico City. When she asks what I'm doing in Mexico, I tell her my husband is a manager of an American-based business."

"What kind of business?"

"The circulation of a worldwide publication."

"Oh," she says, interest peaking. "Which one?"

I imagine she's expecting me to say something like Time or National Geographic. Embarrassed, I say, "The Plain Truth."

I'm relieved when Marie merely questions me with her eyes, then drops the subject. It would seem so out of place to have to confess my connection to a worldwide magazine predicting the end of the world while surrounded by such beauty and playful innocence. A world of Poppy's creation. A world free of Original Sin, for which the God in the Bible says women must pay through obedience and submission to their husbands.

My religious convictions are brought into question. Is this why Poppy warned me, "Never let anyone make you ashamed you're a woman?

I scan the murals—none portraying women in a salacious way. Gazing at the oak around which women are dancing, I tell Marie about our Old Red Mill and how Poppy saved our oak from destruction when the Highway Department wanted to turn the dirt road into a highway. "He told them, 'Why that tree was here before Ethan Allen!' Who the hell do you think you are to take it down?' He was so adamant they not only left it alone, they had to build a marble wall around it to protect it."

Marie smiles as she nods in recognition of the man she knew. "He was a creator, not a destroyer."

The memory of those happy days is too much. I feel myself losing my grip as I struggle to keep from crying.

Marie lays a consoling hand on my arm. "We all miss Poppy," she says with heartfelt sadness.

"I came all this way to see his studio," I whimper, "But Nancy..." Sobs heave up from deep inside.

"I know, dear," says Marie with a gracious smile. "Nancy is quite the recluse these days. It's her drinking. Hardly anyone sees her anymore."

I try to speak the words I've wanted to say all my life but can hardly get them out. "Poppy... he... was my father."

"I know, dear. I think we all knew. We just never spoke of it.

For Mrs. Christy's sake."

CHAPTER TWENTY-TWO

The Grey Tin Box

When people are free to do as they please, they usually imitate each other.

- Eric Hoffer

What was in Mother's grey tin box that her sister Doris considered so worthless that she left it to rust beneath a tangle of vines in her moldering garage?

As soon as I got back to our villa, a thousand feet above Mexico City, I would find out.

* * *

With a worrisome rasp, the 8mm film starts spinning on the rickety projector. I watch with eager anticipation.

A blinding white light flashes across the screen. Then streaks of grey, followed by jerky scenes of Mother and me in swim suits. I'm clinging onto her as she shoves off in an inner tube into the swirling, clear waters of the Mettowee. Poppy is on the bank. In the background, I see the Old Red Mill. There's our American flag suspended between the mill and White Dear Mountain, flapping in the summer breeze. The images move too fast for my liking. Flash to Mother and Poppy being interviewed on Broadway. His huge *I Am An American* poster is about to be launched over Times Square. New York police hold off a gathering crowd. I see women in military uniforms. The camera jerks upwards. A glimpse of a man on a ladder. "I AM" bigger than life is partially obscured by his body. Before I can tell what, he's doing up there, the screen turns white. Brown edges curl inward. I smell something burning.

I scream.

Somehow my husband managed to fix the film, but most of the scene where Poppy's *I Am An American* poster is being hoisted above Times Square has melted.

Only the enormous "I AM" letters are left.

The show begins again.

White letters on grey: *Holly at 3-1/2 months. March 25, 1940, Washington, D.C.* A close-up of Poppy smiling down at me with fatherly love. The camera pans downward to the baby he's cradling in his arms. Doris comes onto the scene wearing a big floppy hat.

"Doris told me she'd never met Poppy," I shriek. "What a liar! Good thing she didn't know she was in these movies, or she would never have let me have Mother's file box."

And there they are again. All three of them—Mother, Doris, and Poppy—fussing over me. The caption reads: *June 28, 1940. Visit from Doris. Washington Grist Mill.*

There I am again at seven months, naked as the day I was born. The caption reads: *Holly's first swimming lesson, Shady Side, Maryland.* I am paddling and kicking with such serious intensity you'd think I was training for the Olympics. Poppy is up to his waist in water as he holds my extended body in the water. He looks up and grins proudly as if to say, "Look at her go." My swimming lesson over, Poppy carries me to the shore and hands me to Hazel, my black nanny.

Seeing Hazel after so many years reminds me of the day Mother took me to visit her in Washington, D.C. I must have been about four. We met in the seclusion of a doorway. I remember Hazel fussing over me. Then we all got on a city bus to go somewhere. Hazel went to the back and sat down while we stayed in front. I never forgot that experience. Hazel had to sit in the back of the bus with the black folks while we got to sit in the front with the white folks. It didn't make a bit of sense to me.

Mother's file box was filled with memories. Hers and mine. There were photographs of Poppy and me; letters between her and her mother; a journal she'd transcribed from shorthand notes taken down while Poppy talked. It was as if she had brought him back to life. Little by little, I began to piece together secrets in Mother's family, kept out of fear for their survival.

* * *

Nanna would have been in her twenties when Poppy's *Christy Girls* became the emblem of American womanhood. I picture her gazing at one of his independent, emancipated *Christy Girls* and wishing she could be like that. But she wasn't. I remember her as a simple, quiet woman in a dust bonnet and a loose-fitting, cotton house dress. However, there was an artist hiding in Nanna that made only two appearances before she put all her effort into helping Mother become everything Nanna wasn't. She had painted two pictures, photographs of which I found in Mother's box. They were small—about ten inches wide. Both heads of women, their hair in pompadours. One a brunette. The other a strawberry blond. They looked like copies of Poppy's *Christy Girls*.

Nanna's mother, Elizabeth Maxmann, was from Germany. Mother seemed determined to impress upon me that she was German, not Jewish. I remember Mother taking me to a church in Harlem to see a plaque that was dedicated to her grandfather. In Mother's grey tin box, I found something that reminded me of that trip. It was an etching of a church with gothic stained-glass windows with an announcement for Sunday Services at St. Mary's Episcopal Church. Below it, Mother had taped a typewritten note describing "a reading desk" in the church dedicated to "Mother's father."

Twenty-five years later, in 1999, I would again come across that crumbling piece of paper pasted in Mother's autograph book and wonder why she felt it was so important. On impulse, I called St. Mary's in New York. As the phone rang, I remember Mother taking me into its dim sanctuary and pointing to the name on a plaque. "Henry A. Maxmann. That was my grandfather," she had said, and I sensed its importance to her.

Henry Maxmann was Nanna's father. Oma married him after she came to the United States. When Oma got to America, she was already a widow.

"*Hullow?*" A woman with a Virgin Island accent answered the phone.

"Is this St. Mary's?"

"Yes."

"Do you have a reading desk there?" I looked at Mother's notes. "Weighing about two hundred pounds? Fashioned in solid brass?"

"Yes, we *doo*. It *hod* a *beeg* eagle over it with its wings spread, but the eagle it is gone now. Stolen. We *hod* some break-ins."

"Is there a large Bible on the desk?" I said, still reading from Mother's description.

"Yes," said the woman whose name was Erica Charles.

"It's a lectern. We read the Gospel from it every Sunday."

"I see. Well, I'm reading this from a note my mother left me after her death. Engraved across the top of that lectern, does it say 'To the glory of God and in memory of Henry A. Maxmann for 17 years a vestryman of St. Mary's Church, Oct. 1, 1889?'"

"Just a *meenute*. I go look."

Erica's echoing footsteps faded as she retreated into the sanctuary.

When she returned, she was breathless with excitement. "Oh, it is amazing!" Erica's voice quavered as if she'd seen a ghost. "This, it make me feel chilly. It says exactly what you said. Oh, it make my blood crawl. You know what I'm going to do? I'm going to tell about this in church this Sunday. Oh, it is amazing."

I told her that Henry Maxmann was my great-grandfather and said, "There's one more thing I'd like to know."

"Of course," said Erica. "Whatever I can do to help, I am glad to do it."

"Can you tell me how old Henry Maxmann was when he died?"

"We have a very old book. You wait. I go see what I can find."

In the silence, I envisioned the lectern standing like a monolith in the center of a sanctuary, silhouetted against the light streaming in through the stained-glass windows.

While waiting for Erica, I did some calculations. Seventeen years a vestryman. That would take him back to 1881. Like Oma, he could have come to this country sometime before that.

Erica's voice interrupted my thoughts. "Oh the book, it looks so old. Yellow and crumbling. So ancient. When I open the book, everything, it was right there on top. Poor *mon*. He die so young.

"How old?"

"Just forty-seven. It say they bury *heem* at the Church of the Intercession."

"Typhoid!" I said, remembering Mother had said he had typhoid.

"Poor *mon*," said Erica, and I could almost feel her shaking her head.

"Are you near Central Park?" I asked, wondering if I could take the bus up Central Park West the next time I went to New York.

"No. We are between Old Broadway and the elevated track. This place, it is declared a landmark now by the government. One hundred and seventy-five years old, it is. You must come and see us."

"Are you in Harlem?" I asked.

"Yes, Harlem, about a mile from Mount Morris Park."

Morris? I shook it off as a mere coincidence.

After I hung up, I looked again at the Sunday Services announcement with Mother's typewritten note taped beneath. Mother had underlined "Mother's Father" with her smudgy artist's pencil. As if to draw further attention to it, she added a check mark beside it with a line pointing to a single word. "German."

Oma had to have been a German Episcopalian. Why else would Mother have made such a point of emphasizing it? Then one day, at an embassy moving sale in Mexico City's Chapultepec district, I came across two books that revealed another one of Mother's secrets. Not just Mother's, but Oma's and Nanna's too.

According to James Yaffe's *the American Jews*, German-born Jews who came to America before the turn of the century went to extremes to hide their Jewish identity. Was that why Nanna was so secretive? And could that have been why Doris scolded me for using the word "rich" because it "sounded Jewish?"

I had to find out.

I wrote Adele Forsberg, my uncle Carl's wife. I hadn't seen Adele since I was twelve years old, so I wasn't sure how she would take it if I started asking questions. I was pleased when I received her response. In her letter, Adele gave me the name of a man I'd never heard of. Gedney Godwin in Valley Forge, Virginia. She assured me if anyone knew anything about Nanna and Oma, he would. So, I wrote Gedney a letter from Mexico City. He sent me a black-and-white photograph of five generations of Nanna's family, starting with my great-great-great-grandmother. Except for baby Carl in Nanna's arms, all five people in the picture were women. Gedney told me that Nanna and Carl were the only ones born in the United States. All the rest came from Saxony, which is Dresden. As I studied the photograph, I wondered, *where are the men? Did all those women come to America alone? If so, why?* Judging by their high collars and long, dark dresses, the picture was taken around the turn of the century.

In the photograph, Oma (Elizabeth Maxmann) looked so stiff and proper in her mounds of shiny satin with big puffy sleeves and high lace collar. If it hadn't been for her prominent nose, Oma would have looked like a Christy Girl with her pompadour. I never met Oma, but I remember hearing Mother and her two sisters, Doris and Audrey, talk about Oma as if she were the family matriarch.

What secrets were these women keeping? I had to know. I called Gedney on the phone and asked him straight out, "Was Oma Jewish?"

Gedney was quick to set me straight. "She was German. From Saxony. They all came from Saxony."

Of course. Oma was German. Mother told me so.

"Oma was a very proud woman," Gedney said as if being Jewish was something to be ashamed of. It was then that I remembered the day Doris scolded me for using the word "rich" because it sounded too Jewish. Fear of being Jewish had apparently been passed down for generations.

"Was she religious?" I asked, wondering if she went to a synagogue.

"She was Episcopalian."

"Did she go to church?"

"No."

"Why?

"She said the rector tried to put his hands on her, and she never went back after that."

"Maybe she joined the Episcopalian Church just to prove she wasn't Jewish," I said, yielding to a nagging hunch.

Gedney's voice went silent. I looked anxiously at the clock. Long distant calls from Mexico to the States were expensive.

"She was very angry with the Jews," Gedney assured me. "I know because I lived at her house for quite some time." I tried to picture Gedney, but I couldn't. I knew nothing about him other than the fact that he was some distant cousin.

"Why was she angry?" I asked.

"She always said it was because of the Jews that her family lost everything. I remember her saying, 'The Jews took our property. God damn the Jews!' She always said it in perfect German."

Perfect German. Yes, she spoke "perfect German." That's

what Mother said. That did it. I was convinced. Oma was a Jew-hating German.

I framed the five-generation photograph anyway and hung it on the wall in the entryway of our Mexico City home. Every time I passed it, I wondered, *where are the men? And what would make a whole family, two of them very old, suddenly leave everything behind and sail to a strange land where they couldn't even speak the language?*

I wish I had asked Gedney more questions, but Doris's stern looks and Mother's impenetrable silence carried an unspoken warning. *Thou shalt not partake of the knowledge of good and evil.*

Years later, I would read another book I picked up in a bookstore. Howard Fast's 1982 book, *The Jews: Story of a People.* In it, I was able to link Oma, her mother, and her grandmother up with what was called the "Great Trek" of Jews out of Eastern Europe that occurred in the mid-to-late-nineteenth century. At that time, there was a great anti-Semitic uprising in Germany. In 1881, "a quarter of a million Germans signed a petition calling for the disenfranchisement of all Jews and their forcible return to the ghettos. In 1882, an anti-Semitic congress was held in Dresden, ...called for everything from incineration to forced exile for the Jews."

Dresden! Exile!

In a way, Oma hadn't lied when she said it was because of the Jews that her family lost everything. Fear had forced Oma to lie about her identity.

The exodus of Jews from Dresden was unparalleled in history. Between 1870 and 1905, more than a third of the Jews in Eastern Europe left their homes. By 1907, Jews made up 28 percent of the population of New York City. Oma had to have been one of them. Nothing else made sense. I asked myself, *how would it have affected Oma, coming from a place like that? Wouldn't she have been proud of her German heritage, rich in refinement, education, the arts, and science? Wouldn't she have provided her children with every opportunity in the New World to pursue a similar cultural life?*

Apparently, it was commonplace for nineteenth-century New York Jews to deny their identity. German Jews wanted to fit in. Although proud of their German heritage, they feared the return of anti-Semitism. Many changed their names to sound American. Stralheim became Stralem; Neustadt became Newton, Soloman to Simson. In Mother's case, Forsberg—a Swedish name that sounded Jewish—became Ford.

How could I blame Oma, Nanna, and Mother for protecting themselves from prejudice and hate? But why would Oma go so far as to say, "God damn the Jews"?

According to Steven Birmingham's 1967 book, *Our Crowd: The Great Jewish Families of New York,* German Jews were alarmed by a sudden influx of "uncouth, unwashed" Jews out of Russia, "...reports of overcrowding in tenements, vermin, garbage, marital disorders, violence, starvation, and crime—were a grievous thorn in the German Jewish side. To be identified as a Jew, along with 'those people,' became increasingly irksome. 'Those people' were loud, pushy, aggressive— 'the dregs of Europe.'" German Jews, like Oma, feared this horde of Russian 'barbarians' would cause an anti-Semitism reaction that would threaten the reputation of all Jews as "good Americans." To ward off persecution, they went to great lengths to identify themselves as different from what they referred to as "kikes," an epithet invented by German Jews in referring to the Russian Jews whose names often ended with "ki." New York Jews became alarmed that "those people" would become a threat to their comfortable life in America.

America—land of the free, home of the brave—was a nation where many were forced to hide their identities to survive. Apparently Mother was one of them. I came to understand why she was so secretive. She was scared.

The more I read, the more I realized that Oma was a typical German Jew. She was willing to deny her identity to protect her loved ones and give them a new lease on life. She had seen what could happen. She had lost everything just for being Jewish. Now she wanted to fit in. Create a new identity. Americanize. Many Jews joined the Episcopalian church or became Christian Scientists.

H. L. Mencken, who lived during those times, observed that to be "fashionable" in American society, you had to belong to the right church. "Fashionable society in America has no room for intelligence: within its fold an original idea is dangerous; it carries regimentation, in dress, in social customs and in political and even religious doctrines, to the last degree." During the nineteenth and early 'twentieth centuries, this regimentation invaded every aspect of human life. According to Mencken, the "right church" was the Episcopalian Church. "Every fashionable Protestant Episcopal congregation in the land is full of ex-Baptists and ex-Methodists who have shed

Calvinism, total immersion, and the hallelujah hymns on their way up the ladder. The same impulse leads the Jews, whenever the possibility of invading the citadel of the Christians begins to bemuse them (as happened during the late war, for example, when patriotism temporarily adjourned the usual taboos), to embrace Christian Science—as a sort of half-way station, so to speak, more medical than Christian, and hence secure against ordinary derisions."

"Christian Science?" I was amazed. There it was. My family's story in print. In light of the facts, Oma's damning of the Jews sounded surprisingly Jewish. Even downright American. And what better icon could these Jewish women look to as an example than Howard Chandler Christy's *Christy Girl?* It was all pulling together.

Like so many German Jews of that time, Oma feared persecution. She wanted to fit in. Start a new life, free of fear. Was it any wonder that years later, Nanna would introduce Mother to Howard Chandler Christy, creator of that all-American *Christy Girl?*

***

A few years ago, I called Adele Forsberg, widow of Mother's brother, Carl Forsberg, at her home in Vero

Beach, Florida. She was ninety-two and spoke with a Long Island accent.

"Do you know if Nanna was Jewish?" I asked.

"I think so. She always covered it up when the subject came up."

"You mean about being Jewish?"

"No. Just anything about the Jews. She must have had something to hide. There were a lot of secrets. I know that. I could never get close to her. You know—to kid around or anything. She was very distant. Reclusive. No company. No friends. There was never anybody there when I went over. They lived a very quiet, private life."

"What makes you think they were Jewish?"

"Because they came over from Germany, you know when there was something going on with the Jews."

"What did Nanna do for a living, do you know?"

"She was a retired school teacher."

"What religion was she?"

"There was never any talk about religion. No religious pictures. I don't think she ever went to church."

"Do you remember Oma?"

"Yeah, I do. Very proud woman. Secretive and

proud."

"Do you think she was Jewish?"

"All I know is, she used to say, 'Gott verdamme die Juden.' God damn the Jews. And she always said it in perfect German. She said the Jews took her father's brewery away from him, and she was very bitter."

Perfect German. There it is again. Oma's curse had become a family cliché.

"Adele," I said, remembering that she too was an emigrant from Europe, abandoned by her mother and raised by her father. "Wasn't your maiden name Feldman?"

"That was my mother's name, yeah."

"Feldman is a Jewish name. You must be Jewish too."

"Probably am," she said, her voice now old and tired. "Probably am."

* * *

Curious to know if anyone else in my family had come to the same conclusion, I called my cousin, Dr. David Leonard, Professor Emeritus in Entomology from

Massachusetts University. David is Uncle Jim's son. I asked him if he thought Oma could have been Jewish, and he said, "Sure she was. I've thought about that for a long time. She was concealing it. I know that."

Then I called David's brother, Tom Leonard, a retired Lieutenant Colonel in the Air Force. He was at his apple orchard in upstate New York, just twelve miles from the Old Red Mill. I asked him the same question. He told me he had come to the same conclusion we had. "Lots of secrets in our family."

CHAPTER TWENTY-THREE

The Soloma

Give me a comfortable seat propped with cushions in the Soloma—a moonlit night and a billowy sea—and I am the happiest most contented creature on earth. Do you think that happiness expensive?

- Letter to Carl T. Forsberg from
Sophie Louise Maxmann,
my grandmother

I slide a black-and-white photo out of Mother's grey tin file box, and what it tells me is worth more than words can say. I see Poppy descending the wide porch steps of my grandparents' two-story, white-frame house. He is holding the hand of a shaky toddler. Me. I can't be more than two years old. The wind from the nearby Long Island

Sound is twisting the long strands of Poppy's white hair. Sitting on the bottom step is my smiling grandfather. Papa looks like Cary Grant, while Poppy looks old enough to be Papa's father. Nanna, in her dust bonnet, is looking up at the camera with a wink.

Nanna's wink says volumes. It sets Nanna apart from the rest of the world, which would have condemned Mother as an adulterer and me as a bastard. Her wink makes me want to know more about Nanna and her family and the times she lived in.

World War II had begun, but I see no sign of fear or stress in this picture. Just one happy family. Nanna's house was the only one on a shady elm-lined street. At the time, the population in the United States was only 134.86 million, and 2.3 billion worldwide—a far cry from today's eight billion and counting exponentially. People had room to stretch like the branches of a tree. Commuting to work in freeway traffic was unheard of. Everything one could possibly need was within walking distance.

For Nanna and Papa, life was slow and easy, even during wartime. After smoking his pipe and reading the morning paper, Papa strolled down the leaf-strewn road to his sleepy dock on Front Street. The only sounds breaking the stillness in the air were the sloshing of water, the occasional screeching of seagulls, and the groan of Papa's Viking Fleet moored to barnacled posts at the head of Woodcleft Canal.

My eyes focus on Nanna.

Her gamy wink. And my uncle Jim's words reverberate in my head. "I blame it all on your grandmother—letting a young girl pose naked for that old goat. She planned it all. She was a very ambitious woman—your grandmother. And, well—damned *arteesists.*"

Nanna is a woman with a story. One I need to hear. As my uncle Jim implied, she had everything to do with my unseemly advent.

***

Carl T. Forsberg was the venturesome son of Nils Olof and Hanna Sofia Forsberg—both emigrants from Sweden. Papa's father was an upholsterer in the shipping industry along the Harlem River. As a boy, it was Papa's job to scavenge firewood to keep the house warm and to cook. Driftwood and lumber scraps were plentiful in the river due to the amount of construction and dock work, so—at the age of ten in 1894—Papa built his first boat by stretching canvas over the ribs of sugar barrels. He used it for gathering firewood from the murky waters of the Harlem River. From this same salvaged wood, he built other boats, which he rowed or sailed on increasingly longer jaunts around Manhattan Island. Eventually, he was navigating his way to New Jersey and on up into the Long Island Sound. Once, he capsized and was rescued by a tugboat that towed him to safety at the Liberty dock.

Papa probably met Nanna on one of his trips because he liked sailing to Belle Island, where my grandmother Oma had a summer cottage on the shorefront. In a short account, typed up by Mother, which I found in her file box, Papa talks about a yacht he built for Nanna in 1905 when she was his fiancé. He named it *The Soloma* after her name: So-phie Lo-uise Ma-xmann. It was the boat he frequently sailed to Belle Island to visit Nanna in 1905.

"Mother Maxmann certainly knew how to prepare a most delicious clam bake," wrote Papa. "We younger folk would dig the clams along the beach and collect driftwood for fuel. The joy of those trips will always be a pleasant memory throughout my life. Sophie and I were married the following year, and before very long, *The Soloma* became more of a problem than a joy. We found that with the wages from my position, we could not afford to support an ever-growing family and a yacht. So, it became necessary to sell the Soloma."

Papa was over six feet tall with broad, square shoulders. He stood as straight as the mast on his schooner. Although both his parents had migrated from Sweden, Papa's dark hair and swarthy skin made him look unlike what most think of as typically Swedish. His father—Nils Olof Forsberg—had married Hannah Sofia Johanson in 1878. From Sweden, they brought a written genealogy dating back to Lapland in the 1600s. Like his ancestors who hunted caribou in snow-swept tundras, Papa preferred the wide-open sea to cramped city life. Papa was rugged but gentle, given to tears when emotionally moved—a Viking without horns. Quite a catch, and Nanna knew it, as expressed in a love letter I found in Mother's file box, which she wrote after returning from teaching school.

What a darling you were to answer my letter so soon. On my way home from school, I wondered what made me feel lighter-hearted than usual, and I didn't stay until 4:30 as I usually do to correct papers, etc. for, I couldn't seem to get done fast enough.

Nanna explains to Papa that relatives were visiting when she arrived home, but his letter "burned" in her hands, so she left her mother and guests "while I, with my hat and coat still on, rushed upstairs to hear the latest news from one who grows dearer and dearer to me and who is going to make me infinitely happy someday."

The letter reveals that Papa built his fiancé a model of *The Soloma* as a decoration for the home they hoped to have together.

And to think that you have worked so hard on our Soloma. I can just imagine how beautiful it will look over our parlor mantel, or perhaps you will be able to suggest some prettier place, darling. Not a single day passes dear that I do not dream of a little place that we can call home and oh, how I hope that I may not fail to make it a haven of rest for you darling; a place to lay your tired head after the toil and turmoil of the day, and be comforted; to be able to tell your perplexities to a ready listener, and best of all, a place where you can study, to your heart's content to become a successful man of the world.

Darling, my aim in life is to be a mistress of a happy little home. It is my life's dream. ...I don't want to attain to anything great myself, but I do want to be an inspiration (willing to stand unnoticed) in order that the man of my heart may triumph, and win the battle.

Everything I do dear will be for your betterment. Self will be out of the question and I do often feel that I will often be glad that I have made myself so proficient in everything pertaining to business, for someday I may play the part of Mrs. Forsberg, (private secretary in private life) but there I am dreaming again."

Then, at the turn of the century, someone struck fear into Nanna. His name was Anthony Comstock, a grim Calvinist who rose up in alarm at the social change brought about by the inventions of the car and the telephone. In the book, *The Century of Sex,* published in 1999, James R. Peterson describes Comstock as bull-necked and stalwart with greying mutton-chop sideburns. According to Comstock, the telephone made it possible to plan secret rendezvous, and the car made it possible to carry out unholy acts. Such "instruments of the Devil" were putting Americans at risk of eternal damnation.

Something had to be done. In keeping with his self-perceived God-ordained mission, Comstock always dressed in "sacerdotal black." As a special agent to the U.S. Post Office and Secretary of the New York Society for the Suppression of Vice (SSV), Comstock pledged to "hunt down sinners like rats."

It wasn't long before Comstock rallied the FBI to his aid in purging America of illicit sex. "For Comstock, sex was a controlled substance," states Peterson in *The Century of Sex*. He was a man who "had the government at his disposal; no one would stand up in favor of freedom for fear of being next on his list."

There it was—the word Poppy fought to promote through art. "Freedom."

These were the times in which Nanna began her life with Papa. And they were anything but free.

As Peterson points out, the big news of the day was the latest dirt on independent women whose views brought them up against Comstock's hard-set jaw. In 1902, Ida Craddock shocked New York by writing *The Wedding Night,* in which she proclaimed it was every woman's right to have an orgasm. Up until Ida came along, nice girls were not thought to have sexual desires.

Female orgasm was labeled "hysteria." Any bouts of irritability, sexual fantasies, or even daydreaming were looked upon with suspicion. Swelling of the vaginal wall and excessive vaginal lubrication were diagnosed as disorders of the mind. A Mary Magdalene-like possession in need of an exorcism. To deal with the problem, the Christian clergy and the American Medical Association (AMA) put their heads together and came up with a cure to release the writhing demons of orgasm. The treatment? Manual manipulation of the vaginal area by a doctor. In the words of one doctor who voiced the religious conviction of the time, "massage of the pelvic organs should be entrusted to those alone who have clean hands and a pure heart."

Comstock slapped the label of pornography on Ida's book, making it a federal crime.

It was a bad time for Ida to stir up trouble, but she was determined to stand up against the penal dictums of her Christian adversary, thus turning the Comstock/Craddock battle over female orgasm into a newsworthy soap opera nobody could ignore. Including Nanna.

Ida called the mutually satisfying union between a

man and a woman a "moment in harmony with Nature." But Comstock came out firing from the hip. He labeled it "indescribably obscene."

Comstock had to put a stop to all this smut before sin broke out in the streets. Through a clever ruse, he framed Ida. Comstock wasn't above lying if it was in the Name of the Lord.

Ida was found guilty before a judge who deemed her book too offensive to show the jury. Ida never showed up for her sentencing. She was found dead with her head in the oven.

No one could ignore this story, which had to have instilled fear in women's hearts.

But the battle wasn't over. Ida left Comstock an open letter in the New York morning news. On October 16, 1902, she wrote:

I am taking my life because a judge, at the instigation of Anthony Comstock, has declared me guilty of a crime I did not commit—the circulation of obscene literature. Perhaps it may be that in my death, more than in my life, the American people may be shocked into investigating the dreadful state of affairs which permits that unctuous sexual hypocrite Anthony Comstock to wax fat and arrogant and to trample upon the liberties of the people, invading, in my own case, both my right to freedom of religion and to freedom of the press. The man is a sex pervert. He is what physicians term a Sadist – namely, a person in whom the impulses of cruelty arise concurrently with the stirring of sex emotion.

The next day, Reverend W. S. Rainsford of New York's St. George's Episcopalian Church responded to her charges against Comstock in the same paper.

"Mr. Comstock: I would not like to be in your shoes. You hounded an honest, not a bad, woman to her death. I would not like to have to answer to God for what you have done."

Could this be one of the reasons Oma and Nanna joined the Episcopalian Church?

Sooner or later, Poppy's *Christy Girls* was bound to get him into trouble. To Nanna, the *Christy Girl* must have seemed like a beacon of hope in a stormy sea of religious fundamentalism as she strove to create a home and raise a family.

It was on *The Soloma* that Nanna and Papa rendezvoused, far from the watchful eye of Comstock's SSV henchmen.

Nanna signs her letter, "All your own, *Soloma*," then adds a postscript that reveals her secretive nature and her fears.

"P.S. I'll write again next week. I would write a great deal more than I do darling, but I'm so afraid you forget to hide my letters. Did I write a foolish letter dear? Your letter made me so glad that I couldn't help reciprocating by telling you how much I really love you more than you will ever know."

How grateful I am that Mother kept this letter. It was one of the many treasures I found in her grey, tin file box that Doris and Wanda left out in the rain seeping in through the decaying roof of their garage. Had I not stumbled upon it rotting away in their moldy garage, I would still be in the dark about Mother's side of the family and why they were so guarded. Who wouldn't have been secretive in a society like that?

Nanna and Papa married, and their first child, Carl, was born in 1906.

Four years passed before the next child, which makes me wonder if there were miscarriages? Infant deaths? Both common at the time. The next three children came in rapid succession. Audrey in 1910, Doris in 1911, followed by Elise, Nanna's Thanksgiving baby.

Mother was born November 27, 1912—the year the Titanic sank. In that same year, President Taft created the Children's Bureau to look into the exploitation of children for cheap labor in factories, fields, and mines. It was also in 1912 that another notorious New York scandal came to an end when Harry Thaw was released from an asylum six years after shooting the famous sculptor and architect Stanford White in front of a large audience in the building he had designed—Madison Square Garden.

The murder was over an artist's model, Evelyn Nesbit.

Accompanied by her mother, Evelyn came to New York at the age of thirteen to model for Charles Dana Gibson. By fifteen, Evelyn was acclaimed as the most beautiful woman in the world. Stanford White, who was married and forty-seven years her senior, became infatuated with her. Evelyn later wrote about their secret world of sex in his West Side "hideaway." She told about a room full of mirrors where he liked to watch her swing naked on a red velvet swing. She also reported that they climbed to the top of Madison Square Garden—the building White designed—and hung naked on the statue of Diana in full view of the city below.

Evelyn told Harry Thaw about her affair with White. After marrying Evelyn, Thaw sought to get even with White by telling Comstock that White had defiled 378 virgins. Comstock marshaled his vice squad to stake out White's house, but no suspicious activity was reported.

On June 25, 1906, Thaw walked up to White on the opening night of a musical in Madison Square Garden. While the band played, *I Could Love a Million Girls*, Thaw drew out a pistol and shot White three times.

Murdering White—an adulterer—made Thaw an American hero. The defense called Thaw, "an instrument of God and an agent of Providence."

These were the stories that shaped the culture Mother grew up in. Of course, she was secretive. According to the Bible, adultery was a crime punishable by stoning, and America was a religious nation. More so at the turn of the twentieth century than it had been after the Nineteenth

Century.

Crowds gathered outside the courthouse to cheer the murderer of the adulterer.

Thaw was found not guilty by reason of insanity and sent to an asylum. A film about the affair was scheduled to open in New York in 1908. Comstock and a group of religious leaders protested, and every theater in New York was shut down.

Every theater shut down? Talk about religion gaining power through government—this was definitely not separation between church and state designated by the Founding Fathers who wrote our Constitution.

America was well on her way to becoming a fundamentalist Christian nation.

I look at Mother's photo of Poppy walking me down Nanna's front porch steps, and I see Papa's passion for the open sea and his Viking Fleet, a refuge from prying prudes. I see Nanna's solitary house on Front Street as a safe haven from the incriminating mores of the times. What I don't see is my illegitimacy and the shame of my genesis. Those thoughts had to be put there by the culture of shame in which I lived. But in that picture, instead of shame, I see innocence. I see family. I see happiness. Far from the ignorant masses in need of someone upon whom to vent their hate, we are as free from persecution as the seagulls soaring in the sky above.

Today, I see Mother as Poppy painted her in his *I Am An American* poster towering over New York's Times Square. As a Jewish girl, she had to keep her identity a secret, just like me. Yet Poppy painted her as the David that Hitler's Goliath could not defeat. Who would have guessed? But in those days, there was anti-Semitism on both sides. Secrets were necessary to protect the innocent.

Knowing this now, I understand Nanna's gamy wink.

CHAPTER TWENTY-FOUR

What Kind of Man?

No virtuous man has ever painted a picture worth looking at, or written a symphony worth hearing, or a book worth reading.

- H. L. Mencken

Someone once asked me, "What kind of man would not tell his own daughter that he was her father? And what did that do to you? That's what I want to know." It would take me almost forty years to find out. All that time, the answers lay moldering in Doris and Wanda's garage.

And how did a beautiful young actress like Mother fall for an "old coot" like Poppy? Was she happy? Or faking it?

And what about Poppy's wife, Nancy? What did she have to say?

The answers were all in Mother's grey, tin file box.

Like me, Poppy married the wrong person, which drove him to drink. Unlike me, their marital battles soon made the gossip columns for prurient New Yorkers, nearly destroying him and his illustrious career.

Right after Poppy returned from the Spanish American War, he was invited to join the Players Club, making him the youngest member of America's creative elite. He recalled with fondness his first day at the club. "Fred Remington walked in. He hadn't seen me since the war and didn't recognize me all dressed up. He looked at me and said, "Is that you, Howard Christy!?' Then he spits on his hands, rubbed them together, and shouted, 'Put'er there!'"

Within the Player's Club was an inner circle called "the Aldine Round Table," and Poppy was invited to join that as well. Membership bestowed the highest honor on its artists and writers. "[Mark Twain] was the idol member of the Club," Poppy said. "I remember his stories, all of which I had read. He looked so comfortable in his suit of white flannel in the winter. He always smoked a half cigar as we sat around the table."

Willard Metcalf, painter of the peaceful pastoral scenes Poppy would later refer to as "Metties," also belonged to the club. Metcalf's Vermont landscapes made Poppy yearn for the day when he could make a living painting landscape. To Poppy, painting tranquil valley vistas was heaven right here on Earth. For him, painting was a form of worship. But he had to make a living, and nobody was willing to pay him to paint landscapes.

At the club, "I was considered just a boy," Poppy said. "So, one night, one of the men fixed me a cocktail. When I picked it up to drink it, it just quivered and stayed right there in the glass. Everyone burst out laughing. They knew it was made with gelatin. They kidded around with me a lot like that."

During this time, Poppy kept his studio on Broadway but moved from his one-room apartment into a place more in keeping with his celebrity status—the fashionable Hotel Marie Antoinette, which was always buzzing with activity. To promote his career, Poppy gave elaborate luncheons for his friends, some of which came all the way from Washington, D.C., to attend. Poppy described one such event. "There was an orchestra assembled on a balcony overlooking the dining room. Every day, they played for luncheon gatherings. Sometimes John Philip Sousa or Victor Herbert would meet me there for lunch. I'd tip the orchestra off that they were coming and hand out beer and cigars to all the musicians. I'd signal the orchestra when Sousa came in, and they'd play one of his stirring marches, and everybody'd sit up and look. A Sousa march will do that to you. And Sousa, he'd bow in military fashion." Poppy would later illustrate a book by Sousa called, *The Fifth String*.

"When Victor Herbert arrived, I'd signal the orchestra, and they'd launch into something like 'Slumber On My Little Gypsy Sweetheart' or the 'Gypsy Love Song.' Herbert was a large, easygoing, carefree man. When he heard his music being played, he'd tilt his head and smile. Then he'd raise his arm and slowly wave it in a wide sweep in time with the rhythm of the music. He was such a likable man."

Some of Victor Herbert's operettas were *Babes in Toyland, Naughty Marietta*, and *The Red Mill*, and later the *Ziegfeld Follies*, famous for its beautiful women. Little wonder that Poppy and Victor Herbert were friends. Victor Herbert was a colorful New York figure who frequented restaurants, cafes, and other meeting places of the theatrical and musical world. "What I love about his music is its buoyancy," Poppy said.

Reading Poppy's account of his youth, so carefully transcribed in Mother's journal, made me realize why he was so patriotic. Comstock aside—there was much to love about living in America. Land of opportunity.

According to Susan Meyer's in *America's Great American Illustrators*, first published in 1968 and still in publication, "Newspapers and magazines would follow [Poppy's] whereabouts incessantly. One week Christy broke into print three times with his escapades: he rode a trick pony at the Circus Ball; drew Miss Motor Corps of America while seated on an old beer case; and ventured to declare to the entire American public that he considered the Venus de Milo poorly proportioned, particularly at the lower extremities."[2]

There was something unique about this new artist in town. He surely must have caught Oma and Nanna's attention. They were undoubtedly enthralled with his exploits and read about him almost daily from the seclusion of their modest homes. At the turn of the century, reading up on the flamboyant lifestyles of the rich and famous was a national pastime.

Poppy's success drew art critics, some of which made their derogatory comments public. This annoyed Poppy. He reasoned, "If a critic can't paint, how the hell does he know enough to criticize others?" Poppy agreed with a French critic who said, "It seems to me, works of art are not made to be judged, but to be loved, to please and to dissipate the cares of real life. It is precisely by wishing to judge that one loses sight of their true significance."

One evening in New York, when Poppy was still in his early twenties, the famous artist Edwin Austin Abbey gave a dinner party to celebrate the completion of the interior design of the Boston Library. Poppy greatly admired Abbey and prized this opportunity to be in his presence at such a noble occasion. Unfortunately, Poppy found himself seated at a table full of the same art critics who had been publicly putting his work down. In contrast, everything they said about Abbey was dripping with syrupy praise and fawning accolades. During the meal, Poppy rose from his seat and held out his menu to Abbey, sitting at the next table.

"Mr. Abbey," Poppy called out above the blather of the critics. "I so admire your work that I would be greatly honored if you would sign my menu."

Abbey motioned for Poppy to come to his table. "To whom shall I sign it?" he asked.

"Howard Chandler Christy," said Poppy.

"I know you well," exclaimed Abbey, referring to Poppy's work. "I will sign your name just as you sign your pictures." And he did. "Splendid work you're doing," said Abbey. "You have a brilliant future. You must come and visit me sometime and my good neighbor, John Singer Sargent. He knows you too."

Poppy returned to his table of critics and showed them how Abbey had copied his own signature to show him how familiar he was with Poppy's work. His critics had nothing to say after that.

That same evening, Poppy returned home to Cad, his deaf roommate. Using sign language, Poppy told Cad how Mr. Abbey had put those "Damned critics" in their place. Then he and Cad "Hooped it up together," playing pranks on one another until they were too exhausted to stay up any longer. As soon as Poppy fell asleep, Cad—who couldn't hear a thing—set the alarm to go off at 3 A.M. so Poppy would have to get up in the cold and turn it off.

The next morning, Cad—wearing an innocent look on his face—asked Poppy with his fingers, "Did you sleep well last night?"

The next night Cad tried to play the same joke, but this time Poppy was ready for it. When the alarm went off at 3 A.M., Poppy knew Cad couldn't hear it, so he reached over and yanked a rope he had rigged up to make Cad's bed jump up and down. Cad may have been deaf, but he sure felt his bed rising off the floor. He leaped out of bed, grabbed the gas lamp and lit it. Then he shook Poppy to get him to open his eyes wide enough to read his frantic sign language. "What happened? Was that an earthquake?"

He found no consolation from Poppy, who merely gave him a ho-hum look from under his snug covers and beckoned to the alarm clock with a lazy swing of his arm. He then gave Cad a wink.

After Poppy became a successful artist, he moved into a place of his own and eventually lost touch with his friend—Cadwallader Washburn—the artist who couldn't hear.

Fifty-five years later, Poppy found out where Cad was and wrote him a letter. Cad wrote back, saying that he was so touched by their friendship which had lasted for half a century and that he was sending some honey from his apiary as a token of his joy. Cad was living in Maine after having traveled all over the world. Poppy and Cad never lost touch after that until one day, in his eighties, Cad ceased to reply, and Poppy said a silent good-bye to his old art school chum with whom he'd had "such a bang-up time" talking with their fingers.

It wasn't long after his return from Cuba in 1898 that Poppy married his most beautiful model. Maebelle Thompson, daughter of an Army officer, was described as having long ropes of raven curls and luminous brown eyes. The original Christy Girl.

From the sunny deck of his transport to Cuba, Poppy had sung *The Girl I Left Behind* along with the Rough Riders. That song had inspired a vision of love and marital bliss with Maebelle, a dream he incorporated into his wartime illustrations as the yearning of battered soldiers in combat. It was the song that inspired his first *Christy Girl*.

Poppy's marriage to Maebelle had everything going for it. Aunt White—a wealthy New Yorker—who had always been supportive of Poppy's talent, gave the newlyweds a charming old home in Closter, New Jersey. The house was situated high on a hill overlooking the Hudson River, with a babbling brook alongside the house. "Bonnie Brook," as it was called, was the perfect spot for Poppy's studio. It was out in the country, and Poppy loved the country. Living there reminded him of his Muskingham boyhood days.

Maebelle hated country life. She yearned for the glamor of the big city, with its lavish parties thrown by famous New Yorkers dressed in high fashion. Now that he was a recognized artist, Poppy preferred the chirp of crickets at night to big city galas and bright lights. These differences only grew worse after the birth of their daughter, Natalie.

Tranquility bored Maebelle to tears. So she invited friends and family to stay at the house. Painting requires a meditative state, but Poppy's studio now buzzed with noisy guests milling about constantly interfering with his work. Forty years later, I would overhear him tell Mother, "I told Maebelle, 'I can't work with all these goddamned people in the house." Maebelle struck back with stinging swiftness. "You call that work? All those models traipsing around *my* house?"

Their relationship deteriorated into constant bickering. Poppy took to the bottle, which only made matters worse. Their marriage grew more and more volatile, with many outbursts, some of them public. Poppy's turbulent marriage soon became the topic of high-society gossip columns.

Seeking solace in the bottle got Poppy into more trouble. It was a time in our history when getting drunk could get you pitched into a mental institution. On occasion, that's exactly where Poppy ended up.

Maebelle and Poppy had other differences besides his preference for painting pretty women. Poppy liked roughing it in the great outdoors. Maebelle preferred the comforts of home. To get away from Maebelle's constant backbiting and partying with her irksome houseguests, Poppy stole away for months at a time to Muldoon's place. Muldoon was a champion wrestler and trainer of famous athletes like John L. Sullivan and Kid McCoy. The men called Muldoon "Professor." Poppy would stay for a month at a time, working out with the wrestlers every day. There were women there too, but they stayed in separate quarters and didn't work out as hard as the men.

So, when things got testy at home, Poppy would take

up residency for awhile at Muldoon's. Thanks to Mother's skill at dictation, Poppy's voice is captured in her journal as he recounts his first day at Muldoon's place. Word for word, it's exactly as I remember it as I listened in while sitting on his knee.

"Right away, Muldoon told me, 'Howard, you're gonna need a horse to ride, so let's get down to the stables.' The stables were quite a distance from the house, down through a lane of maple trees with limbs reaching clear out overhead. "You can ride Shorty," Muldoon said, not mentioning that Shorty didn't like being ridden. "When the men heard Muldoon was going to give Shorty to me, they all meandered down to watch. They knew Shorty threw everyone who was fool enough to get on his back. Then, after Shorty threw his rider off, he'd whirl around and bite him besides."

Throw and bite. Poppy was about to be put through Shorty's initiation rite. It's a story I loved hearing over and over, so I'd get really quiet and listen.

"Well," said Poppy, "when I led Shorty out of the stable, not one of those prizefighters or wrestlers said a word. They all just stood around and watched. Not knowing they were always game for a good prank, I thought they were just being friendly and hospitable. As soon as I swung myself up on Shorty's back, Shorty began to buck and rear up and toss about. Shorty fought with all his might, bucking and twisting and kicking. Everyone cheered and shouted as if it was a major prizefight."

But Poppy knew horses. As a child, he had trained his horse Nellie to come when he blew his bugle. She'd take off running and slide down the steep side of a hill on her rump.

When Shorty's bucking was over, Poppy was still on top.

After that, Shorty was Poppy's horse. He could do anything with Shorty. Even taught him tricks.

Poppy loved the rugged life at Muldoon's and talked about it often. "Horseback riding each morning was done in twos, military fashion, Muldoon clinging to his old Civil War habits. Muldoon liked telling about himself in the Civil War as they rode along through the high snow." Only McClellan saddles were used in Cavalry fashion. Hollow in the middle with edges that made it too uncomfortable to settle down in the saddle and relax. "There'd be no sleeping in the saddle on trips with Muldoon," Poppy said.

Everyone was a little scared of Muldoon. One day, Poppy and John L. Sullivan rode out to visit the roadhouses and taverns and didn't come back till late. When they returned, they were so drunk they had to steady themselves by leaning on one another to get up the porch steps. But they were feeling merry, singing songs and laughing all the way. As they stumbled onto the porch, they found Muldoon sitting on their trunks, which were packed and ready to go. Muldoon jumped to his feet, waving an axe and shouted, "You do that again, and I'll kill you both. Now, you get yourselves together."

Muldoon never let anyone in the house who was drunk after that. And no one was fool enough to try.

The next morning, suffering from a hangover, Poppy forced himself through the daily routine of workouts, knowing full well that if he didn't, there'd be hell to pay. Everyone lined up facing one another in the gym and bounced balls back and forth, keeping them going as fast as they could. Muldoon kept four going at once with Kid McCoy. They called it throwing the "medicine ball", and everyone was supposed to throw it from the same position in which they caught it. If you shifted your position, Muldoon would yell out, "All right, cheat yourself. Pay your money out and cheat yourself." Afterwards, everyone put on flannel robes, drank two glasses of hot water and rested while they perspired. Then they all jumped into an ice shower. On some days, Muldoon led them down to the Hudson River to swim even when there was snow and ice on the ground. I'm sure that's why, many years later, Poppy didn't mind the chill of the Mettowee river.

At Muldoon's place, there was no reason to go into town. Everything anyone needed was right there. However, Poppy and some friends sneaked off one day and brought back some apples and candy. Muldoon found out from the grocer that a bunch of his guys had been in there buying food. That night, Muldoon walked down the hall like a jailhouse warden. Poppy stuck his head out of his room and quipped, "Would you like an apple?" Muldoon said, "Yes, I know about it, what you guys did. I think I will have one. As a matter of fact, I think an apple is the finest thing you can eat before bed. As for the candy." He shook his head. "No good."

Poppy regretted having to leave Muldoon's. He stroked Shorty's soft white nose one more time and told his horse goodbye.

Maebelle badgered Poppy into buying an apartment for her on Riverside Drive in New York while using Bonnie Brook at his studio. Poppy owned a Model T, which he used to pick up models in New York and drive them to his studio in New Jersey. That made him liable for arrest, according to the White Slave Trafficking Act, instituted by Anthony Comstock to keep men from transporting women who were not their wives across state borders in their Model Ts, which he called "instruments of the Devil." It was a law levied to put a stop to prostitution and the "immoral use of rubbers" and other "crimes against society."

Poppy could have ended up in jail.

"There's something fascinating about a fine country home where you can do just what you please," Poppy told reporters. He was thinking of Zanesville, Ohio. That's where Poppy wanted to go. Back to where his parents still lived in the serene beauty of the blue Muskingham river.

Maebelle wanted nothing to do with Ohio. Her strident protests reached the ears of a reporter in Chicago. S. E. Kiser transcribed the Christy battle into lyrics which appeared in the *Chicago Record-Herald*.

Zanesville, Zanesville—I'll never live in Zanesville!

Says Howard Chandler Christy's loving wife:

She might settle in Waukegan or receive her mail in Janesville

And still, get some enjoyment out of life;

But Zanesville, Zanesville!

She shudders at the thought of living there;

So it's up to Zanesville duly

To explain this matter truly—

If it has a reputation, let it keep it in repair.

Zanesville promptly responded in their *Times Recorder*.

So let other cities have her,

For our people wouldn't salve her,

And we hope that never more in all our life

Will we have a greater sorrow

Either past or on tomorrow,

Then we had in losing Howard Chandler's wife.

By 1908, a cloud of despair hovered over Bonnie Brook. Poppy turned to Bena Washington, the "colored" household help, as the only person he could trust. Bena became his friend and confidant. His confessor. In a poem he wrote, Poppy describes his relationship with the woman who remained a part of his family until her death thirty years later.

My Mammy's a Mammy of color I'll say,
With a red bandanna wrapped round her head.
She insists that you eat too much through the day,
And at night when you're drunk she'll put you to bed.
When things seem wrong and day turns to night.
She'll make heaven come singing right out of hell.
And the best of it is, she's most always right.

She can cook a chicken that will melt in your mouth,
With old-fashioned gravy and things that you love.
Because, you see, she comes from the South,
And cookin' down there is a gift from above,
Two birthdays a year, when she goes to the pictures,

And presents besides says this wary old sage.

In the heart of our family, she's one of the fixtures.

What cares she for time, and to hell with her age.

As Poppy's troubles with Maebelle increased, so did his drinking. One day, Poppy awoke, unable to see. Scared that he was going blind, he called the doctor. The doctor told him straight out, "If you don't quit the drink, I doubt if you'll make it through the year."

Poppy called his sister Hope in Ohio. She came right away and brought a woman named Mrs. Stetson, a Christian Science practitioner. Hope told Poppy that Mrs. Stetson had the gift of healing.

There was an aura of serenity about Mrs. Stetson. She was the calm after a storm, and she put Poppy right at ease. From a chair by his bedside, she began to preach the power of positive thinking. Mind over matter. "Know you not that the Kingdom of God is within you?" she crooned in a velvety voice. "You are the image and likeness of God. Therefore you are Divine Love, incapable of sickness, sin and death." She convinced Poppy that the world was spiritual, not carnal. That he had nothing to fear because

"Divine Love alone governs man." Therefore, "Man is incapable of sin, sickness, and death." Poppy found hope in this quote from Mary Baker Eddy's *Science and Health with Key to the Scriptures.*

Mrs. Stetson told him how Mary Baker Eddy, at the age of twelve, had taken issue with the Calvinist doctrine of predestination taught in her parent's church. Poppy didn't much care for those humorless Calvinists either, and he admired Mrs. Eddy for rejecting the Christian doctrine of working out our salvation with fear and trembling. He considered the whole notion of blood sacrifice revolting. Poppy never cared much for religion other than something to crack jokes about. All that damnation stuff got his guff.

More and more, Poppy liked what he heard about Mrs. Eddy, especially when Mrs. Stetson told him how upset Mrs. Eddy had become over a doctrine that condemned her brothers and sisters to everlasting hell—merely by a decree from God. It made her physically ill to hear such a thing. Mrs. Stetson read Poppy Mary Baker Eddy's account of her battle against the doctrine of predestination, "My mother, as she bathed my burning temples, bade me lean on God's love... which would give me rest if I went to him in prayer, as I was wont to do, seeking His guidance. I prayed; and a soft glow of ineffable joy came over me. The fever was gone, and I rose and dressed myself in a normal condition of health. Mother saw this, and was glad. The physician marveled; and the 'horrible decree' of predestination--as John Calvin rightly called his own tenet--forever lost its power over me."

Poppy roared his approval, and—from that moment on—Poppy was a believer in the power of Divine Love.

Mrs. Stetson told Poppy to close his eyes and pray with her. After a few moments of silent prayer and meditation, she breathed these words. "Thy kingdom come; let the reign of Divine Love be established in me, and rule out of me all sin; and may Thy Word enrich the affections of all mankind, and govern them."

Mrs. Stetson stood up. The treatment was over, but before Mrs. Stetson collected her hourly fee—which wasn't cheap—she cautioned Poppy about the future. "You must remain alert and on duty," she quoted a warning from Mrs. Eddy. "It is the duty of every member of this Church to defend himself daily against aggressive mental suggestion and negative animosity. You must not forget nor neglect your duty to God and to mankind."

On April 12, 1937, *TIME* carried an article titled, *Christy's Science*. In it, Poppy is quoted as saying he received his healing on Easter morning twenty-eight years ago. That would have been in 1909. "Previous to this time, I had been partially blind and numb from the knees down," Poppy said. "I had tried all kinds of cures but no help. I tried to forget through drink. The doctors said I could live but a few months." In the article, Poppy claimed that while he was receiving his treatment, "everything in the room began to clear. I could even see the color of her eyes, which were blue. It was as if a fog had lifted. I stood up and wanted to walk out in the clear air and did for a three-mile walk—bought tickets for the theater that night and actually saw the actors clearly for the first time in many months.

"That night, I read three pages of the Christian Science textbook and the next day, I went to work."

Poppy's Christian Science failed to restore his marriage, which continued to spiral downward. Fearing "aggressive mental suggestion and negative animosity" might creep back in and take his eyesight again, Poppy hired Mrs. Stetson as his resident guru.

Angry protests from Maebelle reached the ears of eager

reporters. Poppy had traded his drinking for a cult. "I pleaded that he give up this ridiculous belief and tried to awaken the old love which had made our home so happy," she is quoted as saying in the *Indianapolis Star* on November 26, 1909, "but he merely looked at me thoughtfully and in a far-away manner, as if to say 'Some time you will reach my mental level, and you will see that you are wrong.'"

Maebelle blamed Mrs. Stetson for ruining their marriage by teaching Poppy that life was spiritual, not carnal. Therefore physical marriage was wicked. Newspaper headlines read, *BLAMES STETSON'S CULT FOR TROUBLE* and *Marriage Regarded Unholy - Described as Wicked by Religious Teacher Who Says Life is Unreal.*

Poppy contended that Maebelle's toxic presence in his life had been what robbed him of his sight and almost took his life. More likely it was the wood alcohol in boot legged liquor that was responsible for Poppy's loss of sight that almost took his life.

The angrier Maebelle got, the more she drove Poppy into Mrs. Stetson's aura of Divine Love.

Maebelle was waiting for him at Bonny Brook when

Poppy walked in with his latest New York model. She called him a drunk and threatened to get the police. "But I haven't had a drink for at least two weeks," Poppy later told reporters.

Maebelle called the sheriff.

Poppy grabbed his ten-year-old daughter, Natalie, and drove out of town with the sheriff after him.

In a police chase of Model Ts, Poppy managed to pick up his sister Rose.

All three sailed for Cuba in a grand escape.

CHAPTER TWENTY-FIVE

The Barracks

"Creativity is, after all, the thing that makes us like
God."

- Francis Ford Coppola

Writer, Producer, Director

Through Mother's typewritten notes and newspaper
archives, I was getting to know Poppy, adult to adult.
Something I was deprived of through his death so early in
my life. And, well, maybe he wasn't quite the image of
godlike perfection I had imagined.

Poppy barely made it onto the boat to Cuba with a
posse in hot pursuit. It had been the Spanish-American
War that first took Poppy to Cuba, and "The Girl I Left

Behind" sung by the men aboard the transport that had inspired visions of Maebelle's sweetness. It was his illustrations of her that would catapult him to fame upon his return. Now, he was again headed for Cuba, this time to escape "The Girl I Left Behind," who had soured into a shrieking shrew. Where Poppy's illustrations of romance had been a hot sell, his true-life marital calamity was now what people clamored to buy. It sold on newsstands like the yellow journalism it was.

To escape the Sheriff Poppy's angry wife had sicced on him, Poppy barely made it onto the boat to Cuba with a posse in hot pursuit.

But where was he now?

He had disappeared.

The first Christy sighting, after his flight to Cuba, was in the blue-green hills of Duncan Falls, Ohio, where Poppy had once been a barefoot boy riding his horse and fishing in the clear waters of the Muskingum.

Reporters clamored for the story. Meekly, Poppy told them, "I have decided, on advice of my attorney, to return to New York, and I am ready to answer in court to any charges or proceedings my wife may bring against me. I do not wish a divorce, but if Maebelle so desires, I hope the matter will be adjusted in a quiet way." He then added a few more words, "I haven't drunk intoxicants for 21 months, and I am not afraid of anything that my wife may tell about me. Mrs. Christy says Natalie is not happy with me. That is untrue. She is being educated, wears good clothing and is perfectly satisfied with me."

As it turned out, the battle between Maebelle and Poppy was anything but quiet.

Even Poppy's beloved Bena was drawn into the fray, telling things only the *National Inquirer* would print today. But on January 20, 1910, her statements appeared in the *New York Times* beneath the headline: "CHRISTY GIRL HAS NO CHOICE"—a story about Poppy's daughter Natalie and her reluctance to choose between her parents.

"Bena Washington, a colored maid, formerly at the Christy home in New York, said she often saw Mrs. Christy intoxicated, and that she [Bena] often called Purdy, the chauffeur for her mistress, and that she [Bena] served drinks to both in Mrs. Christy's boudoir.

"On one occasion, the maid testified, Mrs. Christy said to her regarding Purdy: 'I'm crazy about that man. Isn't he handsome?' and 'If it were not for Natalie, I would be with him always.' She also quoted Purdy as saying: 'God only knows how much I love this woman,' referring to Mrs. Christy."

The divorce set off a series of nasty events. Maebelle sued Mrs. Stetson for wrecking her marriage, after which the Christian Science Church "deposed" Mrs. Stetson. Then Maebelle sued Poppy for custody of her daughter, Natalie.

On January 23, 1910, *The New York Times* ran an article with this headline: *Mrs. Christy Loses Child.* It was reported that because of "evidence of many dubious proceedings on the part of each of the child's parents, Probate Judge H. C. Smith this afternoon committed her [Natalie] to the care of her grandparents, Mr. And Mrs. Frank (Francis Marion) Christy at Duncan Falls." This decision was based on witnessed "improper conduct" and "intemperance" of the part of the child's mother.

"Mrs. Christy was not there for the verdict and gave no explanation for her absence, but her counsel, upon the reading of the decision, announced that she would appeal the case..."

As soon as the verdict was read, Poppy "pushed his way through the swarms of congratulating friends and scurried across the street, where Natalie was waiting in a lawyer's office.

"'Here we are, little girl,' he cried and caught her up in his arms. The two left the building together hand in hand."

I am reading these words from *Newspaper Archives* on my computer—something that was not possible until recently—and yet, one hundred years later, it reminds me of how wonderful it was to be Poppy's "little girl."

The judgment of the court was a grand win for Poppy, who set to work building what he called "The Barracks "in memory of the camaraderie he had enjoyed with the Rough Riders. Poppy hired the best carpenters in town and had them camp out on his land. The site was a high bluff overlooking the Muskingum River, as recounted in Mother's journal. Every morning, at the crack of dawn, Poppy roused the men for work by playing taps on his bugle. "The Barracks was built without a blueprint," he said. "I just invented my own ideas."

It was a familiar story. One I had personally witnessed when Poppy renovated the Old Red Mill and built the veranda overlooking the Mettowee.

First came The Barracks barn, which would be

Poppy's studio.

"Sometimes I just guessed how long to cut the boards only later to find in measuring it that it was exactly right," Poppy said. "The workers could work faster with my clear directions and with less waste. I'd just make a sketch to explain how I wanted the finished product to look. This amazed the eight carpenters.

"It took a year to complete my beautiful new barn. A little bridge was the means of entering the second floor, and the door on the lower floor in the back opened out onto a long balcony on a high precipice overlooking the Muskingum river. Oh, it was grand. From the balcony, you could see the steamboats plow up and down the river. These steamboats would blow and whistle as they drew opposite The Barracks, and the band aboard would strike up a Sousa march just for me. To reciprocate, I'd dip the American Flag from the eighty-foot pole. Atop the pole was a gold eagle with a wingspan three feet across."

The barn was Poppy's domain. For his parents, Poppy build a beautiful rambling house as part of The Barracks compound. It must have been enormous because, in Mother's journal, she wrote, "It had many columns and seventy-five windows." It, too, was built without blueprints. True to his love of rustic comfort, Poppy built six outdoor fireplaces as well as big stone hearths inside the house.

"Later, I built a sunporch just for my parents," Poppy said. "It had a large stone fireplace so they could enjoy the outdoor scenery all year round. I built it out of devotion to my mother. I wanted to do everything I could to make my parents happy. At first, they didn't want that porch. Said they enjoyed The Barracks just the way it was. But Mother did enjoy the change after a bit and remarked, 'The sun porch is nice.'

"There was activity about the place and sunlight and joy. It had the feeling of a real home. The long grape arbors connected the two houses, creating a tunnel effect and from the porch, right up between the large pillars, hung a very large iron lamp which illuminated the early evening and night, casting a pleasant light across the green grass and trees. Of trees, there were many. Birch. Fruit. Spruce. And an apple tree which I planted myself.

"We had many pets, and in the evenings, when supper was over, we'd all sit out on the lawn 'till the last ray of light disappeared over the horizon watching the Belgium hares, the yellow and red squirrels and dogs play together.

Oh, yes, there were raccoons, too and peacocks strutting about. There were also about fourteen pigeons which, if called, would alight on my arm.

"I loved my family. But I felt especially sorry for my sister Hope. She came to me once in tears. Said she had failed in a subject at school and wanted more than anything to be a school teacher. I told her not to worry and that it was all probably for the best because I'd heard someone say Oberlin College was the best and I would send her there, which I did. Later, I helped her get a job in the Government Tax Department with my old friend, President Harding's assistance."

Mother's journal had captured Poppy's voice. As I read it, I felt as if he was right there with me, telling me all about the things that happened there the way he had when I was a child.

"Hope had a lot of boyfriends," Poppy said of his sister. "And my mother, well, she had a vivid imagination. So, every time Hope went out of sight, my mother would reach over and ring the damn dinner bell as hard as she could. I'd laugh out loud. I knew what she was doing. Then I'd call out to her, "Now, Mother!""

"I'll bet your mother didn't do that to you. And by the

way, Hope isn't going to hear you way down there in Gaysport where she's going."

"Mother very often didn't have success with that dinner bell because she told me one day that she rang it and Dad didn't answer it. I asked her why and she said, 'He was thinking she's not calling me for dinner. She wants me to haul a bucket of water.'

"How do you know that's what he was thinking?" I asked.

"Cause he admitted it later."

"That evening, I asked my Dad how he knew Mother wanted him to fetch a bucket of water. He said, "I could tell by the way she rang it. Hard. Like she was calling me to work."

Apparently, the water for drinking at The Barracks was gotten the same way we got our water at The Old Red Mill. By hauling it back in buckets from a spring.

"There was so much of it," Poppy said about the spring water. "We could fill the swimming pool with it, and it was still overflowing with ice-cold water. That pool felt good. But Oh, was it cold! But after a good day's work, it was mighty welcome."

It was at The Barracks that Poppy had a large order of illustrations for Sir Walter Scott's, *The Lady of the Lake,* and Alfred Lord Tennyson's *The Princess,* which would require a model who would be willing to live at The Barracks until he finished. So he went to New York to find a girl to "work with him" on the books, as he put it.

Mother didn't shrink from transcribing Poppy's stories about his models, one of which was a French girl named Jeslain.

"I went over to Mrs. Brown's home where this girl, Jeslain, was living to find out if she could go to Ohio to pose. Jeslain was French and spoke very little English, but Mrs. Brown agreed, and Jeslain was tickled with the idea. I told Jeslain to be ready at 6 a.m. the next morning to leave. That's when her face dropped. She gave a heavy sigh and told me it was too soon. She had no trunk and nothing to put in it, for the Chinaman wouldn't have her clothes ready at the laundry. I told her, 'Never mind. You come with me,' and I bought her a whole new wardrobe with a brand new trunk to put it in."

She stayed at The Barracks as Poppy's model for two years. But when she first arrived, they had some trouble understanding one another because she spoke very little

English and that with a heavy French accent.

"Sometimes I couldn't understand a damn thing she said. She sure as hell didn't understand me either, but it got better with time as she began reading my sign language and expressions.

"After she settled down in the house with my family, each day, for several days in succession, she would run down the hill at about four o'clock in the afternoon when the steamboat was due to come down the river. I got very curious. One day I asked her why she was doing this, and she answered me in French. By this time, I could get the gist of what she was saying. I could even speak a little French. 'Well, I sent away for something at Montgomery Ward that cost two dollars.

"I explained to her, 'You can't expect to get it this soon. It has to come all the way from Chicago.' She finally received the package. It was a pair of sandals.

"When I asked her why she wanted a pair of sandals, she told me it was so she could look like a Greek goddess. Oh, I got such fun out of her girlish dreams. There were lots of them like that, but my family, well, they just missed out on it all. Hope was not very nice to her, but Dad, he was a good sport. He liked her. He was the only one who did.

"Jeslain was thrifty with her money. She'd buy a dress and then ask me in her snappy way, 'How much you think I pay?' After guessing very high, she exclaimed triumphantly, 'One dollar, forty-nine cents!'

"Oh, I had lots of models back then, and they all enjoyed posing, but the one who enjoyed it the most was Jeslain. She was herself artistic. I think that was why.

"That Jeslain. She was such a character. One time she was putting on perfume upstairs and accidentally spilled the whole bottle on the floor. She came running downstairs all in a tizzy to find me catching it with my hands as it seeped through the ceiling and rubbing it all over myself. She stopped. Gave me one of her looks, tossed back her head and snapped, 'You owe me *exactly* one dollar ninety-eight cents!'"

"One day, while I was walking down the street, I passed this little shop with canaries in the window. I stopped to look. There they were in their little wooden cages. It made me so mad I marched right in and bought the whole kit and caboodle of them. Took 'em back to The Barracks and let them fly free. Why hell, those birds were so glad to get out of those damned cages. They just sang to beat the band. I fed them, and they hung around, flying in and out of my studio at random.

"I asked Jeslain if she wouldn't like to feed them. She got so she really enjoyed calling them out of the rose bushes. They'd fly over to her and alight on her arm and shoulder. There were quite a few because every time I came across another bird in a cage, I bought him and set him free. Jeslain would cry if there was one missing. She really loved those birds.

"In winter, inside the studio, these birds would swoop down between me and my canvas while I was painting. It was like a game with them to see if they could make it. Then they'd perch in a row along the top of the canvas and watch me work."

Poppy incorporated his love of Nature into all his art. He preferred to be outdoors and was very brown from the sun, coming inside only to paint, which he did for four hours a day.

"One day, quite a few women visited the studio," Poppy said. "In fact, visitors were always welcome on an equal basis—refreshments included for all and often day parties came with their lunches, and when they left, there would not be a speck of paper left to mar the landscape."

One thing Poppy wouldn't stand for was "marring the landscape." God forbid he catch someone tossing a bottle in the bushes. There'd be hell to pay.

Poppy instilled in me our stewardship of the Earth. That its beauty was proof of God's love, and it was "our job to keep it that way."

"But to get back to these women visitors," as Mother quoted Poppy saying in her journal. "They gibbered a lot in high-pitched voices. But one of them had a voice that sounded like a bass drum. No one even noticed Polly the parrot all this time, she was so quiet. But after the ladies left, Polly started in with all this high-pitched gibber, then suddenly burst out with a bass voice. Dad heard it, and it struck him so funny. He really had a good laugh over it.

"That parrot was then thirty years old and had the distinguished reputation as a wise but ornery old bird. Sometimes guests would stay too long at The Barracks. Finally, after many goodbyes and the last visitor had left, I'd sing out, 'Goodbye, goodbye, goodbye, for Christ's sake.' Polly picked this right up, and you can imagine my embarrassment when she used it on visitors.

"One day, I heard Polly call out, 'Give me ma' coffee'. Bena whirled around and laughed with her hands on her hips. 'Now what do yo' think o' dat?' she said with a big grin, but I suspected she'd taught him that. Then one day, Polly was missing for two days. The whole household was searching for him all the way to the edge of the woods and back many times. It was Bena who came running in, yelling that she'd found him. How'd you find him? I asked, 'I heard him calling 'Howard, telephone!' Howard telephone!' from the direction of the woods. Well, Polly was out on a limb swaying over the precipice that dropped into the Muskingum River. I called, 'Come on down, I can't go out and get you,' but, as it turned out, I had to, and when I picked her up, she bit me terribly all the while, she answered, 'All right, all right.'

"That bird was so comical, but when I had to leave her with my parents and return to New York years later, she never talked again."

Wherever Poppy went, his love of animals and the environment created beauty and happiness.

For that, I will always love him.

* * *

Poppy also hired male models, one of which was a young man named Raymond Crumbaker, who said he was a bit scared when he first went to pose for Poppy at his Muskingum studio. "But when I got to The Barracks and met Howard's mother [Mrs. Mary Matilda Chandler Christy] everything was fine. She was a wonderful person," he said as quoted in the July 18, 1971 full-page article that appeared in the Zanesville *Sunday Times Recorder* in which an interview with Crumbaker, a Duncan Falls native, appeared. His paternal grandfather had been Poppy's doctor. His maternal grandfather, Skelton Waxler, had been Poppy's blacksmith.

Crumbaker told how he had been tutored by Poppy's two sisters, Rose and Hope, Poppy's daughter Natalie, and Nancy Palmer—who would later become Poppy's wife. They all pitched in, and when the young Crumbaker went back to school, he was "way ahead of his class." He told how he would sometimes get bored posing for Poppy and would sneak off and go fishing. "Howard was very exacting about posing on time and wanted to work when the light was just right. He could be stern... but he was never unkind." Once Poppy had his sister fire a canon to liven Crumbaker up.

"Poppy always road around in a horse-drawn buggy," Crumbaker said. "There were lots of models that would live at The Barracks for months at a time. At Christmas, Poppy would play Claus "heaping presents" on everyone.

"Howard was so kind that when he wanted me to look angry for a pose, he would have someone else needle me. He wouldn't do it."

As I read Crumbaker's account of what a strong swimmer Poppy was, it was exactly the way I remembered him. I could just see him swimming the Muskingum river every day after he'd gotten through with his work. I could see him stripping down, tying his clothes into a bundle and putting it on his head as he swam to Philo to catch the train. That was something Poppy would do.

But all was not perfect at The Barracks. There was a stigma attached to illustrations that Poppy didn't like. He had always wanted to be a fine arts painter. It was Nancy, one of his models at The Barracks, who encouraged him to give up illustration and follow his dream.

When Poppy was clearing out The Barracks to move back to New York, he told the young Crumbaker and another boy to take what they wanted of his paintings and to pile the rest in the middle of the driveway. This they did. Poppy lit a match, and a "great number of originals disappeared" into the fire and smoke of the bonfire.

"I knew him as a warm, kind human being," Crumbaker said.

CHAPTER TWENTY-SIX

Nanna Knows Best

"Beauty quickens. It adrenalizes. It makes the heart beat faster. It makes life more vivid, animated, living, worth living."

- On Beauty by Elaine Scarry

No mother wants to see her daughter suffer. And neither did Nanna. So, when she was faced with raising her youngest child, Elise, through grievous times, she hatched a plan to lift the young woman, who would become my mother, above the struggling masses that were facing ordeals, the likes of which none of us has had to face today.

What started out as nothing more than a happy family gathered around Nanna at her piano led to Nanna's recognition of Mother's talent for voice. In an effort to develop her daughter's talent, Nanna enrolled Elise in New York's Alviene Academy, which was responsible for Fred Astaire's fame. By the age of ten, Mother was already appearing on the New York and New Jersey stage as an Irish street urchin, impersonating a boy. She did a solo skit in which she tap danced, sang and told jokes with a cigar clenched between her teeth. When my daughter heard that, she exclaimed, "She smoked a cigar?" I assured her it was fake, that Mother never smoked, nor did she drink. Her naturally blithe spirit made it unnecessary to seek artificial means. With Nanna acting as a stage mom, it wasn't long before Mother was winning acting awards. To all appearances, she was heading for stardom. A letter from a producer at Paramount Pictures reads:

My Dear Little Friend, I received the two photographs of you which are exceptionally fine, also the newspaper article which is very interesting and describes you as I know you are. Some of these days I anticipate you being a screen star and think that if you keep up your practice and persist in your endeavors you will finally accomplish what you most wish. My kindest regards to your mother."

The letter was written when Mother was about ten because it was addressed to her parents' home in Mountain View, New Jersey. As usual, Mother tore the date off the upper right side of the page so no one would ever be able to determine her age.

Two years after Mother's birth, Margaret Sanger fell victim to the Comstock Act. She was arrested for publishing *Women Rebel* in 1914. As with Ida Craddock's *Wedding Night*, Sanger's book was deemed obscene. Rather than face 45 years in prison, Sanger escaped to Europe. Before leaving, she printed *Family Limitation*, a pamphlet that told everything she knew about birth control. In it, she committed the unpardonable sin. She called a satisfying sex life "health-giving" to both males and females and birth control as female liberation from sexual slavery.

In 1915, Anthony Comstock died. Perhaps his death had something to do with Poppy and Nancy, his then-common-law wife, moving back to New York in that same year. They were among the first tenants to move into the newly constructed Hotel des Artistes—an ornately carved, castle-like structure with menacing gargoyles keeping vigil above its iron gate.

Poppy remained legally separated from Maebelle for ten more years. Because divorce was illegal in New York, this made Poppy an adulterer, a distinction he managed to retain without incident.

These were contentious times. "Comstockery," a term coined by British philosopher and social critic, Bertrand Russel, was a serious threat long after its namesake died, especially from those fomenting change, such as Poppy, who saw all of God's creation, including the human body, worthy of celebration. Not shame.

When World War I broke out, Poppy raised more money for the war effort than anyone else by painting posters such as *Fight or Buy Bonds*. This he did free of charge, auctioning them off at rallies to the highest bidder. It was at one of these rallies in New York City that people suddenly fell ill. Strong, young men and healthy children turned purple and oozed bloody foam from their eyes and nostrils. Within hours, they were dead. No one had ever seen anything like it. At first, it was thought to be a new form of German biological warfare. Then came the horrific news: a worldwide epidemic. No one dared leave their house. Those who did venture out wore face masks. In

New York, a heavy fine was levied on anyone who didn't. Streets became deserted.

Mother was just four years old when the Flu Pandemic of 1918 struck. It killed far more people than the Black Death and World War I put together. An estimated 20 to 40 million people died worldwide. By comparison, the war only killed 9 million. The flu had a profound effect on its survivors. Watching bodies being carted away in wagons to be buried in mass graves must have made Nanna and Poppy think *life's too short. If I make it through this, I'm going to live life to the fullest.* I suspect Nanna made a life decision, one which would eventually affect Mother and me.

In 1919, immediately following the Flu Pandemic, Poppy married Nancy Palmer. Nancy's close friend, Jocelyn, tells me that it was right after he got word that Maebelle, who had finally divorced him, remarried. "Well, everyone else is getting married," Poppy told Nancy. "We might as well get married too."

Major social changes followed the end of World War I and the Flu Pandemic. The '20s became the Age of Decadence. Women cut their hair, hiked up their skirts, wrenched themselves out of their straight-laced corsets and shimmied onto the dance floor, kicking up their heels to the Charleston. Freedom was in the air. But it didn't last long. In 1920, a constitutional amendment made Prohibition the law of the land. Saloons were shut down.

Prohibition didn't faze Poppy. He had given up booze for Christian Science. He gave up smoking after I was born but never did give up coffee, a habit frowned upon in Christian Science.

As for Oma, my great-grandmother, she rebelled. No silly American law was going to keep her from enjoying her favorite German beverage. Uncle Jim told me she set up a brewery in her closet. One day, the bottles exploded-blowing the door off.

In 1921, women finally got the right to vote. Mother was nine years old. States in which women had organized for Prohibition were the first to grant women suffrage. At least something praiseworthy came out of all the fuss and fury. That same year, Poppy officiated in the first Miss America contest, which I saw recently for a brief TV second in a documentary. He looked just as Norman Rockwell had described him: wearing a white suit and a white Stetson. As usual, he was as happy as could be.

Women may have gotten the right to vote, but in no

way were they considered equal to men. The only respectable jobs open to them were waitress, hairdresser, secretary or schoolteacher. And those—only if you were Christian. Nanna saw Vaudeville as Mother's ticket to freedom. Besides, an actress had a better chance of snagging a successful man. Women who took to the stage were called Gold Diggers, but epithets never stopped Nanna. It was Nanna who led Mother onto the stage, and it was Nanna who took Mother to Poppy's studio. When it came to promoting Mother's success, Nanna pursued every avenue. In that day and age, modeling for Christy was great publicity. He was, after all, considered the American connoisseur of beauty and the sole judge of the first Miss America contest.

Nanna focused all her attention on Mother. By this time, Nanna's oldest daughter, Audrey, had married Jim, a fireman. As for Doris, she showed no interest in anything other than primping in front of the mirror, a habit which eventually transformed her from a gangly kid with sawed-off bangs into the seductive glamor queen she became. Adele Forsberg, my uncle Carl's wife, told me they used to call Doris "Dodo." I suspect it was because Doris showed no interest in anything other than flaunting herself around as if she thought she was a movie star.

By contrast, Poppy saw beauty as strength. He never could tolerate the notion that women were dumb and frail, not after growing up with a pioneer mother in Ohio. It seems Nanna must have been catering to Poppy's praise of strong women when she put together Mother's portfolio. Why else would she create a collage of photographs of Mother dressed as a boy, playing sports with boys and rolling down a hill in a hoop? What was she trying to prove? That a girl could do anything a boy could do and better? If so, she hit a chord with Poppy.

Mother was quite an athlete. I remember seeing rows of gold and bronze medals encased under glass. She once told me she had earned them in athletic competitions with boys. Women didn't play sports in those days, so Mother cut her hair short and wore boy's clothes to compete. I don't know what happened to those medals. Maybe they were buried beneath Doris and Wanda's garage when it finally caved in beneath a tangle of weeds.

Nanna knew that posing for Poppy would further Mother's career by placing her picture on the covers of major magazines. It was the best way to become noticed. And—as any stage mom knows—getting noticed is the key to success in the world of entertainment.

As for *Nude with Cat*, it's unlikely that Mother posed for that picture without both Nanna and Nancy present. According to Olga Steckler and Judy Thomas, Poppy's two models with whom I spoke personally, it would have been out of character for Poppy to have done otherwise.

The human form was starting to reclaim its rightful place as a worthy subject in art. Women were emerging from their cultural closet of shame. No wonder Poppy repeatedly warned me, "Never let anyone make you ashamed you're a woman." He'd heard enough about shame from Comstock.

In 1927, at the invitation of Benito Mussolini, Poppy and Nancy sailed for Europe on the USS *Leviathan*. I doubt if Poppy would have gone had he known there was an attack on art going on in Rome. Mussolini's best friend and co-conspirator, Marinetti, had already begun riling up the masses against the beauty in classical art by convincing them that it was the means by which the rich deluded them into thinking life was good. Under Il Duce's regime, realistic art was banned, but — when it came to immortalizing his own image — Mussolini chose not to be depicted as a blockhead by some cubist. He chose Poppy as his artist.

When Poppy got to Rome, Mussolini had been in control for five years. While Poppy was Mussolini's guest, it's quite likely Poppy met Marinetti, architect/designer T. H. Robsjohn-Gibbings describes as "...aggressive and pretentious, and masculine to the point of overacting. [H]e strutted and ranted his aesthetic doctrines like a major leading himself. Wearing gigantic goggles and driving an enormous white racing car with glittering exhaust pipes, he could be seen behind a cloud of dust speeding between Paris, Rome, and Milan."

I imagine Marinetti, with his narrow-eyed, down-in-the-mouth, I'm-so-macho glower brandishing his contempt for everything Poppy loved most—freedom and beauty. Marinetti's "advent-garde" was nothing more than an anti-intellectual movement that called for the banishment of all skill and quality in art and turned culture on its head. Ugliness was in. Beauty was out. Graffiti was praised as depicting the rage of discontent.

In spite of Marinetti's hatred of fine art, Poppy was welcomed as a celebrity not only by Premier Mussolini but Prince Victor Emmanuel, Crown Prince Umberto and Prince Philippe of Hesse. But Poppy must have sensed something sinister was going on. The tension around him must have been great. Perhaps this is why he fell off the wagon and broke his Christian Science vow to never take another drink. One night, he got so drunk he forgot where he was and stumbled down the spiral staircase of Crown Prince Umberto's palace, stark naked. This is something Nancy confided in Jocelyn, her next-door neighbor. And Jocelyn told me. "You know," she said, "Winston Churchill did that too?"

Poppy never told me about his getting drunk. But he did tell me that he and Nancy had to dress up to see Mussolini. I don't remember if Poppy said Mussolini was sitting on a throne or not, but that's the way I visualized it, the way Poppy looked on his frayed, red-velvet throne when he told me this story.

"I bowed the way I was supposed to," Poppy told me with a mischievous grin. "Nancy lifted her skirt and gave him a low curtsy. As she bent over, she let one fly under all those crinolines." The joke was on Nancy, and Poppy and I laughed till my ribs hurt.

A few years ago, I met an eighty-year-old relative of Poppy's in Indiana, Mary Bone. Mary told me how much she loved to visit Poppy at The Barracks, but when she tried to visit him in New York, Nancy told her he was busy. "She dropped a few famous names of people he was supposed to see," Mary told me. "She made me feel like I was just a country girl. That was the last time I ever tried to see Uncle Howard. If he had answered the phone, it would have been a whole different story. He would have said, 'Well, I'll be damned. Come on up.' But Nancy... well, let's just say she was a name dropper."

And there certainly were plenty of names to drop. Crown Prince Umberto sat for Poppy in the Palace at Turin with a retinue of attendants clad in long red coats, but the thing that impressed Poppy most was the Prince's interest in all things American. While Poppy painted, the Prince sang Stephen Foster songs and talked about stories he had read by Mark Twain.

Twenty years later, Poppy told Mother, "While I was in Italy, I carried a camera with me and took pictures all over the place—of troop movements, buildings, Fascist gatherings—and Mussolini just said, 'Go ahead, take whatever you like.'" Poppy confessed to Mother that he actually liked Mussolini. They had some good laughs.

When Mussolini saw Poppy's finished painting, he said, "This is the best portrait ever done of me." Mussolini then gave Poppy a bronze bust of himself as a gift to take back to America. Poppy placed it on his grand piano, and there it stayed, next to where Winky ate his canned fish––until Poppy's death in 1952.

After Italy, Poppy and Nancy went to France. The smell of freshly turned sod and the picturesque beauty of the fertile valleys in Normandy must have been a welcome respite from all the pomp and ceremony. Poppy loved Normandy almost as much as he loved his Ohio homestead. "Of course, you would love Normandy," Nancy told him. "This is where the Chandlers in your family are from."

While in Normandy, Poppy saw his Coat of Arms. He later described it to Mother. "It is unlike any other coat of arms I have seen as it stresses the strength of the feminine rather than the masculine. A steel gauntlet symbolizing strength is combined with a mother swan plucking the meat from her breast to feed her young. The inscription read, 'Faithful unto Death.' Up on the left-hand corner was a single rose."

Before returning to the United States, Poppy and Nancy were received by Queen Marie of Romania at her spectacular Peles Castle on the steep, forested slopes of the

Bucegi Mountains in Sinaia. Queen Marie must have been a kind soul. She believed there was far more sorrow in the world than wickedness, and—if only we could come to understand this—perhaps we would be kinder to one another. She begged Poppy to stay at her castle and paint portraits of young King Michael and other members of the royal family, but Poppy didn't want to stay any longer. He told the queen he wanted to go home. "You see," he explained to Mother years later, "Over there, it's like this. They consider an artist above royalty. But the queen understood. If there's anything they dislike, it's an American who tries to act like them."

To European royalty, Poppy was another Benjamin Franklin. They loved him as another "rustic American."

In 1931, after Poppy returned home to his Hotel des Artistes, a little boy named Honnie came down for breakfast one morning to find his parents dead. The murder of his mother and the suicide of his father left Honnie an orphan. One more tragedy of the Great Depression. Poppy took the little boy in and sent him to a private school. When I overheard Poppy tell Mother this story, it left me wondering if I was another orphan like Honnie that Poppy had taken under his wing.

Poppy wasn't famous for his finesse. Nanna alludes to this in a letter she wrote to Mother about a radio broadcast in which Mother and Poppy were interviewed together. "Dear Elise, Well, I'm glad the broadcast is over. I know one thing, I couldn't take you by the hand... the way I did years ago. I was never nervous, but just took it as a part of my life, I guess. ... Dad sat there and wept as usual. Also wept when he heard Mr. Christy. You know Dad is that way, and you can't change him. But Mr. Christy did better than he ever did before on the radio, and it was so natural and interesting too."

In a world fraught with peril, Nanna and Papa saw Howard Chandler Christy as their daughter's savior. And that was cause for tears of joy.

On August 5, 1945, Nancy Palmer Christy gave this statement for a full-page article on her famous husband in the *Zanesville, Ohio, Sunday Times-Signal.*

"He has the most marvelous personality in the world. He is an ideal person to live with because he is always good-natured, and what temperament he has, he puts on canvas."

CHAPTER TWENTY-SEVEN

The Promise

"Life is mean and petty to most people, because they
lack the artistic instinct".

- Elbert Hubbard

I ignored it at first. It was too cryptic to understand.
Then, one day, I took another look at the note Poppy had
written to Mother in 1938. It didn't make sense. But, if it
didn't make sense, why did Mother carefully paste it into
her gold-leaf, gilded scrapbook that I found in her grey,
tin file box? In reading it again, I saw something that was
meant for Mother's eyes only. And it sent me into a frenzy.

I called my now-grown daughter in Palos Verdes,

California. By then, Christina was the mother of two boys and a baby girl she'd named Elise after Mother.

"Mom! What's wrong? You sound very upset," she said when she heard the anguish in my voice. "Are you alright?"

"It's one thing to lie about your own age," I said, "Quite another to lie about mine!"

"What are you talking about?"

"Christina, I'm older than I thought."

"What? How do you know that?"

"Just listen to this note Poppy wrote to Mother. 'If I could find words to express to God the gratitude swelling within. Of the glorious vistas which offer to view. And the door which shuts out all evil. There I would give thanks for the joy in life. And <u>Thy</u> <u>will</u>, <u>not theirs,</u> be my prayer. Though I find not the words—God understands. Love filleth all space. Everywhere.'"

"What's wrong with that?" asked Christina.

"I'm not finished. At the bottom, he writes this little afterthought: 'Dear Elise, Something I thought of in the train coming down. Love to you&Holly, Poppy.' Christina, it's dated July 26, 1939! I wasn't even born yet."

"Oh."

"Mother must have lied about my age on my birth certificate. It was filled out a year after I was born. It says so right on the certificate."

"Mom, why would she do that? It would mess you up in school. I really don't think a mother would go that far."

"Why not? She lied about everything else!"

"So what if she did? What's one more year?"

"What? That would mean I'm sixty!" I ranted on about how Mother only thought of herself.

"Mom. Is this the first time you've seen this note?"

"No."

"So why is it such a big deal now?"

"Because I could never read what it said before. Poppy's scrawl is awful. Then, just now, as I was looking at it, the words popped out at me, clear as day."

Being a thoughtful, insightful woman, Christina contemplated the matter and then got excited. "Mom, Mom! Don't you see?"

"See what?"

"Poppy named you before you were born. The way

you did with me, and I did with Elise." She asked me to read the part about *Thy will be done* again, and I described exactly how Poppy wrote it in detail. I told her he had underlined <u>*Thy*</u> <u>*will,*</u> <u>*not*</u> <u>*theirs*</u> ... Again, I read, "Though I find not the words—God understands. Love filleth all space. Everywhere."

"Mom! Don't you see? He's talking about you in your mother's womb. *Love filleth all space.* She was five months pregnant!"

"Wait a minute," I said, noticing something I'd missed before. "I see something I totally missed."

"What is it?"

"The 'you&Holly' are joined with an ampersand. No spaces between."

"Oh, Mom. Somebody must have been telling her to get rid of you—maybe get an abortion or give you up for adoption. Don't you see? *Thy will, not theirs, be my prayer.*"

I remembered my Uncle Jim's words. "She threw her life away on the old goat." *Yes. Uncle Jim was one of the first people to know. He probably told Mother to get an abortion.*

"You think so?" I asked my counselor daughter.

"I know so," Christina assured me. "Think about it. Poppy refers to the *door which shuts out all evil*. He's talking about her womb. Then he gives thanks for the *joy in life*.

That "joy" in "life" is you. They wanted a little girl just like you wanted me, and I wanted my third child to be a little girl too. But your mother was scared. Mom, he is reassuring her that everything will be alright. He's promising her *glorious vistas* ahead. And it was the truth. Have you forgotten the Old Red Mill?"

The year was 2000. My granddaughter, Elise, was a year old, a beautiful child with blond hair and big blue eyes. Christina had given up a career as a bank administrator to become a stay-at-home mom, something she never regretted.

"Your mother didn't lie about your age."

***

After sorting through the many things in Mother's file box, there remained a gaping hole in my past. One only Mother's voice could fill. Try as I might, I could not remember her voice. Only the silence. Nor could I conceive of how she might have acted in certain circumstances— especially when she was alone with Poppy. I began to wonder if she really loved him. He was, after all, forty years her senior. There remained many unanswered questions. I knew so much about Poppy and almost nothing about Mother. This bothered me, especially when Christina asked me if I thought my mother was happy with the life she'd chosen for herself.

Then, what seemed like a miracle happened.

I got an email from Elaine Stomber, Project Archivist for the Skillman Library at Lafayette College in Easton, Pennsylvania. After Nancy's death, all Poppy's things—left over after the auction—were donated to the library by the family of Nancy's late husband, Robert Coneen. Elaine had found a cardboard box marked "Elise" among Poppy's possessions.

Elaine's email read, "There are photographs of your mother throughout, and I'm sure you'll enjoy looking at this material as well. Quite a few of the letters are undated, but if you read them, you may be able to help us date them. ...I know how important it must be for you to see these letters." She said she would send photocopies of everything.

Her message brought sobs of joy. Until that moment, I did not realize how much I missed Mother and how much

I wished I'd gotten to know her better. The sound of her voice. Her laughter and her cheery whistle while she painted. Eagerly I awaited Mother's letters, feeling as if her spirit was returning to fill the void left by so many years of silence.

The manila envelope arrived a few days later. I tore it open and read the cover letter—dated November 2, 2000—from Elaine.

"Dear Holly, It gives me great pleasure to enclose photocopies of the Elise Ford letters to Howard Chandler Christy..." I turned the page and saw Mother's sketch of Cupid with a paintbrush and palette. On his canvas, Mother had written a poem. Her voice resonated in my ears as I read it.

"I've heard say, On Valentines Day, we send our wishes True. So here is mine, And I just say I Love you! And what you Do."

Mother came alive. And years of anger fell away at hearing it.

I came to realize I'd missed her happy, playful spirit. And now, her own written words had brought her back. The letters that had dates were written between 1936 and 1937. All were sent—strangely enough—from Poppy's studio in the Hotel des Artistes while he was in Washington, D.C., trying to get a bill passed through Congress that would commission him to paint *The Scene of the Signing of the Constitution*. The bill took three years to pass. Meanwhile, Mother, who was Poppy's protégée— used Poppy's studio to paint her own portraits.

But where was Nancy?

The letters tell the story.

July 24, 1936. Mother is twenty-four years old. Poppy is sixty-four. "Dear 'Poppy,'" writes Mother with Poppy in quotes. "So happy after reading your letter. I read it over and over. ...You're the only one that understands. I miss you so and will be so glad to see you. How could you finish a portrait in so short a time?" Mother is copying a portrait of the Pope by Diego Velasquez. "Yesterday, worked hard all day long on the Pope. Thought all the while, if he could have seen it, he would have turned over in his grave. First he looked like a Chinaman. Then all he needed was a knife between his teeth and he would have taken a prize as a pirate. Then all night long, I dreamed of mixing paint for the highlight on his nose. Almost lost interest in him, but am determined to get him now. I think him a most magnificent type and almost fell in love with the bird. It's interesting to see where Velasquez loses the form, then accented it in other places. It's hard to feel the form, isn't it? ...

"..Loved your letter so—read it over and over. Can't help think how good you are and tonight I saw a photo of you at Bena's which only made my longing to see you stronger."

Bena? I knew Bena. Or at least I felt like I did after hearing so much about her from Poppy. I pictured Bena—Poppy's trusted friend for thirty-seven years—looking like Margaret with natty, grey hair pulled back in a bun. Apparently, Bena and Mother became close friends because Mother writes, "Wanted to look at some cars. Bena didn't want me to go alone, so she went with me. ...Saw a wonderful car. $335. However, you can see."

I found myself wondering if this was the Studebaker—that dictator sedan—we rode in during our many trips to the country. In the next letter, Mother writes about another car she and Bena found for $330. And I wonder if Nancy—Poppy's wife—knows what they've been up to. Mother refers to Bena often, divulging secrets only the three of them know. Little by little, Mother's letters fill me in with the details of her life.

February of 1937. Poppy is still in Washington, D.C., and Mother is still using his studio while he is gone. She has now completed three life-size portraits. One of Poppy's black maid, Callie; a black man named George and a copy of Velasquez's Pope. Mother is eager to show Poppy her accomplishments. "Enclosed are some pictures we took of Callie and Geo's pictures and the one of the Pope."

I turn the page and find photocopies of the portraits. Mother is sitting in front of the painting of George with her paintbrush and palette in hand. I'm dazzled by her beauty. And the images on the canvas are so lifelike. I remembered seeing those pictures tucked in the back of our studio on 54 W. 74th Street.

"I just laid him in in ½ day and tomorrow he will be all dried up so I can work all day," writes Mother about George's picture. "I know he's all wrong now, but this is just to show you what we've been doing. I did old Geo's in ½ day too—but Callie's 2 as she would fall asleep on me. I told her to keep the lights in her eyes up long enough for me to paint them.

"Wink and Scoot are just fine, and when I first went in, I called 'Wink?' and he answered me on his way down the stairs to see me."

Winky! I knew who that was. But Scoot? *Oh, that must be the Fox Terrier the magazine interviewer talked about.* I read on. "Winky's so sweet and when he wakes up from his nap, he cries like the Devil till someone picks him up and pets him. I tried to paint him today. Coaxed him to sit for me. Propped him up with a pillow then he'd stay a while longer. Just got his head in. That's all he'd stand for.

"Bena posed all day for me." I pictured Bena's pleasant, round face. "A fly kept wanting to stay on my arm and old Bena said, 'Someone wants to see you.'"

I chuckled. "Old" Bena sure knew what was going on. I felt as if I was right there watching everything that was going on.

"Every time I paint, a thought of thanks goes up to you for those brushes. They're great!

I miss you!!! Always, Your Side Kick."

Mother adds an afterthought about Poppy's portrait commissions in Washington. "I'll bet your portraits are just beautiful!" I realize that this is probably when Poppy was commissioned by President Roosevelt to paint his presidential cabinet.

As I read each letter, I relived my childhood, listening to Mother and Poppy talk. Mother's voice was exuberant. Filled with the joy of life and zeal to capture its beauty on canvas.

"Dear Poppy, Couldn't wait till tonight to tell you how happy I am, and when you're happy you want someone to share it with. Finished Callie this morn. And did a head of Geo. This aft. I've been so happy painting away and the music on the radio was so beautiful and being there in your studio—It is all so great!

"Why—for a minute—I thought I was a great artist. And when a man on the radio—while speaking about great musicians—said, 'Genius belongs to everyone,' I almost signed my life away right then and there.

"You're so wonderful. How can I ever repay you? But if good thoughts can do any good—you're walking on air right now and always.

"Guess there'll be a letter from you tomorrow. Hope so. Anyway, if it goes home, Mom will forward it."

Was Mother actually living at Poppy's studio? Another letter answered my question. She is staying at Doris' place on Central Park South, walking distance from the Hotel des Artistes.

Mother's letters disclosed an abiding love for art and the man who had taught her how to paint. Painting was her dream. Nothing else mattered.

"Dec. 13, 1937. ...Bena comes tomorrow. What a thrill! We talk about you from morning till night about how good you are. Mom says she never knew a man so good and wonderful.

I wasn't surprised to hear that Nanna approved of Mother's relationship with Poppy. "Thanks so much for that darling poem," Mother tells Poppy. "It's just beautiful and I just love it. I read it to Doris just to make her jealous and show her Taddy up. She thought it was so cute. I said her Taddy couldn't write her poetry like that, and she said, 'Oh, well. Not everybody can write poetry.' It thrilled me with the thought of how many attributes you really have. I love all those poems and will paste them in that beautiful book."

Ah ha! So there was *competition between Mother and Doris—with their two world-famous artists.*

"Tomorrow Bena will talk her head off about how wonderful 'you is', and 'how good you was' to her when she was sick, and how she could ask you anything about the Bible and you could answer it, and she's just going to make me miss you more."

The more I read, the more vivid Mother became in my memory. Her enthusiasm for life and its expression through art, each painting an offering of gratitude to God. I could hear her voice in my head. "Oh, isn't life wonderful!" She lit up my life with her face, so gentle and sweet. *How could I have hated her?*

In my head, I heard her laughter. I saw her silly Vaudeville antics that made Poppy and me laugh, like when she dried a dish on the backside of her swiveling hips. All had been eclipsed by my suspicion that she had lied to me about my identity. For years, it had allowed anger to darken my soul.

As I read Mother's words, the sun broke through the clouds of darkness—the way it was at the Old Red Mill after a storm, with a rainbow arching over the mountain, fresh and clean in the dewy mist. Memories returned in intricate detail down to the hollow in the brown bar of Castile soap Mother used to scrub her brushes in. The fragrance of freshly cut lilies in a crystal vase and the scent of linseed oil mixed with the sharp odor of the turpentine-soaked rags as she wiped her brushes clean.

What was there to hate about that?

In my mind, the scent of wet paint on canvas fused with the smell of two pairs of white canvas sneakers—side by side—bleached white by the sun on the back porch of the Old Red Mill. Our mountain hideaway. Never could I have wished for a better life.

They were the two happiest people I'd ever known.

It takes me days to read all of Mother's letters. Every day, I shared them with my daughter, and we rejoiced in connecting with the past that is us.

I read Christina a letter written on February 20, 1937, which began with "Dear Poppy, After talking with you on the phone, being so near and yet so far, I'm all filled up with such love and admiration for you. You said you dreamed of losing me. You need never worry. ...besides, I'm so like you. All I want is to be able to paint... and when we go to the country, to sit side by side and paint. When you're not here, I realize the value of the talks we have together. Such beautiful harmony. I'm keeping the fireside warm till you get back. I'm not going out at all except with the dogs. Just devote all the time to work.'"

In her letters, sent from Poppy's studio in the Hotel des Artistes, Mother shares everything she does with Poppy. She talks about the books she's read and sends him quotes for them she likes. One from Shakespeare. "Arent' these just great!?" she writes.

"Did you say your mother was using Poppy's studio to paint in?" asked Christina.

"That's what her letters say."

"Where's his wife?"

"Oh, that's another thing. Listen to what it says in this one," I told Christina as I thumbed through the stack of letters. "Ah, here it is. 'Doris came over with both Stykas the other night.' She's talking about Tade's brother, Adam. 'They saw the pictures and were quite thrilled. They both felt my muscle and said I must be pretty strong to cover a canvas like the one of the boy in so short a time. Then they asked me if I wouldn't go to dinner with them downstairs, but I refused. Later in the eve, Mrs. Christy walked in with her Jockey and saw them.'"

"What's that mean? 'Her Jockey?'" asks Christina.

"Well, I wondered about that too, so I called Jocelyn and read her the letter. She said it had to be Robert Coneen. He was quite the horseman. Worked across the street in the stable and always wore jodhpurs and riding boots. Everyone in the Hotel des Artistes called him the

Gentleman Jockey. Later, after Poppy's death, Nancy married Coneen, *so-o-o*... maybe they were seeing one another on the sly."

"No wonder Nancy didn't care what Poppy did," said Christina.

I read more from Mother's letters to Christina, all in praise of Poppy, signed, "Lots of Love and Yours Always, Elise."

With each letter, bits and pieces of Mother's dreams came together. Mother did not want to be tied down to a house and family as her mother, and elder sister had been. She wanted the freedom to pursue more creative goals. "...If we could just grow like a flower in the field, with dignity, breathing the cool breezes...."

"The cat is sitting on my lap just gazing up at me and purring," writes Mother. And I think *She must be talking about Winky*. Winky was alive then.

Mother uses the word "wonderful" over and over again. She tells Poppy, "I'm the happiest girl in the world." She talks about what fun it is to paint Callie's portrait. The thrill that runs through her as she observes how the north light illuminates Callie's face, revealing her kind soul. "Such beautiful light," she raves. "I have one love," she says about her art, "and to keep it beautiful is the nearest thing to heaven. God put us on Earth to love. To love the thing He has made, the trees, Nature... Oh! The power to express the beauty I see so that others might enjoy!"

Mother's letters reveal a young woman enamored with the artist she holds in awe. Poppy is someone she wants to emulate. Through him, she has discovered her dream. To be a great artist. And Poppy was willing to nurture her talent to fruition.

To Mother, the most exciting thing in life was to see. The way an artist sees. The greatest thrill? To be a creator. It is, after all, to become like God.

The French sculptor Auguste Rodin had the same feeling, for he said, "The only thing is to see. The mediocre man 'looks without seeing.' His world is 'flat and without character.' ...The artist, on the contrary, sees; that is to say, his eye, grafted on his heart, reads deeply into the bosom of Nature."

Poppy had given Mother the gift of sight.

A true artist loves the object painted. This absorption in the Other is totally selfless and is the source of great joy. Mother's love of Nature was the secret of her happiness.

No one can be happy in a world he wants to see destroyed by an angry god.

Wherever Mother goes, Poppy is always on her mind. Even on the train. On December 13, 1937, she wrote, "A darling little boy just came on the train. He has just opened a package and is playing with its contents. A truck with ice, an icepick and tongs. Makes me think of what we said—"

What did they say? I want to know. I keep reading.

"Now people speak of getting married and all this. Why should I give up all and take on another man's life— for how could I paint and go right along with him to make a success of either, when, I know the most wonderful man in the world who is …doing things to better humanity?"

She talks about feeling the "gypsy in me" that wants to "throw off" traditional ties and be an artist like him. In another letter, she signs off with "Love to you always, Madam X." I realize this is the name given to the woman in a black velvet dress painted by John Singer Sargent. The gossip surrounding it almost ruined his career.

Mother shares details of her visit with her sister Audrey in the country. She says, "We had a bang up time skating on a lake," and talks about her sister's elkhound as if he is part of the family. "Tauser couldn't understand what ice was, cause he couldn't run, so he hung onto the sled and wanted to be pulled around. It was great exercise and good fresh air."

It was because of Mother that Poppy's greatest dream—the *Signing of the Constitution* came to be. What he called "a message of Truth."

As I was to find out, the *Signing of the Constitution* is also how I came to be born.

Was Mother happy? I'll let her say it in her own words.

December 13, 1937

DEAREST "POPPY"

Closest to my heart—in fact—all that is in my heart is what you put there. You and painting. And an abundance of love of the beautiful, which you have showed me. And an intense desire to express it in painting, which you have taught me. And, no matter how you fix it, it all points and centers around you.

So, is it any wonder that I am completely at a loss without you?

Lots of Love to you again,

Your Side Kick.

CHAPTER TWENTY-EIGHT

The Summit

"'What is it you are aiming at?' I asked. 'What are the
dreams of a monk like you?'

"And for the first time I heard the word: 'Satori.'

"'Meaning what?'

"'A moment of great clarity. The moment when you rise
above everything.'"

- *A Fortune Teller Told Me*
By Tiziano Terzani

After my divorce, I remained single for thirteen years
before I met Jim Longuski, a professor of Astronautics at
Purdue. We met while working on the Galileo Mission to
Jupiter at Jet Propulsion Laboratory in Pasadena,

California. In 1988, Jim accepted a position as a Professor of Astronautics at Purdue, University in Lafayette, Indiana. One day, in 2001, I picked up the little foldout frame Mother had given me before her death, with photographs of the two paintings I had grown up with in Mother's art studio in New York. I turned the pictures over and read the following typewritten note on the back:

"Flag Day, June 14, 1962, DEED OF GIFT." *Isn't that just like Mother—to choose the day commemorating the symbol of the nation she and Poppy loved?* "You may want to see these again someday," I remembered her saying. "And, when you do, this is where you'll find them."

Now brown with age, the typewritten paper identified the paintings as: "*Elise,* and *Mother and Child,* by Howard Chandler Christy. Accepted as Gift by the Ohio Historical Society, signed and witnessed by Erwin Zepp, Director, Warren Charles Klein and Elise Ford."

That night, I told Jim, and he said, "I think you need to see them."

That same day, I called the Ohio Historical Society. Knowing that artists often leave messages in paintings, I was wild with anticipation. *Maybe Poppy left me a message in those paintings.* They were, after all, a memorial of his love.

I described the paintings I was looking for to the person I spoke to at the Ohio Historical Society and was asked to wait. I became apprehensive. Finally, she returned. "We do, indeed, have a painting by Howard Chandler Christy. It's called *Elise*."

"That's my mother," I cried out like a lost child. "And the other one? The big one of me and my mother?"

"I'll have to get back to you on that."

"What do you mean? Is it there, or isn't it?"

"I'm sorry, I'll have to have someone call you back."

"My mother gave it to your museum. There was a Deed of Gift."

I hung up feeling angry and distraught. *How could such a massive painting disappear?*

I called my daughter in California and told her what had happened.

"Mom," Christina said, "You have to see that painting. I dreamed that Poppy left you a message written on the back. Mom, didn't you say White Deer Mountain held a mystery for you?"

"Yes."

"Poppy painted you and your mother on that mountain? What other mountain would it be? Mom! There's a message in that painting. I'm sure of it. Just like he said, he had done with the *Signing of the Constitution.* He loved you too much not to leave you a message."

The idea that Poppy may have left a message left me feeling that somewhere out there, he was waiting to tell me something he couldn't tell me before.

Later that same day, the phone rang. "Hello, I'm calling on behalf of Governor and Mrs. Voinovich. *The Summit* is on loan and is hanging in the stairwell of the Governor's mansion in Columbus, Ohio. The Governor and his wife have invited you to come and see it."

The Summit?

Was this the same painting as *Mother and Child?*

From Lafayette, Indiana, Jim and I took the scenic route through the blue-green hills of Poppy's home state of Ohio.

We went first to the Ohio Historical Society, where we were directed to the basement. Crammed with relics from bygone days of the first railroad, it looked like a man cave. A mechanic's den. Not the sort of place I expected to find

Mother. Then, upon walking around a rusted-out engine, there—at the far end of the room—I saw Mother lit up and glowing like a vision. I rushed toward her. Gazing up at her life-sized image was like stepping back in time. There she was—exactly as I remembered her as she had posed in her blue satin gown. On her finger was the large topaz ring Tade Styka had given her for rescuing him and Doris from an Atlantic riptide. On her wrist was the pink-and-yellow-gold bracelet Poppy bought her at Tiffany's at the same time he bought me the pink-and-gold love-knot ring. The 17ᵗʰ-century Flemish tapestry is in the background, which I recognize as the Archangel Gabriel hovering over her.

As I looked into her lovely face, I was filled with agonizing remorse. *If only you could have shared the fear of persecution that drove you and your family into secrecy. But you couldn't. I would have put us all in jeopardy. You knew I would have crowed it to the heavens that I was Poppy's little girl. In so doing, I would have subjected us all to the tyranny of sexual politics. During and after World War II, had it been known that the symbol of the I Am An American poster was the mother of Howard Chandler Christy's illegitimate child, all of us—especially you—would have been branded as politically disloyal, feebleminded and a sexual deviant. During and after World War II, communism and sexual transgression were considered equal threats to the survival of our nation.* What would have happened to Poppy's *Signing of the Constitution* painting had the US government known the truth? To put it in the words of Senator Joseph McCarthy: "Once the people of a Nation become complacent about moral degeneracy in its leadership, then that nation has not long to live."

No wonder Mother took her secret to her grave. The world wasn't ready for the truth—including me. We all lived under the tyranny of ignorance.

As I stood before her lifelike image, I ached to tell her, "I never got a chance to tell you how much I admired you. Or how much I loved you. In light of what I now know about history, I realize you did the right thing to take your secret to the grave."

How well I understand the meaning of Paracelsus's words, "He who knows nothing, loves nothing." To know History is to love and understand.

To know is everything.

I yearned to embrace her and tell her, "I'm sorry."

But it was too late. She had died without my love and appreciation.

Jim folded me in his arms as I melted into uncontainable sobs of regret.

The two of us were alone in that basement as I cried my heart out before Mother's portrait. When, at last, I gained control, through my tears, I saw something I'd missed before. A gold plate at the bottom of the frame gave the name of the painting as *Elise, My Side Kick*. I could hardly believe my eyes. How did they know that's what Poppy called Mother? It was their little secret.

I raced upstairs and confronted the curator. "How did you know that Howard Chandler Christy called Elise 'My Side Kick?'"

"We couldn't miss it. It was painted in big black letters on the back of the canvas."

***

After Poppy's open admission that Mother was more to him than "his Boswell," as Doris had said, I was even more tense with anticipation as we drove through the big iron gate of the Governor's mansion. Two police cars were waiting in the driveway. An officer got out and strolled up to my '66 Mustang and asked for identification before allowing us to approach the door where a retinue of attendants was waiting to usher us into the Governor's Spanish colonial mansion.

Mrs. Voinovich, a slender woman with statuesque elegance, graciously stepped forward to greet us. We chatted for a few minutes in the foyer. Then she said, "Well, I suppose you want to see *The Summit*."

As Jim and I followed her up a wide spiral staircase, the light from the towering windows above us flooded me with memories: the deer trail up the side of White Deer Mountain; the trickling of spring water around the mossy rocks; the scent of pine, the cheerful murmur of the Mettowee in the valley below; the tapping of the woodpecker on a near-bye tree; most of all—the patches of light filtering through the leafy ceiling above, the abode of the two white deer at the clearing at the summit.

As we reached the stairwell, the immensity of *The Summit* drew me. I was rendered speechless as I looked up at it. Poppy's love for Mother and me was in every brush stroke. It brought me face to face with a past which is no more. The wild Poppy wanted me to experience when he said, "I want you to run wild and free on the mountain, the way God intended it."

Sitting beside me on the summit, Mother was pointing to something beyond the clouds, her lips parted. *She is telling me something important. But what?* What is she trying to tell me?

"How old were you when you posed for that painting?" said Mrs. Voinovich, breaking my spell.

"Maybe three or four," I said, choking up with emotion.

"Do you remember posing?"

I nodded. "Poppy lifted me onto a piano bench on top of a modeling stand. I didn't like posing and put up a fuss.

Observing my emotional state, Mrs. Voinovich gave me an understanding smile. "That book you're holding in the painting, I have always wondered what the picture is on the cover. I've never been able to make it out. Can you tell me what it is?"

"It's a cow. A brown Guernsey cow with a white face."

"Of course," exclaimed Mrs. Voinovich. "I see it now."

I could stand it no longer. All the years of anger at Mother for her secret and my sudden remorse came out in a flood of tears.

"I know it must be a very emotional time for you," said Mrs. Voinovich. "Shall we go downstairs for tea?"

Too distraught to answer, I nodded, and Jim and I followed her down the stairs.

As we sat in the living room sipping tea, Jim moved the conversation to *The Signing of the Constitution* in the United States Capitol building—its giant proportions and the amazing quality of each and every life-sized signer responsible for instituting our democracy.

Then something extraordinary happened.

"What a strange coincidence this is," said Mrs. Voinovich. "Just yesterday, a woman called asking permission to see *The Summit*. Her name is Helen Copley. She's coming here tomorrow to see *The Summit*. When she heard that you were Howard Chandler Christy's daughter, she asked me for your phone number. She's writing a book about your father. Would it be all right if I gave her your phone number?"

***

Two days later, Helen, Jim and I were sitting at my dining room table, which was piled with the contents of Mother's grey, tin file box: photographs, Mother's journal, her album filled with autographs from some of the world's most important people; poems Poppy had written to me and photographs. Lots of photographs. All telling stories that took me almost fifty years to unfold. Stories I would never have known had I not found Mother's grey tin file box in a heap of moldy leaves in Doris's dilapidated garage.

Helen closed Mother's scrapbook and looked up at me across the dining room table. "Why, Holly, this is a miracle, don't you think? What are the chances that two perfect strangers would suddenly feel the urge to see an obscure painting called *The Summit*? A painting hidden away in the governor's mansion in Ohio? And what are the chances that those two strangers would be invited to the Governor's mansion within one day of each other?"

I shook my head. By then, Helen and I had been on this earth for over fifty years. Yet we'd never met. Then one day, out of the blue, Poppy's *Summit* brought us together.

It *was* amazing.

Helen had already begun research for her own book, *The Christy Quest*, now published. In the years that followed, she would accumulate a coterie of people, all of whom accepted me into what Helen called "our Christy family." In the years that followed, all would play a role in bringing Poppy back to life. The world-famous artist Ray Kinstler told me how Poppy always gave him enthusiastic encouragement, something Kinstler's teacher James Montgomery Flagg never did. Olga Steckler and Judy Thomas, two of Poppy's models, shared inside stories, some of which are in this book. Through Helen, I met Judy Goffman Cutler, the New York art dealer and owner of The National Museum of American Illustration in Newport, Rhode Island. I also met George Lang, owner of the Café des Artistes who gave me a signed copy of his book, *"The Truffles I've Known*. And, most of all, I am so grateful to have met Paula and Geanfranco Sorrentino, the present owner of what is now called Leopard at Café des Artistes. Through their loving care of the murals, they have restored Eden to its life-like brilliance and clarity after years of suffering beneath a veil of yellowing smoke from cigarettes.

Today, the description of Poppy's murals by New York's legendary author and critic, Brendon Gill, takes on new meaning as they fill us with joyful expectations. Today, Christy's "pinkly silken hamadryads instruct us by their wanton rompings in how far we have come from those dour Dutch burghers and buttoned-up Britishers of the seventeenth century.

"We are lucky to visit here on West Sixty-seventh Street, to find ourselves among artists and writers whom their fellow New Yorkers regard not with suspicion but with adulation."

***

"Holly, honey!" crooned Helen in her Texas accent. "Just look at all this memorabilia, Poppy and your mother left you. All these photographs. Helen laid a loving hand on several of Mother's type-written sheets of paper. "And just look at all these poems he wrote you. He loved you like only the most loving father could.

"Holly, you've got to write a book about Poppy.

"He wants you to write a book. I just know it."

***

To reduce our short existence on this Earth to simplistic ideas of right and wrong is as foolish as trying to paint a picture without light and shadow. Like the morning light that comes to show you things, there were mysteries in its shadows, but my childhood with Poppy and Mother glistens and dances on in my memory. As Poppy would have put it, *Life. Yes, life is what we want—Life!"*

There are only two kinds of people on this Earth: Creators and destroyers. Eden belongs to the Creators.

As for the mystery of White Deer Mountain, its meaning is as clear to me now as the memory of the chattering blue Kingfisher that awoke me every morning as he perched on the line that held the American flag out over the Mettowee river. To me, Poppy and Mother were those two white deer on the summit. Through their love of the beauty and tranquility of Nature, they filled my life with ecstasy. In so doing, they harmed no one, yet they had to hide from the public eye lest they be hunted down as being different and destroyed.

For a brief time on this Earth, they reclaimed Eden and left its memory shining in my heart.

The End